The Churchill Deception

The Churchill Deception

The True Story of Peter Churchill in World War II

PETER JACOBS

Greenhill Books

The Churchill Deception
First published in 2024 by
Greenhill Books,
c/o Pen & Sword Books Ltd,
George House, Unit 12 & 13,
Beevor Street, Off Pontefract Road,
Barnsley, South Yorkshire S71 1HN

www.greenhillbooks.com
contact@greenhillbooks.com

ISBN: 978-1-78438-957-4

CIP data records for this title are available from the British Library

Edited and designed by Donald Sommerville
Typeset in 11.7/14 pt. Adobe Garamond Pro

Printed and bound in the UK by CPI Group (UK) Ltd,
Croydon, CR0 4YY.

Contents

Plates

Peter Churchill in uniform. *UK National Archives (TNA) HS 9/314*

Wanborough Manor training school in Surrey. *Courtesy of the Puttenham & Wanborough History Society, via Patrick Yarnold*

Orchard Court in London's Portman Square – SOE headquarters. *Author*

Parachute training included a course at RAF Ringway in Manchester. *Courtesy of the Dallow family*

Maurice Buckmaster, the head of F Section. *Imperial War Museum (IWM)*

Photograph of Churchill taken in 1941 for use on identity cards. *TNA HS 9/314*

Churchill's identity card in the name of Pierre Chauvet. *TNA HS 9/314*

The MS *Batory*, on which Churchill travelled to Gibraltar at the start of his first mission. *Skyfotos, Kent*

Virginia Hall, a highly successful SOE agent despite her disability. *TNA*

Georges Duboudin, codenamed ALAIN, Churchill's main contact in Lyon during his first mission to France. *TNA HS 9/452/3*

Memorial in Antibes marking Churchill's landing from HMS *Unbroken* in April 1942. *BE&W agencja fotograficzna Sp. z o.o./ Alamy Stock Photo*

The submarine HMS *Unbroken*, from which Churchill landed two wireless operators during his second mission. *via history photography*

Alastair Mars, the brilliant commander of HMS *Unbroken*. *IWM*

Henry and Alfred Newton, SOE operatives known as The Twins. *Author's collection*

Westland Lysander, used to transport agents to and from occupied Europe. *Air Historical Branch*

Churchill's Lysander Training Report. *TNA HS 9/314*

Odette Sansom, codenamed LISE. *TNA HS 9/648/4*
Francis Cammaerts, codename ROGER. *TNA HS 9/258/5*
Members of Vichy's Milice Française. *Author's collection*
Hugo Bleicher. *IWM*
SOE agent Maurice Pertschuk, codenamed EUGÈNE. *TNA HS 9/1172/7*
German personnel carrying out a vehicle search in France. *Author's collection*
No. 84 Avenue Foch, the SD's headquarters in Paris. *Author*
Sachsenhausen gateway. *Image by brownphoto from Pixabay*
Churchill with Odette and her daughters, after receiving their gallantry awards from the King. *SuperStock/Alamy Stock Photo*
Churchill's DSO on display. *Combined Military Services Museum*
Churchill and Odette at their wedding in 1947. *Trinity Mirror/Mirrorpix/Alamy Stock Photo*
Churchill at Dover harbour in 1955. *via barrelorgan*
Peter Morland Churchill, 1909–72. *Pictorial Press/Alamy Stock Photo*

Acknowledgements

Books like this would not be possible without help and so first, I would like to thank the staff at The National Archives, Kew, and the Imperial War Museum, London; we are so lucky to have these marvellous national institutions.

Also, I would like to acknowledge all the authors who have written about the Special Operations Executive over the years, and those who run the websites and chat forums that have now appeared. These books, websites, and chat forums have all helped keep the SOE story alive.

On a more personal note, I would like to take this opportunity to thank Stephane Bogner who kindly gave me access to the notorious No. 84 Avenue Foch in Paris; Keith Turner for his help with locating the whereabouts of Peter Churchill's Distinguished Service Order; Poppy Walker (Operations Director, Dreweatts), and Richard Wooldridge (Trustee) and Julie Miller (Curator) at the Combined Military Services Museum at Maldon, Essex. And, of course, my personal thanks to Michael Leventhal and all at Greenhill Books for enabling this story to be told.

Finally, I would like to pay tribute to the men and women of SOE who bravely went into the field. Without their courage there would be no such stories to tell.

Introduction

In fact, rather than fiction, it is rare for remarkable accounts of bravery and personal endurance, coupled with political fascination, double-dealing, and betrayal, to be part of the same story. But that is the story of Peter Churchill.

Whenever I have read or written about the Special Operations Executive, SOE, during the Second World War, the name Peter Churchill has often appeared, and so this is a story I have long wished to tell. I simply wanted to know more about the man and what he did as it was recorded at the time, rather than be swayed by the post-war opinions of others. Churchill was one of the pioneers of SOE and his story is unique in some ways, but was he a great officer whose luck simply ran out – or did he become too complacent and allow his personal feelings to get in the way of his professional judgement?

It is difficult to say how Churchill's life would have turned out had it not been for war. He was from a privileged background and was a highly educated man, and for a while he even followed the family footsteps into the diplomatic service. But he never seemed to stay in one place, or in any one job, for very long. By the time war came in 1939, Churchill was in his thirties and perfectly suited to the role of an Army intelligence officer, which he became. But he clearly wanted to do more and with a flair for languages, particularly French in which he was fluent, and with his physical fitness as an accomplished athlete, he was ideally suited for the newly formed Special Operations Executive. And so began Churchill's service with SOE.

From the official files and reports now available to us we have the facts as they were recorded at the time. And from the personal recollections of some of those who served with him during the war, and with reference to Churchill's own accounts in his three books written after the war – *Of Their Own Choice* (1952), *Duel of Wits* (1953), and *The Spirit in the Cage* (1954), all published by Hodder & Stoughton – we can follow his movements that are not recorded on file.

Way back in the 1950s, though, books such as Churchill's could not reveal certain things; either because of the sensitivities at the time, the Official Secrets Act, or simply because the author was not aware of all the facts. Inevitably, I came across some inconsistencies in what I read in Churchill's books and what I discovered elsewhere. For example, in his first book, *Of Their Own Choice*, which covers his first mission to France, Churchill wrote about how he learned of the loss of the submarine *P.36*, which had dropped him off along the Côte d'Azur (French Riviera), and its commander, Lieutenant Harry Edmonds. According to his book, Churchill was in Gibraltar on his way back to Britain at the time, which we know was in mid-February 1942, but he could not have heard the news then because *P.36* was sunk, without casualties, in harbour at Malta at the beginning of April and Edmonds was lost at sea in May while travelling in another submarine, nearly three months after Churchill had passed through Gibraltar on his way home. Another example is in Churchill's second book, *Duel of Wits*, when he wrote about his own wireless operator, Adolphe Rabinowitch, travelling to a farm near Montréjeau to help a colleague, Marcus Bloom, fix a radio set. In the book, Churchill places this event before the arrival of his courier, Odette, but Odette and Bloom arrived in France together, and so the event at the farm must have happened later than described in his book. And in his third book, *The Spirit in the Cage*, when writing about the time he was being held at the Gestapo headquarters in Berlin, Churchill recalls a large air raid against the city on the night of 27 February 1944, yet Bomber Command records show no operations that night. The large raid against Berlin that Churchill was likely referring to in the book took place twelve nights earlier, soon after he had arrived in the German capital. And another example relates to 1964, when Churchill applied for financial compensation for his time in captivity. When including the dates of when he was held at various camps, there are minor discrepancies from the dates included in his mission debrief report, which was completed in May 1945, nearly twenty years earlier. But whether Churchill was held at Flossenbürg for ten days or eight days, or whether he spent the night of 13/14 April or 16/17 April at Dachau is irrelevant. It was April 1945 and that is accurate enough.

Such inconsistencies are not surprising given the time elapsed between events that took place during the war and May 1945 when Churchill's mission debrief report was completed after he had returned home, and again when books were written in the 1950s and forms filled out in the 1960s. However, none of these inconsistencies affect the overall story of Peter Churchill, but the point of highlighting some of them here is to show the difficulty we now face when trying to piece together a sequence of events that happened eighty-plus years ago. In such cases, I have corrected inconsistencies as best I can, although when quoting from records and documents on file I have kept the dates as officially recorded at the time.

Another point worth making is that in his series of books Churchill consistently refers to himself as Michel, which provides the reader with continuity and avoids revealing anything that might have been considered classified at the time. But from his personnel file we know that Churchill's codename was OLIVIER during his training and for operations it became RAOUL.

It is also worth remembering throughout this story just how big the south of France is. Because of a shortage of petrol during the war there were few private cars about and so agents had to rely on the rail network, which, incidentally, the French Resistance were constantly trying to disrupt. To travel from Cannes to Lyon, for example, is a journey of 450 kilometres, which even today is a long train ride lasting several hours. Or to go along the coast from Cannes to Marseille – a regular journey for agents operating along the Côte d'Azur – is nearly 200 kilometres. In modern times the train journey can take three hours, but back then it could take all day. Regarding measurements, I have used kilometres (or metres) when referring to distances overland in continental Europe, which seems appropriate, but have used miles or yards elsewhere, unless quoting from contemporary sources when I have left the unit of measurement as recorded at the time.

When quoting from sources, official or not, I have kept the spelling, grammar and so on as written in the original document, although at times this might mean the content lacks clarity or there are inconsistencies in the spelling of names. And, after introducing an agent and their codename, I have used the agent's real name throughout the rest of the book (unless quoting from a source). So, for example, Georges Duboudin, codename ALAIN, is referred to as Georges Duboudin in my own text in the remainder of the book rather than ALAIN, and to help avoid any confusion, I have also included a summary of codenames used by agents in France at the end of the book.

Since the public release of personnel files at the National Archives, several books have appeared in recent years about SOE and its agents during the Second World War. They have all added to our overall understanding of the organisation and its people. We know, for example, the true identities of the agents who worked with Churchill and we know far more about what happened in France during that time. Having access to this new and more in-depth material means we can now add substance to Churchill's accounts written seventy years ago and put his story into a more meaningful context that we can better understand.

What I was not prepared to do, however, was deviate from what has been placed on record by those who were there at the time. It would have been all too easy to stir the pot by suggesting things that simply might not be true just to make the story more dramatic than it already is. For example, Churchill and his courier, Odette, clearly began a personal relationship while operating together in France, but to suggest exactly when it started and to what extent would be speculation. Both told their stories after the war but disclosed little about their relationship while they were active agents. Indeed, on the night the two were arrested, they and Hugo Bleicher (the German 'spy catcher') have all gone on record stating that Churchill and Odette were in separate rooms at the hotel, even though they were using the cover of being a married couple enjoying a holiday together in the mountains, and so it would be wrong to suggest anything else. Besides, Churchill and Odette's relationship is not the focus of the book – it is but one, albeit important, part of the story.

And so, we can add Peter Churchill to the distinguished list of SOE names to have their story told. It is based on how it was recorded by those who were there at the time, although telling it under one cover has been a significant challenge. It has not been done before. Deciding what to leave in or to take out was never going to be easy, particularly when trying to verify events that took place all those years ago. And on that last point, it is always important to remember that only those who were there at the time were ever in possession of all the facts.

I hope you enjoy the book.

Chapter 1

The Firm

Staring down through the hole in the fuselage floor, RAOUL could see the wintry landscape of the Alps rushing past below him. With the moonlight glinting off the snow it presented a most tranquil scene. At any other time of his life, it would be a most welcoming sight. But this was April 1943 and Europe was in its fourth year of war.

On the ground, the small reception committee lay excitedly in wait. Everything was in place and with the moon lighting up the snow-covered plateau it was a near-perfect night. Even the wind, which had picked up a short while before, had now dropped. There had been little time to prepare. Only a few hours earlier they had eagerly gathered around the wireless set to listen to the evening's messages from the BBC. Then had come the announcement they had all been waiting for – RAOUL would be returning that night. They had immediately set off, not knowing at what time the drop would come. Now, after all that had gone before, they could hear in the distance the unmistakable sound of an aircraft approaching. It was time for the bonfires to be lit.

On board the aircraft – a modified RAF Halifax bomber – the Belgian observer, lying on his stomach in the nose, could see the bonfires in the distance, marking the drop zone – a bleak spot on the slopes of a mountain peak high above Saint-Jorioz in south-eastern France. RAOUL heard the change in sound as the pilot reduced power to the aircraft's four engines. It could only mean they were getting close. He had connected his static line to an anchoring point on the floor next to the hole only minutes before; now he checked it for the last time.

The aircraft speed reduced further still as the pilot lowered the flaps. They were now just above the speed at which the Halifax would stall. Across the dimly lit fuselage the dispatcher raised his right arm and a red light illuminated above his head, signalling to RAOUL that it would soon be time to jump. As he dangled his legs through the hole in the fuselage floor, he could feel the slipstream of the aircraft and he could see Lake Annecy pass below. RAOUL was about to return to France.

* * *

Timing is everything in life and no date is more fundamental than the era of one's birth. For example, men born in the late 1920s were fortunate to be just too young for service during the Second World War, and they would enjoy their early adult years in a secure peacetime Britain soon to be at the epicentre of the swinging sixties. But for those born earlier in the twentieth century fate offered a quite different prospect. For their generation was called upon, quite literally, to save the world in a total war unleashed by Nazi Germany.

One of this latter cadre was Peter Morland Churchill. Born in Amsterdam, Netherlands, on 14 January 1909, he was the second of four children and fortunate to have been raised in a well-educated, well-travelled and extremely well-connected family. His father, William Algernon Churchill, was a British consul and his grandfather, Henry Adrian Churchill, was an archaeological explorer of ancient Mesopotamia and a British consul at the age of twenty-eight, while two of Peter's uncles, Sidney John Alexander Churchill and Harry Lionel Churchill were also British diplomats. William had married Hannah Violet Myers in Worcester in 1906, and the couple's first child, Walter Myers, was born the following year. Next came Peter, then his sister, Flora (born 1911), and finally his younger brother, William Oliver (born 1914), by which time the Churchill family had moved to Sweden where they lived for six years until Peter was aged ten.

Fortunately, all four children were young enough to avoid the horrors of the First World War, but all three boys would later distinguish themselves next time Britain went to war, although Flora was sadly to die after a major operation at the age of eighteen.

Peter Churchill was educated at Malvern School (1923–7), Chillon and the University of Geneva in Switzerland (1928–9), and Caius College, Cambridge (1929–32), where he read Modern Languages. Not only was he bilingual in French – his French was faultless – but he could also speak Spanish and Italian, and he had a good understanding of German. He also possessed an abnormally powerful physique and excelled in sports. By 1932, his final year at Cambridge, he was captain of the university ice hockey team; his service record shows he earned fifteen international caps. He was also an excellent skier, a diver, a very good golfer – playing off a six handicap – and a competent piano player.

Although Churchill first tried his hand as a publicity agent for a hotel advertising magazine in Switzerland, he inevitably followed the family footsteps and, in 1935, he moved into the British diplomatic service, serving as Pro-Consul at the Vice-Consulat Britannique in Oran, Algeria. But he did not stay overseas for long and soon returned to Britain, first working in a bicycle factory in Birmingham and then writing sporting articles for newspapers and working in the fur business.

By 1939, Churchill was thirty years old, living in London, and working as Under Secretary to Sir Norman Birkett, a senior lawyer and Home Office adviser. But the outbreak of war in Europe, for the second time in living memory, meant Churchill's life was about to change.

Like so many of his contemporaries, Churchill did not wish to play a passive role in the war. On 23 August 1940 he joined the Army and for the record he was described as having a tall frame (he was 5 ft 10 in. tall), an olive complexion, brown eyes, dark hair, and no distinguishing marks. His time at university had made him something of an idealist, albeit a practical and matter of fact one, never starting a task without seeing the steps that were needed to carry it out successfully. And he was quick to grasp the complexities of a problem.

Churchill spent four months at No. 169 Officer Cadet Training Unit, Aldershot, after which he was posted to York as an intelligence officer with the rank of second lieutenant and service number 162707. Then, in March 1941, he was posted to Headquarters Northern Command and was immediately sent to Farnborough to attend No. 29 Air Photo Course, which lasted two weeks. As an intelligence officer, Churchill could have tried to see out the war in some quiet way, but he was not prepared to do that, nor was he prepared to accept the comparative uneventfulness of an 'ordinary' life in the Army. He was convinced his language skills could be better used elsewhere and it was just a matter of finding out where that would be. The answer was the recently formed Special Operations Executive, SOE.

SOE had been established in July 1940, after the fall of France, following an order by the British Prime Minister, Winston Churchill, to 'Set Europe Ablaze'. The Prime Minister simply wanted the ability to hit back at the enemy in Nazi-occupied Europe in whatever way possible and was convinced that SOE operations would divert vital enemy resources to guard against SOE's work, and that any attack, no matter how small, would raise the morale of those under occupation.

In the words of its founding charter, SOE was to 'coordinate all action, by way of subversion and sabotage, against the enemy overseas'. However, while the direction was clear, there was no blueprint to follow and there were certainly no rules. And thus SOE would become an unorthodox organisation set up to fight the Nazis. But to fight a successful clandestine operation would require huge support from elsewhere and, although SOE sat alongside Britain's armed forces, it gained little support within Whitehall during its early days and was kept separate from existing military and intelligence organisations.

SOE set up its main headquarters in a greyish five-storey building at 64 Baker Street. For a long time, its very existence remained little known. Those attached to the organisation from other departments were discouraged from referring to it by its full name, and so they tended to refer to it as simply 'The Org', 'The Racket' or 'The Firm'. If it had to be referred to in any official correspondence, then the designation Inter-Services Research Bureau, or ISRB, was used to allay unwelcome curiosity. Furthermore, outsiders were rarely invited to Baker Street and meetings were usually held elsewhere.

As SOE grew, it spread its operations far and wide but, for several reasons, France offered the best opportunities to foster sabotage and subversion. It was just across the Channel and so could be supplied and re-supplied with relative ease. There was no shortage of places where agents could be dropped or picked up, either from the air or by sea, and the terrain in many parts of the country, particularly in the vast areas of rolling hills and dense woodland, proved ideal for conducting guerrilla warfare. Furthermore, French-speaking agents could be found without too much difficulty and once on the ground they could merge into the local population with credibility and relative ease.

In one way at least SOE was like a club, for membership was by invitation only. There was no recruiting system as such, but every potential member was carefully scrutinised before those considered suitable were invited to join. There would never be a typical SOE type. Recruiting officers had to rely mainly on their personal judgement, but volunteers came forward in good numbers, not only from within the military – men like Peter Churchill – but from all walks of life. The principal recruiting difficulty, security apart, was the need for a wide variety of characters and skills. It took a special kind of person to become an SOE agent in France. First and foremost, he – for there were no female agents in the early days – needed to be fluent in French. This meant far more than just being able to speak the language. He would have to appear native to the region that he was operating in to avoid attracting any attention, and he would need a new identity with a lifelong story that could credibly be passed off at any time, even when under extreme stress.

The main body for organising French subversion was F Section (F being for French), which was set up to work closely with resistance movements in France. When France fell in June 1940 this left the country's proud military reputation in ruins and its government divided, and it was given to a First World War hero, Marshal Philippe Pétain, to sign a humiliating armistice with Nazi Germany. While Hitler would always be suspicious of the French, the total occupation of France was considered an unnecessary liability and, given that France had delivered a government that was willing to cooperate, dividing the country seemed an ideal solution. France was therefore left with an Unoccupied Zone, called the Zone Libre (Free Zone), in the south of the country and inland from the Atlantic coast, which was administered from the spa town of Vichy, while the Germans occupied and governed the northern zone, the Zone Occupée (Occupied Zone), from Paris.

This arrangement gave those in the south of France a certain feeling of freedom and independence, but many ardent patriots owed their loyalty to Pétain. Consequently, there was initially no organised resistance. But the fact that the south was, for the moment, unoccupied did not mean that SOE would have total freedom to operate in the Free Zone; far from it. Guarding its integrity was the security service and Vichy police, and later the Milice Française (French Militia), all employed and directed by the Vichy government. Nonetheless, it did mean there were very few Germans about in the south of the country, and although the insertion of agents into the Free Zone provided SOE with an obvious place to start, operating in the south of France would not be without its difficulties. Furthermore, the legitimacy of Pétain's leadership was challenged by an exiled and at that time little-known French officer, Brigadier General Charles de Gaulle. De Gaulle claimed to represent the legitimacy and continuity of the French nation and from London had broadcast his message to the French people at home to continue to resist the Nazi occupation of France. He also set about building the Free French Forces from personnel outside France, and so RF Section was set up to work specifically with de Gaulle and his staff.

It was a complicated situation, as complicated as French politics at the time. There were plenty of people in France who were prepared to resist the Nazi occupation, but not all were supporters of de Gaulle. The British were keen to support them, too, but F Section had the difficult task of having to recruit agents against the constant opposition of the Free French. The result was that F Section had little contact with RF, and was not supposed to. F Section remained separate from RF but was not anti-Gaullist; it simply worked independently. In any case, the two sections pursued different aims. F Section's objectives were more limited than RF's and laid down by the SOE chain of command to suit outline directives from the British Chiefs of Staff. Not surprisingly, there was always friction between F and RF, as there was between SOE and the other services, but eventually each section simply accepted the existence of the other.

And so it was against this background that SOE began undertaking operations in France, although it was still some way short of being ready to fight a subversive war. F Section's early missions were exploratory; it was only a few months since the first agents had been inserted into France, and they had been left battling against an enemy who seemingly held all the trump cards.

While F Section's agents were struggling across the Channel, those back in London were busy formulating a plan for the construction of circuits (otherwise called networks) in France. The number of agents in the field would soon increase to around fifty, a figure that would more than double in the year after that and reach around 200 by the beginning of 1944, with circuits spread far and wide across France. While Europe was not yet ablaze, it was beginning to smoulder and men like Peter Churchill were just what SOE was looking for.

Churchill's interview to join SOE was on 19 April 1941. Not surprisingly, he was considered an ideal candidate. Churchill's interview report assessed his linguistic skills as 'perfect in French, some Italian and Spanish', and under 'Recommendation' it states, 'Excellent type if he will play', while under 'Remarks' it describes Churchill as 'Pleasant, competent, mature, physically very fit, good brain, good experience of life, gets on well with others.'

With his interview over and knowing that he was just the type of person that SOE was on the lookout for, it took no time at all for Churchill to decide that he did want to play. He was off to SOE.

Chapter 2

Becoming Pierre Chauvet

Built in 1527, Wanborough Manor is near Guildford in west Surrey. Although its exterior has long remained unchanged, the manor house is now divided into privately owned dwellings, but during the Second World War it was requisitioned from its owners and for four years it was a school for secret agents. Designated Special Training School No. 5 (STS 5), Wanborough briefly became home to those brave men and women of SOE who were destined to go into the field.

For SOE recruits, there were three phases of training – Preliminary, Paramilitary, and Finishing – with Wanborough providing the Preliminary phase. Essentially, the school had two main tasks – to provide basic military training and student assessment. By the time Peter Churchill arrived in June 1941, the first training courses had already passed through. His course was designated Party 27F – the number 27 identified it as an F Section course and the F identified it as the sixth course in the series. Churchill missed the first couple of days of the course, but this was not an issue given that he was already commissioned. It was several weeks before Party 27G was due to start and so it was decided to get him into training as soon as possible, rather than wait for the next course.

Not all records of those attending Churchill's course have survived, but the number of students could have been as high as fourteen, as Churchill later recalled in *Of Their Own Choice*. Whatever the number, there had been three significant changes since the school opened. Firstly, Wanborough had become the exclusive preserve of F Section, whereas earlier courses had a mix of students from the different sections of SOE. Secondly, the course length had been increased to three weeks from two; the extra week being added to allow for the teaching of clandestine techniques. And thirdly, a new man had just arrived to run the school. This was Major Roger de Wesselow, a fifty-something former officer of the Coldstream Guards, and Churchill's course was to be his first as commandant.

Students were instructed to say very little about themselves and not give anything away about their personal histories. The less they all knew about each other the better it would be for everyone should they ever be captured in the field. Instead, they were given a codename by which they were to be known during training, after which they would be given another codename for operating in the field. In the case of Churchill, he was to be known throughout his training as OLIVIER, with the student number nine.

Even though some of the students were undergoing basic military training for the first time, the atmosphere at Wanborough resembled more the country manor that it was, rather than that of a military establishment. Both English and French were spoken on the course, although de Wesselow insisted that only French be spoken around the table during meals. Fluency was an important factor when determining a student's suitability for further training, although this was never going to be a problem for Churchill.

The long daylight hours of June meant the day started early with reveille at 6 a.m., followed by physical training on the lawn in front of the manor. It was not how most would have chosen to start the day, but it was never intended to be a physically demanding course. Students had been recruited because of their specialist skills and so PT sessions were more about getting them into shape. After breakfast, the rest of the day was spent in a succession of classes, many conducted outdoors in the fine weather, during which the students were taught several new skills. The syllabus included: basic weapons training on all types of light weapons, including French and German; unarmed combat; signalling, wireless operating and coding; demolition techniques; fieldcraft and cross-country navigation; and physical training. All the time the students were being assessed to determine their potential for further specialised training, such as becoming an organiser, a wireless operator, or a saboteur, or whether they should even be employed at all. The day was broken up for lunch and then again for afternoon tea, and then there was another hour of lessons before dinner, after which the students retired to their dormitory for the night.

Behaviour was also closely monitored at Wanborough to see how the student behaved in everyday occurrences, such as when under stress or the influence of alcohol or while asleep at night. It was important to know, for example, if a student talked in their sleep, what language they spoke. No stone was left unturned. Sifting out students not considered suitable, for whatever reason, was one of the school's key responsibilities. Anyone could be rejected at any time, although it was F Section, rather than the school's staff, that ultimately decided whether a student was acceptable for further training or not.

The training tempo picked up during the three weeks as students became more familiar with their new skills. Night navigation became easier, as did the PT, so too the Morse code, more weapons and heavier explosives were introduced, and the exercises became more complex. SOE demanded a combination of qualities far beyond the requirements of the ordinary fighting man – unselfishness, moral courage, a level head, and steady nerves. Ordinary people were about to be asked to do quite extraordinary things.

The preliminary training records of early F Section students are less informative than the more comprehensive records of students who joined SOE later in the war, but there is enough to suggest that Churchill did well during his time at Wanborough. In his first Weekly Progress Report, dated 26 June, one of the staff, Lance-Corporal Edgar, wrote:

> Missed 2½ days of the course, owing to late arrival. However, is catching up very well. Excellent physique and fitness. Very humorous and most popular. Keen to learn and fascinated with practical demonstrations.

In the next weekly report, dated 3 July, Edgar wrote of Churchill:

> Has picked up well on the subjects he missed the first few days and is doing very well at Morse. Has a lot of common sense and cheers up the others with his humour. Has not attended P.T. and some of the schemes, owing to an injured foot, but nevertheless is fit. Loves the open air life and is very fascinated with the course.

The injury to Churchill's foot referred to in Edgar's report had occurred in the swimming pool, with de Wesselow having reported the incident to F Section on 2 July:

> No 9, OLIVIER. This student damaged a foot in the swimming bath last week. I sent him to the local hospital to have it X-rayed with negative result. While out on night march he broke down. Today he attended hospital and was sent on to an orthopaedic hospital at Pyrford, where they said treatment was

> essential and that after five days electric and manual massage they could express an opinion. I am, therefore, sending him there daily on a motor-cycle. He is entirely dependable and will be unaccompanied unless I am instructed to the contrary.

Churchill's injury was clearly not enough to prevent him from completing the course, for in his end of training report, dated 9 July, he was assessed as:

> HEALTH – Robust, an athlete;
> CHARACTER – Excellent;
> PHYSICAL TRAINING – Out of action owing to foot injury;
> FIELDCRAFT – Missed all schemes except last when he did well;
> CLOSE COMBAT – Very good;
> DEMOLITIONS – High standard;
> COMMUNICATIONS – Very good;
> SPORTS – Good;
> MAP READING – Good.

Edgar also wrote, 'Was best at Morse test. Good at all subjects. Has a lot of common sense. Still cheerful and humorous', while under COMMANDANT'S REMARKS, de Wesselow wrote:

> Full of self-confidence. Extremely intelligent and able; combines with these gifts abnormally powerful physique. Has been out of action owing to an accident in the bathing pool. Though I have seen a good deal of him I don't feel I know the extent of his powers, but he seems to be gifted with a strong personality without perhaps being so likeable as one or two of the others. Perhaps he is more Latin. I am pretty sure he could take on a big job and do it well. 'A'.

In *Of Their Own Choice*, Churchill recalls four students being turned away at this stage, while those remaining on the course caught the train to London and then on to Scotland to undergo the next phase of their training. After changing trains at Glasgow, they arrived in the coastal town of Mallaig, where they were met at the station and then driven in trucks to a small country house by the sea.

Inverness-shire has always been a popular destination for trekkers and salmon fishing, but during the Second World War the War Office requisitioned several properties in the Highlands – mostly shooting lodges and holiday homes – with each being large enough to accommodate a dozen or more people. Officially, they were declared to be for 'unspecified military purposes', but they were all part of a paramilitary training school under the watchful eye of Lieutenant-Colonel J. W. Munn.

Churchill had arrived at one of these establishments – Garramor House in South Morar, known within SOE as STS 25. There to welcome the new arrivals was the Commandant, Major Jas Young. This was to be their second phase of training and for the next three weeks they were to be assessed in a physical and rugged environment.

Although it was summer, it rained. In fact, it would rain for most of the course. Training began with a hard slog over rugged terrain. There would be more hard slogs to come, some covering more than twenty miles, with few roads and other navigational features to help, and much therefore depending on map-reading skills and good compass work. The students were also taught more general fieldcraft, which included learning how to live off the land, and there were further sessions on elementary Morse code, with the requirement for receiving a message being a minimum of twelve words per minute. There was also more weapons and demolition training, including laying dummy charges on selected targets, and more sessions on close combat, during which the students learnt new techniques such as silent killing.

In his report on Churchill's progress, dated 17 July, Edgar wrote:

> Still shows plenty of interest and is extremely interested in demolitions. Doing very well at Morse. I have noticed that his eyesight affects his reading of compass-bearings. Every time OLIVIER took a bearing it was checked by two others, and his reading was found to be out by a good margin. He mentioned that he considered his eyesight was probably causing the mistake. I am certain he knows how to use the compass. I mention the latter for what it is worth. Will leave S.T.S. No. 25 on 2.8.41 and proceed direct to S.T.S. No. 51 for parachute training.

The following week in his next report, dated 24 July, Edgar wrote:

> Very fit; full of humorous imagination and always in good spirits. Still doing well at Morse. Is enjoying the course and shows no lack of interest.

Then, a week later, Edgar added:

> Has been altogether very enthusiastic about the course. Like PHILIPPE, good all round. Unlike the others has combined the serious and the comic. Had good control over his men when made leader of a scheme. Would be suitable for a leader or an individual job.

In Churchill's end of course report, dated 1 August 1941, his character was noted as 'charming, always alive and amusing, but lacks depth' and he was assessed as:

> PHYSICAL TRAINING – Very good;
> FIELDCRAFT – Good;
> CLOSE COMBAT – Good, above average;
> WEAPONS TRAINING – Good, but poor in dark due to eyesight probably, and did not handle pistols and revolvers as well as expected.

Churchill scored 92 per cent in the Explosives & Demolitions test with an assessment of 'very good', and he achieved eleven words per minute in his Morse Communications with the comment 'could do better with practice'. Under the Commandant's Remarks, Young wrote:

> This student has done well in everything but should have done better. Except in games he does not exert himself sufficiently. While apparently game enough there is something lacking in him which I find difficult to define. Having strong arms and a good toss his legs are weak and generally his physique is not as good as it looks. Grade C.

Munn, meanwhile, was more positive about Churchill's potential:

> A very intelligent man with a quick decisive manner who is capable of leadership. He is cultured and a good mixer with all classes. He has shown great keenness and is clearly capable of working as an organiser. Category 'B' possibly 'A'.

It was not unusual for assessments of an individual to vary. After all, the students differed in age and experience and came from all walks of life. No one was perfect, that was for sure, and much of the assessment process was subjective. How an individual was seen by one instructor could, and often did, differ from how he was seen by another. This was quite evident in Churchill's latest assessment where Young had made the comment 'there is something lacking in him' and marked him as a Grade C student, whereas Munn was full of praise.

The reality was it was never going to be easy to assess someone in a training environment for what they might experience in the field. The instructors were always on the lookout for obvious weaknesses and many who were initially considered to be suitable candidates had not made it that far. SOE clearly had no intention of pushing anyone through the system and sending them off to occupied Europe unless they were up to the task, as shown by the high number of drop-outs during training.

Churchill had done well overall up until this point. Comments might have been mixed on occasions, but he was certainly suitable for the task, although his poor eyesight had now been commented on several times. This was something he would have to work around, rather than be failed in training because of it. Churchill had the personal qualities that were needed for the SOE, particularly his grasp of the French language and his organisation and leadership skills, and so his poor eyesight was something he would have to deal with, just as he would have done throughout his life.

By the end of their second phase of training in Scotland, Party 27F was down to five members. Next stop was Dunham House in Altrincham, Cheshire, to undergo parachute training at nearby RAF Ringway in Manchester, known as STS 51.

Before conducting their first jump, students were taught how to land properly by performing a series of rolls – rolls to the right and rolls to the left, and then somersaults backwards and somersaults forwards, using their hands to support them and then without. These were done on rubber mats, after which the students were introduced to the giant trapeze, which gave them a better feel for what it was like to land under certain wind conditions. They were also taught how to vacate an aircraft through a hole in the fuselage floor, using a mock-up airframe inside the hangar.

Each student was required to complete five jumps to qualify for their parachute wings. These were a mix of jumps from a tethered balloon from a height of 800 feet, in daylight and at night, and from an aircraft, a converted twin-engine Wellington bomber. The number of jumps would later be reduced to three as more agents were recruited by SOE and because F Section wanted students to qualify as quickly as possible. Weather and aircraft availability were always factors and there was often much wasted time sitting around, either waiting for the weather to clear, or the wind conditions to be in limits, or for an aircraft to become available.

Churchill, however, had to wait longer for his first jump. Just two days into the course he again hurt his ankle and so the medical officer declared him unfit to jump. Churchill instead went to London for a few days of leave and had to return to Ringway to complete the course later. In his report on Churchill, dated 7 August, Edgar wrote:

> Left party on leave 4th August. He failed to pass the doctor, owing to a foot injury and was advised to rest. Before coming to this school he had rested his foot as much as possible in order that he might be able to jump and was, consequently, very disappointed.

Churchill's parachute training had to wait, but within days he was certified fit to travel and on 16 August he met up with his course colleagues in London and boarded the morning train for Brockenhurst. They were heading for the depths of the New Forest in Hampshire for their final phase of training at the SOE's Finishing School at Beaulieu (STS 31), the ancestral home of the barons Montagu set in a quietly beautiful and inaccessible part of the forest.

Agents often described Finishing School as the hardest phase of them all, not because it was physical in any way, because it was not, but because the focus was on security and there were many carefully prepared traps into which they could fall. This final phase of training was more about mental agility and preparation for going into the field. It was all about clandestine operations, communication, concealment, and security. Above all, though, it was to make sure the soon-to-be agents learned how to be French – to look like them, to behave like them, and to eat like them. A Frenchman, for example, would eat all his food and then use bread to mop up his plate, and he would certainly not neatly align his cutlery at the end of a meal. It was all about learning how to avoid drawing unnecessary attention to themselves when in France.

The students were accommodated in the large house at Beaulieu, and much of the training took place in the great hall. Staff outnumbered the students, with fifteen specialist instructors at the school, each an expert in their own field. One was the security expert. His task was to teach the students how to behave inconspicuously and what to expect in the way of local curfews and customs. Once inserted into France they would instantly have to fit in with the local population. The clothes they wore had to be French, as would anything in their pockets, such as a used train ticket or a cinema stub. Every item carried had to be current and relevant. Everything had to be just right.

Then there was also an expert in German uniforms. This was for recognition purposes when intelligence gathering in the field. There was also a coding expert. Communications would always be important, and everything should be sent and received in code. The students were also taught how to set up a resistance circuit by using cells. These were small groups of people, maybe no more than six, only one of whom was allowed to contact the circuit organiser's deputy who, in turn, would be the only member of the group with access to the organiser. Such a secure system would be vital when in the field, particularly as the larger resistance groups would grow into hundreds of people. There were also experts in the outdoors. They taught a range of things, such as how to bury a parachute without leaving a trace, not only their own parachute should they be dropped into France, but those of containers when receiving supplies from the air. There were also lessons on what to expect should they be captured and suffer interrogation. The Gestapo (an abbreviation of Geheime Staatspolizei, Secret State Police) already had a reputation for inflicting various tortures on captives to extract information. Learning about their techniques did not make easy listening. And, of course, there was more PT.

The students were also given exercises to lead, called schemes, with the staff assessing each student's potential as a leader. One task took Churchill into nearby Bournemouth where he had to identify various points of interest, such as a telephone exchange or factory, while having to shake off one of the staff who had been told to follow him. This had to be done discreetly and without Churchill making it obvious that he knew he was being followed. Then, having identified a building of interest, he had to make a report on it and then hand over the report to another member of staff waiting at a nearby hotel. This hand-over had to be done at a specific time and in a manner that would not be obvious to anyone else.

Churchill spent four weeks at Beaulieu. Because it was the final phase of training, there were regular visits from SOE staff who travelled down from London. Following one such visit from London, conducted at the end of the first week, the staff officer raised a concern he had about Churchill:

> OLIVIER – This man I would not entirely trust but I think he has no real evil in him and he has an extremely good brain. My chief objection to him is that he has only spent some four months in all in France and has no contacts or specific knowledge of any region. On the other hand, he does know ORAN and MERS-EL-KEBIR very well, having been pro-Consul there for some time. His training should be continued and I would suggest that he might be more usefully employed in North Africa than in metropolitan France.

At that stage, nothing had been decided about any of the students, but it was now getting towards the end of their training and decisions would soon have to be made as to where and how individuals would be best employed – if at all. However, while there was some concern about how little time Churchill had previously spent in France, there was no doubting his ability as a potential organiser, with comments on his personnel file such as 'is the best organiser of the party' and 'has not an outstanding brain, but always makes sure that he understands his facts before going any further'. There is also the following observation:

> OLIVIER – Good man – wide experience of life – when he dislikes somebody he finds it hard to control himself – needs a lot of sleep in order to be able to work – does not look very English, specially now he is very brown after the beautiful sunshine of Wanborough and relaxing air of Scotland – French is good, he has a slight accent at times – has nice manner and does not drink much, knows how to make himself pleasant – had bad luck throughout the courses with ankle injuries – during schemes proved to be a good leader – confidence in his own ability.

As Churchill's time at Beaulieu was coming to an end, he was given a written brief. It was his new French identity – Pierre Marc Chauvet – and associated cover story, which used parts of his real pre-war life wherever possible to reduce the amount he had to learn. The story was that Pierre Marc Chauvet was born in January 1909. His father was Jean-Louis Chauvet, a French citizen and businessman who had worked in Buenos Aires, and his mother English. Pierre had left Buenos Aires when he was young, after his father had died in 1913, and settled with his mother, being educated in England and Switzerland. Pierre Chauvet supposedly did his military service in 1929, the details of which Churchill had to memorise:

> Started his military service on 15th April 1929 and it finished in 1930. Your service was in the 19e Train. In Cannes at the outbreak of the present war and reported immediately (i.e., on 3.9.39) at the barracks of the Ecole Militaire. Your military life was a simple one. You did your classes but not very well, having skipped everything you could. Your class consisted of some foot drill, instruction on driving cars, because you went into that side. You had the usual classes on gas, the theory of the internal combustion engine, maintenance of motor vehicles and so on. After six months your classes had finished. At the end of your classes you managed to get the job of driving officers around Paris from the 'Ecole de Guerre' to the 'Ministère'.

The brief continues that Chauvet was then sent to Le Mans:

> At Le Mans you were billeted at the barracks of the 4ème Train. You were posted to the C.R.E. 2nd Corps Troops. You worked with Colonel Foley. You spent the war up to the time of the push into Belgium in his office. From the LAVAL neighbourhood you went to Libercourt (Carvin) – the nearest town of any size is Lens. You stayed there until the push into Belgium.

The brief then goes on to say that Chauvet was attached as the '*agent de liaison*' to the 2ème Détachement de la Mission Militaire Française auprès de l'Armée Britannique, commanded by Captain Ciriez and based at Phalempin, near Carvin, but that Chauvet rarely went there. He also 'remembered' a Captain Meric.

> When the flap came you went up with the C.R.E. to Brussels. There orders were given to various English detachments. You went back to Lille, back again into Belgium and out through Dunkirk on Friday, May 31.

The cover story then goes on to describe what happened to Chauvet after his evacuation at Dunkirk – how he landed at Dover and went to Tidworth before he was sent back to France to join another unit, landing at Cherbourg on 12 June. He then went to Brulon, a village not far from Le Mans, and from there proceeded under the orders of Commandant Chocquet to the south of France. After the Armistice, Chauvet was sent to Perpignan where he was demobilised in July. Then, with little money and nowhere to stay, Chauvet made his way to Corsica, where he stayed with friends, before returning to Marseille to look for work. After having no success in finding a job he made his way to Lyon. His brief then included a list of several so-called friends with whom he had stayed.

It was a plausible cover story, but it was one that Churchill had to learn. He was tested several times, but it was vitally important that he remembered every detail should he ever be stopped and questioned while operating in France.

At the end of the course, the Commandant's Report summarised Churchill's performance at Beaulieu:

> A very intelligent man with a quick decisive manner who is capable of leadership. He is cultured and a good mixer with all classes. He has shown great keenness and is clearly capable of working as an organiser. Category B (possibly 'A').

In *Of Their Own Choice*, Churchill recalls only three students on his course being accepted as agents, but from what is now known, at least five of the original members of Party 27F, including Churchill, subsequently went into the field. One was a Frenchman, 35-year-old Marcel Clech. He had suffered an injury to his foot early in the course at Wanborough and was temporarily withdrawn from training, but he joined a subsequent course and went to France in April 1942. He was later arrested, and died in Mauthausen concentration camp in March 1944. Another member of Party 27F was 23-year-old Jean Philippe Charles le Harivel, a British subject who had been born in France. He parachuted into France, but was also arrested, although he escaped back to Britain via Spain. Having then given up his commission in 1944 due to ill health, he remained with F Section as a civilian. Another was 27-year-old George William Abbott who went to France in February 1942, but was also captured. Fortunately, he was treated as a prisoner of war and saw out the war in Colditz Castle. And then there was 29-year-old Jack Thorez Fincken.

Like Churchill, he was already an Army officer and had transferred to SOE from the Royal Fusiliers. He parachuted into France in June 1942, was soon arrested and was another to be fortunate to survive the war in Colditz.

It was late September 1941 when Churchill left Beaulieu. He next spent a few days at Brickendonbury Manor in Hertfordshire, another specialist training school known as STS 17 (or Station XVII). Set in beautiful countryside and just a short drive from the town of Hertford, this impressively grand Jacobean mansion had been requisitioned by the government at the outbreak of the Second World War and was being used by SOE for training saboteurs. But because Churchill was not going to be a saboteur there was little for him to do. A note was written on Churchill's file – 'he was getting demoralised doing nothing down at XVII while everyone else was doing something'.

There was no point in Churchill staying at Brickendonbury any longer, and so he was soon on the train back to London for a few days of leave. He went to stay with a French friend, Madame Fol, at her home in Flanchford Road, W12. Churchill was a great friend of the Fol family. Charles Fol was living in Paris under the Nazi occupation while his brother, Pierre, was serving as a captain in the Royal Engineers, and Pierre's wife was living in London. Churchill would often stay with her when he was in London, and she is listed on his personnel file (along with Churchill's father) as someone who should be kept informed should things ever go wrong.

On 12 October, Churchill left London for Manchester to resume his parachute training at Ringway. He caught the afternoon train to Wilmslow and from there was driven to Dunham House. But he left Manchester just four days later having completed only one jump, from a tethered balloon, which was conducted on the 14th (from 800 feet and with a variable wind of 15 knots), during which he injured his chest on landing. Churchill's report, signed by Major Edwards, commanding STS 51, states:

> The officer concerned carried out his ground training on the first day and showed interest in the work. He was however rather short sighted and owing to the general confusion which existed that day he was unable to get the detailed individual instruction which is normally given to the students on their first jump with the result that he landed heavily on his chest.

> I very closely questioned this officer about his eye, and he was confident he could judge the approach to the ground without glasses. He came provided with special lenses which fit over the eyes inside the eyelids, but did not think it necessary to wear them on his first decent. He was one of the casualties due to circumstances that I have already reported, and a victim of the general confusion which prevailed that morning. Excellent at P.T., and of athletic build, there is no reason why he should not make a first class parachutist and from my knowledge of him I am confident that he would be a valuable officer on operations; intelligent and good company.

With his parachute training cut short for a second time, Churchill went back to Beaulieu before returning, once again, to Manchester. This time everything went well and being the only student at Ringway at that time, he successfully completed the remaining four jumps – three by day (on 11 November from 800 feet, and two from 500 feet on the 12th and 15th) and one simulated at night on the 15th. His end-of-course report, dated 16 November 1941, and again signed by Edwards, reads:

> This officer in spite of the handicap of his eyes successfully completed his five descents, and was one of the first to use the tinted goggles to simulate a night descent, which proved quite satisfactory. A highly intelligent officer with a good personality, inspires confidence and should prove extremely valuable.

It was now the end of November 1941. Churchill was thirty-two years old, earning £7 a week, and fully trained. In his own words he was 'fully equipped to start anything from a whispering campaign to guerrilla warfare'. But he also considered that his chances of a safe return from operating in France were evens at best. His only hope was that he would avoid capture for as long as possible, as with all the knowledge he now had it would be such a waste if he was to fall at the first hurdle.

Chapter 3
Time to Go

As he approached Orchard Court, Churchill felt good. From the outside the tall building appeared little different to any other in Portman Square, but the residential apartments within had since been taken over by SOE, and the flat allocated to F Section, number six, had been completed to a luxurious standard. It was the late afternoon of 2 December 1941 and one of those rare occasions when he was required to wear his best uniform, that of a lieutenant in the Intelligence Corps, now with the addition of his parachute wings. Not that anyone in London noticed. Britain had been at war for over two years and there were plenty of uniforms about.

Churchill had moved into one of the many SOE apartments in London, near Haymarket, and had just returned from leave, having spent a few days with his parents at their home in Malvern. He was not going to be able to spend Christmas with them, but it was the best he could do. He often wondered about what they must be going through. Walter, his older brother, was a fighter pilot in the RAF who had fought over France and in the Battle of Britain. By late 1941 he was a highly decorated wing commander with a Distinguished Service Order and the Distinguished Flying Cross and a recognised 'ace' with seven confirmed victories. Oliver, meanwhile, the youngest of the three brothers, had been commissioned into the Worcestershire Regiment, but he had swapped life as an infantry officer to follow Peter into SOE, and was about to leave for Malta to train Italian partisans in the Mediterranean and Middle East.

Despite the air raids, Orchard Court had remained untouched. Churchill was met on arrival by an elderly porter wearing a dark suit and tie. Known to the agents as Park, he had worked in the Paris branch of the Westminster Bank before the war and was now working for the new head of F Section, 39-year-old Major Maurice Buckmaster, who would lead the section for the rest of the war. The appointment of Buckmaster had been an inspired choice. As a former reporter with a French newspaper and a senior manager with the French branch of the

Ford Motor Company, he had useful and extensive contacts in France and knew the country well.

Buckmaster had a handful of trusted individuals to help him run F Section. The briefing officer, 34-year-old Major Jacques de Guélis, was a former publicity agent in Paris. He had been captured whilst serving as a French liaison officer with the British Expeditionary Force in France but managed to escape to Britain and had joined SOE. De Guélis was one of the first agents to go into France and, although his stay was brief, he succeeded in recruiting several volunteers in the south of the country whom London could work with in the future. Buckmaster's general staff officer was 37-year-old Captain Nicolas Bodington, a former Paris correspondent of the *Daily Express* who had been with F Section since its earliest days and would go into France on four occasions, usually to resolve difficult situations in the field. The planning officer was Major Robert Bourne-Paterson, a Scottish chartered accountant and peacetime solicitor who knew France well and understood the importance of planning if agents were to be given the best chance of succeeding once in the field. There was also Captain Lewis Gielgud, forty-seven years old and the brother of the actor John Gielgud, who had served in France during the First World War. He was F Section's chief recruiting officer. And there was Buckmaster's very capable assistant, Vera Atkins. She quickly became the heart of F Section. In her orderly mind she stored an encyclopaedic knowledge of resources and regulations concerning the day-to-day life of an agent in the field. Vera was a perpetual source of information, and dealt closely with the agents in the final days before they went into the field.

Churchill and Buckmaster had met before, during the final phase of Churchill's training. Buckmaster had been impressed by what he had read in Churchill's training reports but made it clear that he did not have to take a mission on. F Section's operations were, as Buckmaster reminded him, to be conducted voluntarily and so Churchill could refuse, although the thought of pulling out now never entered his mind.

The two then briefly discussed Churchill's proposed mission, called Operation WILLOW. Using the codename RAOUL, Churchill was to be flown to the south of France in a Westland Lysander and landed in a field to the north-west of Montpellier. He was to take with him a large sum of money – 2 million French francs (equivalent to £10,000 then and at least £600,000 today) – and then go to Lyon, Cannes, and Marseille.

In each city he was to meet SOE's local organiser to discuss and try to rectify any troubles, issue them London's new directives, distribute the money amongst them and make financial arrangements for the future. Churchill was also to arrange for the release of arrested members of the French Resistance. Then, having done all of that, he was to make his way back to Britain via Spain, by crossing the Pyrenees on foot.

It all sounded straightforward enough. To Churchill, it was a case of slipping quietly into France, meeting a few people, issuing them directives and handing out the money, and then getting out. If all went well, the Vichy authorities would not even know he had been there. As for when he would go, Churchill was warned to be ready to leave London in two days, although the actual night of departure would not be known until the day itself. But when the call did come, he would be taken by car from Orchard Court with one of Buckmaster's staff to STS 61 (Audley End, a country house near Saffron Walden in Essex) where he would wait until it was time to go. He would then be driven the twenty miles to RAF Newmarket in Suffolk, from where he would take off under the cover of darkness at 6 p.m., and he could expect to be in France by around 10 p.m.

After leaving Buckmaster's office, Churchill went through the detail with de Guélis. Although the idea had sounded simple enough, the mission was far more complex than it first appeared and, again, there was much to learn. Churchill's instructions were written in a brief for him to read and digest, although he could not take the written brief with him. Everything would have to be learned and committed to memory.

Under the title of SUMMARY OF INSTRUCTIONS GIVEN TO LT CHURCHILL BEFORE HIS DEPARTURE, his mission is recorded on file, with Para A relating to instructions for Lyon, Para B for Cannes, C for Marseille, D for leaving France, and E for when he first landed in France. Para A is included here to give an idea of the content:

> 1. When he reaches (a), he is to go to the Hôtel de Verdun near the station. He should then get into touch with V. H. at the Grand Nouvel Hôtel, introducing himself by the Marcel formula, and ask her to get in touch with JULES. If V. H. is not there, leave her a note bringing into the text '*nouvelles de Marie*'. Should V. H. not be able to contact JULES, Churchill should write to Fox, at the Credit Lyonnais, bringing in the words '*Nouvelles de Véronique*'.

2. When Churchill sees JULES, he should immediately supply him with news of his wife, and money. Then give him the new neutral Portuguese post-box, inform him that W/T communications have at present broken down, and give him any new passwords, names, etc., to pass on to any men working under him. He is to tell JULES to continue normally with his activities, and bring back any messages or information of use.
3. JULES should be told to send a courier to CLAUDE's cut-out address, note to be handed personally to the cut-out, addressed to M. Etienne, containing a request for news and asking him to fix a reception committee for the end of this month. The courier will take some money to be handed over.
4. JULES should be told that another W/T man will get in touch with him. If the W/T man does not show up, JULES should tell ETIENNE (representing CLAUDE or LUCAS) to expect a visitor.

Paragraphs B and C contained similar orders for Churchill on what to do on reaching Cannes and Marseille respectively. Paragraph E (instructions on landing in France) was short and essentially told Churchill to go straight to Lyon, while Paragraph D, which covered his exit, was more complex:

1. Churchill was then given instructions for getting out through Spain, either by contacting a man in (c) or by another route known to us.
2. If he cannot get satisfaction from the man in (c), he should go to (d) [identified elsewhere as Perpignan] and see a woman [named elsewhere as Madame Dasque] owning a small shop at 36 Chemin des Eaux Vives. To contact her, Churchill must say he is '*en voyage*', she will ask '*d'où venez-vous?*' and Churchill must reply '*de Suisse*'. She will then ask '*où allez-vous*', the reply to which is '*aux Etats-Unis*'. Tell her that he would like to see M. Edouard, and if she turns him down flatly, he is to leave immediately, as this will mean something is wrong.
3. He is to use the same procedure if he is in (f) [Toulouse] or (g) [Pau], asking for different people in each town. Any of

these people will put him in touch with M. Edouard whom Churchill will contact with a pre-arranged password.

4. To contact the man in (c) he will have to introduce himself as a friend of F.L.1 [Jacques de Guélis]. He should tell this man that it is extremely urgent for him to get to Barcelona within an agreed space of time, and this man's brother will then help Churchill to do this, getting him Spanish money, etc.
5. Churchill has been shown by F.L.1 the route which he used to escape from Spain. He has studied this in detail on the map and is only to use it in extremis if the other two concrete methods indicated to him should have broken down.
6. Once he has reached Barcelona he will have to contact the Consulate-General where he will get full protection. He is to use a special contacting password, either 'phoning or calling in person.

Churchill was also given instructions on how to keep in touch with London, the use of coded messages, what to do if he got into difficulties, and a list of hotels in Cannes, Marseille, Nice, Perpignan and Montpellier where it was considered safe for him to stay. He was also given instructions on what to do with the 2 million French francs he would be taking with him, specifically that Frs. 500,000 was reserved for an agent codenamed ETIENNE and Frs. 500,000 reserved for JULES, although if he thought it advisable, rather than give the full amount to JULES he could split the latter as Frs. 300,000 to JULES and Frs. 200,000 to another agent known as OLIVE. The rest of the money was to be used for helping prisoners as and when they were released, and once that side of business had been taken care of then the remaining money could be managed as Churchill thought best.

It was now a matter of being patient and waiting for the right weather and an aircraft to become available. But the aircraft of No. 138 (Special Duties) Squadron at Newmarket were in high demand. Most were converted bombers, adapted for the dropping of agents and supplies, and only three Lysanders were available at that time. The situation was not helped during the week that Churchill was due to go when a Lysander drop-off in Belgium resulted in the pilot being shot and the aircraft damaged. Not only that, but the weather was bad, and the squadron was in the process of moving to Stradishall, all of which resulted in Churchill's drop being further delayed and then finally cancelled.

Churchill's mission could not wait any longer and so arrangements were hastily made for him to go by sea. He would first travel to Gibraltar, from where he would be dropped by submarine at a suitable location along the Côte d'Azur. Then, under the cover of darkness, he would paddle ashore in a small lightweight foldable canoe, known as a folbot. It was to be F Section's first insertion along the coastline by submarine and something of a trial, but if successful it could be done again, assuming, of course, a submarine could be made available.

The revised plan meant juggling Churchill's itinerary once in France, but that was easily done. By 15 December, arrangements had been made and it was finally time to go. He was to set sail for Gibraltar from Glasgow the following night, which meant he would be leaving London that evening on the overnight train.

At Orchard Court, Churchill went through his mission one final time, before thoroughly checking the documents he had been given. There was his new identity card in the name of Pierre Chauvet and a demobilisation certificate from the French Army. All that was needed was Churchill's thumb prints to authenticate the card as belonging to him. Should he be stopped by the authorities, the documents would hopefully keep him out of any trouble. And with that, Buckmaster wished Churchill good luck and bon voyage.

Churchill then discussed with de Guélis how F Section could follow his progress once he was in France. He was to send a series of telegrams to different addresses in Britain. The first was to be sent from Antibes soon after he arrived, in which he was to talk about the health of an aunt. The second telegram was to be sent from Lyon and mention his sister, and the third was to be sent from Marseille and mention a fictitious brother. London would then warn the Consulate in Barcelona that Churchill was on his way there.

It was midday by the time Churchill left Orchard Court. The sun was shining and as he had nothing to do for the next couple of hours he decided to stroll down to Hyde Park. Walking along the Serpentine on such a beautiful and crisp December day was a real pleasure, although the heavy anti-aircraft guns and the row of Nissen huts lining the eastern edge of the park were harsh reminders of war. He then caught a bus back to his apartment. It was time to check through his clothes and other small items that he was to take with him. Everything fitted neatly into a single suitcase, which he could easily carry, and every item was French – his shirts, sweater, trousers, underwear, socks, pyjamas, toothbrush, razor, and cigarettes. He then placed a small attaché case inside the suitcase; this was for any small items he needed to take with him. Finally, he checked the contents of his wallet – his French identity card, his demobilisation certificate, his French money, a part-used book of tram tickets, and an old photograph of an unknown French couple who, if asked, were his parents. He then checked through the items that he would need before he got to France – his British money, War Office identity card, and train ticket to Glasgow. Any British items that he still had on him before sailing for France would have to be left in Gibraltar. Nothing could be left to chance.

Later that afternoon, Churchill returned to Orchard Court to pick up the money belt he was to take with him to France. He was now a French millionaire, twice over. There were still a few hours before his train was due to leave London and so he decided to go to a cinema in Leicester Square, where he settled down to the epic *Gone With The Wind*.

Finally, after three hours and forty minutes of Clark Gable, Vivien Leigh, Leslie Howard, and Olivia de Havilland, it was time for Churchill to leave. When he stepped outside the cinema it was completely dark. London was in blackout. He waved down a taxi and headed for Euston Station.

Although it was late, Churchill arrived to find the station extremely busy. He boarded the crowded Glasgow train and found his reserved seat. He looked around the dimly lit carriage. There were uniforms and ranks of all types. They were all going somewhere, but he had no idea where and he knew better than to ask. As the train pulled out of the station his thoughts turned to his mission ahead, mulling a multitude of things over and over in his mind. Churchill was on his way to France and there was no turning back.

Chapter 4
Gibraltar

The Firth of Clyde on the west coast of Scotland has the deepest coastal waters in the British Isles. Sheltered from the Atlantic Ocean by the Kintyre peninsula, the Firth was strategically important to naval operations during the Second World War, with Glasgow and the Clyde becoming one of the main entry and departure points for merchant shipping, military personnel and equipment, and for the assembly, dispatch, and control of ocean convoys.

Churchill arrived in Glasgow on the early morning of 16 December 1941. Christmas was just over a week away, not that it made any difference. There was no time to take in the festive scene. He had to get to the docks as quickly as he could, where a troopship was waiting to take him to Gibraltar.

Churchill's passage to Gibraltar was to be on board the MS *Batory*, a Polish pre-war ocean liner and the flagship of the Gdynia–America line. At just over 14,000 tons, she was the pride of the Polish maritime marine and among the country's best-known ships of all time. Named after Stefan Batory, a sixteenth-century king of Poland, she had been launched in 1935 and had spent her peacetime years sailing between Gdynia and New York. Then, following the outbreak of war, she was mobilised and had already shipped valuable Polish treasures to Canada, taken part in the evacuation of Dunkirk, and had transported much of the UK's gold reserves across the Atlantic when Britain faced the threat of invasion. Now, she was about to sail for Gibraltar.

The reception Churchill received on board from the crew was more of a frosty than a welcoming one. As the embarkation officer explained to him, their departure had been delayed for several hours because they had been told to wait for him. Churchill's mission debrief report, written on his return to Britain, reads:

> Churchill was put on the boat at Glasgow by an embarkation officer of the R.A.F. who introduced him to a Captain in the Intelligence, the two went on board, leaving Churchill high

> and dry amidships to make his own arrangements for his room, and would have left him there if he had not collared them. They took his identity card off him to send back. In fact, the whole affair was rather vague.

With Churchill finally on board, the *Batory* slipped its moorings and headed out into the Clyde. At that stage, Churchill was still Churchill, as he would be in Gibraltar. His War Office identity card was in the name of Churchill, and he would continue to wear his uniform up until the point he sailed for France. Only then would he become Pierre Chauvet.

The *Batory* was an ideal troopship for the run to Gibraltar. With a maximum speed of 18 knots, she was too fast for a convoy as merchant ships laden with stores would be much slower, and so the quicker troopships stood a better chance on their own. Sometimes troopships were given a naval escort, although in *Of Their Own Choice* Churchill makes no mention of a naval escort, and so presumably the *Batory* made the run alone.

Churchill would not be afforded the luxury of simply being a passenger. Being one of only a handful of Army officers on board he was allocated to the ship's defensive guns. These were placed at every possible position on deck to offer the *Batory* some form of defence. There were Bofors 40-mm guns, Oerlikon 20-mm cannon and a heavy 4-inch naval gun on a platform at the stern, all manned around the clock by a mix of Army and Navy gunners. Churchill was to supervise the gun crews, working a 4-hour watch cycle, starting with the 8 p.m. until midnight watch later that day. Churchill knew nothing about the different types of guns, but there were twenty separate units spread across the upper decks and so he was keen to learn about them all.

First, though, there was a mandatory lifeboat drill, after which Churchill was able to familiarise himself with his new surroundings. Dinner provided an opportunity for Churchill to meet other British officers on board who were not on duty at the time. They were a chatty and likeable bunch, and all listened respectfully to each other's story as to why they were going to Gibraltar. One, a naval commander, was to take command of a ship while another, an intelligence officer, was posted to Gibraltar for his next tour of duty. As for Churchill, he came up with a long-prepared cover story as to why he was temporarily being sent to Gibraltar, which they all seemed to accept. They all knew better than to question each story being told.

After dinner it was time for Churchill's first shift of duty. Despite it being winter, many preferred to spend their time up on deck; they felt safer there than down below. It was a cold and windy night, but he was keen to meet the gunners and he was keen to learn as much as he could about the guns. He decided to start on the sun deck, the highest point of the ship, from where he would work his way down. From the stars shining bright against what was a dark, clear sky, Churchill noticed the ship was heading north, and not south towards their destination.

The route to Gibraltar initially took the *Batory* northwards towards Iceland before she turned west out into the North Atlantic, as if heading towards Canada or the United States. She would then turn south to pass to the west of Ireland and run the gauntlet of the North Atlantic, zig-zagging all the way and maintaining best possible speed. This would make it as difficult as possible for any prowling U-boat commander wishing to prosecute an attack, and by keeping far out into the Atlantic she would hopefully avoid detection by German reconnaissance aircraft operating from bases in France. Finally, the *Batory* would turn eastwards towards the Strait of Gibraltar.

The passage to Gibraltar took seven days. When not on duty or asleep, Churchill used the time on board to rehearse in his mind the countless names, addresses and codewords he would need for his mission. Nothing could be written down and taken with him to France. Fortunately, it was a quiet trip. Everything seems to have been in their favour. The weather and sea conditions kept any hunting U-boats at bay – either that or they were more interested in the Atlantic convoys carrying supplies to Britain rather than a lone troopship heading to Gibraltar. Whatever the reasons, the *Batory* successfully completed another run.

It was early morning when the *Batory* crept into Gibraltar. Churchill gazed at the armada of warships around them. He could see an aircraft carrier, a battleship, a cruiser, and several smaller ships. Gibraltar was home to the Royal Navy's Force H, crucial for the re-supply of the fortress island of Malta, which had been under siege for eighteen months and was strategically too important to lose. The war in the Mediterranean had reached a critical point, and Malta held the key to the door of the desert war being fought in North Africa. But everything needed to fight a campaign – people, food, fuel, ammunition, medical supplies, aircraft, and spares – had to be delivered to the island in sufficient numbers, and on a regular basis.

The *Batory* dropped anchor just outside the breakwater. It was soon Churchill's turn to board the tender and leave the ship. He expected to be met ashore and hoped his stay in Gibraltar would not be very long, but things got off to a slow start as detailed in his mission debrief report:

> At Gibraltar, according to instructions, Churchill asked for Quennell, was told he was not there, after waiting four hours he was put in touch with a Lieutenant Commander who had taken Quennell's place, and he put Churchill in touch with Morris. MORRIS impressed Churchill very much as being a man of great intelligence, looks after people coming out there excellently. Churchill was put up at the Rock Hotel, and Morris helped him in every way in sending messages back here. He has working with him a man called Captain Constance, who was also very helpful and introduced him to the Admiral.

Staying at the Rock Hotel was typical for SOE. Built in the 1930s, the hotel is majestically situated near the foot of Gibraltar's famous rock and has since become a magnet for the rich and famous. Churchill was to stay there until leaving for France, and the admiral referred to in the debrief report was almost certainly Vice-Admiral Sir Frederick Edward-Collins, then Vice-Admiral Gibraltar, as the boats of the 8th Submarine Flotilla based at the Rock came under his overall command.

Given that Churchill's drop-off along the Côte d'Azur was to be the first time a Gibraltar-based submarine was used to insert an SOE agent into the south of France, the admiral understandably wanted to know more about what was going on – or at least as much as Churchill was able to discuss with him. Churchill expected the meeting to be a delicate occasion. He knew he would have to convince the admiral that his drop-off was important to the war effort and worth diverting a valuable resource from carrying essential supplies to the besieged island of Malta.

At their meeting, the admiral wasted no time in making it clear that his submarines were highly valuable assets and in great demand. Churchill's solution, though, was simple. He explained to the admiral that all he needed was a lift to a suitable drop-off point for him and his canoe. He was happy to bunk down anywhere on board and to occupy as little space as possible, and as soon as he had been dropped off the submarine could proceed to Malta with its full cargo of supplies. All he was asking was for the submarine to take a slight detour from its normal route.

It was a reasonable request and one to which the admiral agreed, but only on the understanding that the submarine would not go within five miles of the coast. Churchill would have to paddle to the shore from there. And with that, Churchill got up, saluted smartly, and left before the admiral decided to change his mind.

With the meeting over, Churchill took a stroll through the beautiful Fortress gardens before returning to the dockyard once more. There was still one more person he needed to call on – Captain 'S' on board the submarine depot ship, HMS *Maidstone.*

Captain 'S' ('S' being for submarines) was 43-year-old Captain George Voelcker, the lean and versatile Captain (S) 8th Submarine Flotilla. Voelcker was also in command of the *Maidstone,* a relatively new ship built in the late 1930s to support the increasing number of submarines operating away from the UK's home waters.

Churchill had to wait for his meeting with Voelcker to take place. In the meantime, Morris and Constance arranged for him to practise entering a canoe from the side of the ship. As expected, it was not easy. Churchill would later write:

> Have today practised entering canoe from side of ship. It requires great strength and control to descend rope and lower oneself gingerly with legs at right angles so that total weight is equally distributed.

When it was time for Churchill's meeting with Voelcker, Constance accompanied him on board the *Maidstone.* They were met by one of the ship's officers and escorted down a steep gangway and along the deck to the captain's quarters near the stern.

Voelcker's greeting was a warm and pleasant one. He even recognised Churchill from their previous meeting before the war, some six years or so before, when Voelcker had visited Oran while in command of a submarine and Churchill had been working at the British Consulate. Churchill also remembered their meeting. It was a happy coincidence and it bade well for getting his mission off to a good start.

Over a glass of sherry, Voelcker explained he would be providing a submarine, HMS *P.36.* They then talked about what Churchill had discussed with the admiral, although Voelcker insisted the submarine would drop him off closer to the French coast than the five miles the admiral had agreed; something more like a couple of miles should be possible. Not only that, but there was also a period of no moon coming up and so it would be very dark, making conditions ideal for such a landing. And with that Voelcker sent for the captain of the *P.36*.

It did not take long for 28-year-old Lieutenant Harry Edmonds to arrive. He was wearing the ribbon of the Distinguished Service Cross, which he had been awarded the previous year, and after brief introductions, Voelcker told Edmonds that Churchill would be going with him on his next trip. It was only then that Churchill found out there would be other passengers on board the submarine, firstly a Czech wireless operator called Schutz, but known as FELIX, who was to be landed somewhere near Perpignan. There would also be at least two other passengers travelling on to Malta.

They moved across to a table where a naval chart was laid out. It covered the French coastline between St Raphaël and Cannes. Churchill was asked to point out where he would like to be dropped off. It was a stretch of the coastline Churchill knew well from his days before the war. Studying the chart in more detail, he identified the Pointe de l'Esquillon near Théoule-sur-Mer, at the western end of the Bay of Cannes. He knew of a tiny bay there, near the Hôtel St Christophe Mirano d'Estorelle, where there was a suitable landing spot hidden from the coast road by a wall. It was about 20 km to the west of Cannes. He had been there before the war and used to dive from the rocks into the sea. There were even steps out of the water, and the rocks would make it easy to dispose of his canoe. He could even spend his first night at the hotel. That, Churchill said, would be a perfect spot for him to land.

As for the plan to drop Schutz, Churchill's mission report reads:

> It was arranged with Captain Volcker of the Depot Ship and Captain Constance and Churchill that this other agent should be landed near Perpignan, that in case of bad weather he should be given the chance of landing on the night scheduled and if not successful, on the following night. That if on the following night the weather was unfavourable, he should be sent straight through to Malta, in order to give Churchill every chance of landing near Antibes, for which Churchill was to be given three operational days, depending on the weather.

With a plan in place and the landing spot agreed, Voelcker insisted Churchill dine with him that evening, after which he could spend the night in one of the cabins on board. He would arrange for Churchill's belongings to be brought across to the ship, including the suitcase containing the money belt with the 2 million francs. It was, after all, New Year's Eve, and so it was only right that Churchill did not spend the evening alone. Besides, there was no knowing what 1942 had in store – for any of them.

Churchill's meeting with Voelcker had been a success, but it was already clear from his discussions with senior naval officers in Gibraltar that securing a submarine for the dropping of agents was never going to be easy. Before leaving for France, Churchill took the opportunity to write to Jacques de Guélis back in London. Dated 31 December 1941, part of the letter reads:

> My transport is leaving on the night of January 1st and the senior Naval Captain has been obliged to take another man of my sort from another organisation. There will also be two passengers. When you consider that it will take five days to drop the first man with 24 hours' grace for very probable bad weather, and that from there to my spot near OLIVE requires two more days with 48 hours' grace for the same reason, it is quite possible that I shall have been in a confined space without a bed for anything up to ten days. If I do not get claustrophobia after this lot, I never will. Although the naval authorities have been extremely helpful, it is quite obvious that they consider Mediterranean straffing of far greater importance to the balance sheet of our war effort than playing at taxis for us. I think you will agree at home that there is a great deal in what they say.

The letter concludes:

> You will note that this mode of transport is quite beyond the pale. I had seriously contemplated suggesting returning by plane and starting again, but owing to bad weather this time of year and further risks of poor moons, I gave up the idea. M [Morris] and Capt C [Constance] and their staff have been most helpful to me. Do not anticipate my arrival telegram until January 10th.

With the letter written and sent, Churchill enjoyed a wonderful evening dining on board the *Maidstone*, although he declined the offer to see in the new year with the rest of the crew. He needed a clear head as he would be leaving Gibraltar the following day.

Chapter 5
Aboard HMS *P.36*

Churchill woke early the following morning. It was New Year's Day. The suitcase containing the money and his belongings had arrived as promised the previous evening and he was now dressed in his French civilian clothes. He was excited at the thought of what might lie ahead, but he was also wondering about what it would be like on board *P.36*. How would he feel when they closed the hatch? He had never been underwater in a submarine before. In fact, he knew very little about them. He did know, though, that he would have to overcome any fear, like he had always done when placed in a new and uncomfortable situation. Being on a submarine was presumably no worse than, say, dropping from a tethered balloon. But there was no point thinking about that now. He had things to do. Everything connected to his British way of life had to be packed away in a case and left in the cabin. Then, at 6 a.m., there was a knock on his door. It was Edmonds. It was time to go.

It was cold and dark outside. Edmonds led them down to the lower deck and along a gangway to where four submarines were waiting. Being the next to depart, *P.36* was the outermost of the four and so they had to cross the decks of the others to get on board. Churchill followed Edmonds up the outside of the bridge, carefully placing each foot in the small recesses as he went, before lowering himself through the hatch of the conning-tower.

HMS *P.36* was a new U-class submarine. Built by Vickers Armstrong at Barrow-in-Furness and launched only eight months before, she had been commissioned in September 1941 and had just returned from a patrol in the Bay of Biscay, during which she had attacked a German U-boat near Belle Isle off the coast of Brittany. Churchill was given a brief explanation of the layout of the control room and shown the area allocated to him – on top of a pile of kit bags. It was all that Edmonds could offer. The submarine was full. There was no space anywhere. It seemed like there were pipes everywhere, and where there were no pipes there would be something else.

Edmonds then led him down a narrow corridor to the small wardroom where Churchill was introduced to the other officers on board. Like him, three were hitching a ride, but in their case they were new submariners straight out of training school and on their way to Malta to join their own boats.

Under the cover of darkness, *P.36* slipped quietly out of Gibraltar and into the Mediterranean. As it would soon be getting light the crew prepared to dive to avoid anyone reporting the submarine's departure. The diving routine was a hive of activity. From his vantage point on top of the kit bags, Churchill watched the crew as they went back and forth in response to incomprehensible commands. There was nothing else he could do. And just as soon as *P.36* was safely down, the control room quickly emptied, leaving only a handful of the crew at their stations.

As the day went on different crew members replaced those who had been on watch from the start. It would then be their turn to rest, and so it went on. Every now and then the officer of the watch would scan the horizon through the periscope. There was generally little sound, other than a constant buzzing noise, and little or no sensation of them moving through the water.

For the next few days life settled into a routine as *P.36* crawled along just beneath the waves. Breakfast was at 10 a.m. and an evening meal was taken at 8 p.m. Daylight and sunshine were never seen, except by those lucky enough to use the periscope. The daily pattern was to dive at dawn and surface at dusk, and only during the hours of darkness could the crew smoke and stretch their legs over a tot of rum.

The submarine's batteries were recharged at night. With its batteries fully charged *P.36* could stay submerged for up to twenty hours. Fortunately, though, it was winter and so each twenty-four-hour period was evenly split, with half of the time submerged and the other half spent on the surface. Night was always welcome. Powered by its two diesel engines the submarine could make better speed, up to a maximum of eleven knots, and with the top hatch open the cool and salty night air was a pleasure to breathe. Churchill was allowed up top and was always grateful for the fresh air while talking to the duty officer and lookouts. However, when beneath the surface, progress was slow as the silent electric motors meant *P.36* could average little more than a few knots.

Churchill quickly adapted to his new surroundings and was full of admiration for the crew and how they lived on board. He played bridge with the officers and drank cocoa with the petty officers, although much of his time was spent asleep. Not only did it pass the time, but it also meant he kept out of the way. Conversation was minimal when the boat was submerged, but there was fun, wit and humour on board. Morale seemed to be good, but he did find carrying out everyday activities – such as eating, washing, brushing teeth, and going to the toilet – like nothing he had ever experienced before. And, like the crew, he soon learnt to give up on trying to shave. He even found that he was starting to enjoy the way of life.

Unfortunately for the Czech wireless operator, Schutz, the weather was not suitable for him to go ashore at his planned dropping-off point near Perpignan. He would have to wait his turn, as detailed in Churchill's mission debrief report:

> As the weather at Perpignan was unfavourable, FELIX was unable to land, and since he seemed so keen to carry out his operation, Captain Edmunds of *P.36* and Churchill decided that every effort should be made to put him off near where Churchill was to land. When they reached the section of the Côte d'Azur which Churchill knew, he pointed out a little bay to Captain Edmunds most suitable for the landing of FELIX with his radio set. It was arranged that Churchill should land some three kilometres further along, at the Hôtel St Christophe, Mirano d'Estorelle, Alpes Maritimes, and that an hour after leaving the submarine, FELIX should be taken back three kilometres and landed at the prearranged spot.

Finally, after nine days at sea, *P.36* approached Churchill's drop-off point. It was time to make his final preparations. He had a shave and got dressed ready for his arrival in France, took a couple of Benzedrine tablets to help him keep awake, and then checked his documents and the contents of his small case for the last time.

Through the periscope Edmonds identified a headland. Churchill also looked to see where they were. They were in the right place, but Edmonds was keen to get Churchill as close to land as he possibly could. The thought of him trying to paddle ashore from two miles out, with a strong current and in a choppy sea, was too much to ask. Churchill could end up landing miles away from his intended spot or, worse still, not make land at all.

The two men had got to know each other well during the past nine days. Churchill learned that Edmonds had been born in British Guiana on Christmas Day 1913. He had joined the Navy before the war and at the outbreak of hostilities had been living in Kent while serving in HMS *Sunfish*, an S-class submarine. He had married Phyllis, who came from Edinburgh, just before the announcement of his DSC, which he had earned during an attack on a U-boat and the sinking of two German merchant ships while in Norwegian waters. There was clearly a mutual respect for what each other did. Although Churchill had coped well with being under the surface, there was no way he wanted to spend the rest of the war operating in that way. Equally, as far as Edmonds was concerned, the thought of wandering around France and often having to work alone, never knowing who to trust, did not appeal.

With the submarine still far enough out to sea for it not to be seen or heard from land, *P.36* surfaced once more. It was very dark, perfect for the landing, and it was still early evening. Churchill had the whole night ahead of him. Like everything that had gone before as far as the planning was concerned, the drop-off point and timing were perfect.

Edmonds slowly took *P.36* towards the shore. From the bridge he and Churchill had a spectacular view of the Alps in the distance, the peaks silhouetted against the night sky. They could see the lights of the Hôtel St Christophe, close to where Churchill planned to go ashore. Finally, when they were as close to the shore as they dared, just half a mile or so from Churchill's landing point, the submarine came to a stop. It was time to go.

The two men said their farewell. Churchill climbed over the ledge of the bridge and carefully made his way down the outside of the conning tower to the hull of the submarine. His mission debrief report describes the conditions:

> There was a big swell, the boat was taken out of its bag, the suitcase was put under the front seat, well '*calle*', Churchill climbed down a rope at right angles and got into the boat, was shoved off and rowed away.

Churchill started paddling as quickly as he could to get away from the submarine, before slowing down to maintain a sustainable rate, all the time focusing on making sure he kept heading towards the Alps. But with the swell of the sea and occasional loss of sight of the shore, he felt an enormous sense of being alone. At times it was as much as he could do to stay upright. He turned round to look back towards the submarine, more out of curiosity to see what it looked like against the night sky, but he could not see it at all. Either he had gone so far already, and it had been lost in the dark, or it was no longer there.

As Churchill got closer to the shore, he could see the waves breaking over the rocks. He faced a difficult landing, although the sound of the waves would mask any noise he might make. But as he got closer to the rocks, he lost sight of the hotel's lights. He realised he must have drifted and was now probably a mile or so further to the west than where he wanted to be. Rather than be left with an even longer walk than originally planned, he headed towards the other side of the bay. Soon he could see the waves rolling in on a sandy beach and from there he found the inlet that would take him to the hotel's private cove. Churchill had arrived. All he needed to do now was to find the steps out of the water, assuming they were still there, and then remove any evidence of him having been there at all.

The steps out of the water were still there and although there was quite a swell, Churchill eventually made it to the rocks. He was exhausted, but there was just one more thing he had to do before moving on – to get rid of his canoe. However, that was not as easy as he had hoped, as his mission debrief report explains:

> After resting for a bit, Churchill went down to the canoe and gashed the canvass at the bottom in three or four places, tipped it up, and pushed it under the water having taken the air chambers out, and after all this, the boat did not sink. Churchill eventually had to leave it turned upside down to float into the little cove, having done everything he could to make it look as if it had been capsized and the inmate drowned.

There was nothing more Churchill could do. Besides, he would soon be moving on. The submarine, meanwhile, had remained about half a mile out to sea. Edmonds kept it there for as long as he could until he was certain Churchill had made it safely ashore. Sadly, though, Churchill would not see *P.36* or Edmonds again. *P.36* was sunk in Malta harbour three months later during an enemy air raid. Edmonds was ashore at the time and so he was transferred to another submarine, HMS *Olympus*, but just a month later, on 8 May, the *Olympus* hit a mine off Malta and sank. She had just left for Gibraltar and was fully laden with personnel. Only nine of the ninety-eight on board survived. One of those lost at sea was Lieutenant Harry Noel Edmonds, DSC. His body was never found, and his is one of the 24,654 names commemorated on the Portsmouth Naval Memorial.

Chapter 6

Making Contact

As he was sitting on the rocks, taking in the cool night air, Churchill's memories of happy and carefree days before the war at that same spot came flooding back. He looked at his watch. It was nearly 10 p.m. It had taken him two hours to get ashore. It had been extremely hard work, but it would soon be time to move on. He had decided against trying to stay overnight at the hotel just in case his canoe was found the following morning. Instead, he would walk to Cannes.

He knew of a large villa there, which before the war had been owned by English friends. They had long left, but their gardener and his wife were almost certainly still living at one of the small cottages. They could be trusted and so he hoped to be able to stay there until he went on to Antibes.

Before leaving the rocks there was time for a quick coffee from his flask and to change into some dry clothes. Churchill then made his way to the road and headed off up a long, winding hill. He knew the road well from before the war. Little seemed to have changed and there was nothing too unusual in what he was doing. He was, after all, like any other Frenchman going about his business, although it was starting to get late.

After two hours, Churchill reached a sharp hairpin in the road. He was approaching the village of Théoule-sur-Mer. The overnight curfew was between the hours of 11 p.m. and 5 a.m. and so it would already be in force. He still had to pass through the village and did not want to push his luck by being seen wandering along the road late at night. He saw a gate leading to a house and settled beneath some trees where he could not be seen. He would spend the night there.

It was a cool but otherwise calm night. Churchill wrapped himself in his raincoat as best he could and settled down, using his case as a pillow, to try and get some sleep. But it did not work. Hours later he was still awake, and it was getting colder by the minute. Churchill's mission debrief report records the moment:

> A storm came up at about 2 a.m., which started off with lightning and hail. It was very cold and Churchill decided that owing to the freak conditions, the police would probably not be out, so chanced walking through the village, and in fact there was no one about.

The hailstones turned to snow, but that was not a bad thing. It would keep people inside. Churchill had started to warm up, but rather than follow the coast road all the way to Cannes, which passed alongside the main airfield and would most likely be patrolled, he decided to take a detour inland to pass along its northern side. It would take him further out of his way, but at least it should be safe.

Daylight came. The snow turned into rain. Churchill was soaked, but still he plodded on. Having got clear of the airfield and past the district of La Bocca, he returned to the coast road once more. No one had challenged him so far, and with it being light again he felt more at ease as there were now more people about. He decided to make his way through the town centre where he could blend into the crowd. It also gave him the opportunity to see what life was like in southern France in January 1942. The food shops were near empty and some of the luxury shops abandoned. There were queues for this and queues for that. Some of the streets were near deserted, although he noticed there were still Vichy police about. An area once bustling with foreign vehicles and tourists now presented a quite different scene. The hotels were empty, there were very few cars about because of the shortage of petrol, and people seemed quiet and subdued. In Churchill's own words 'the spirit of Cannes had sunk'.

It was mid-morning by the time Churchill reached the district of La Californie. He found the cottage where he hoped to stay. An old man was stood there. It was the gardener, Joseph. Rather than be seen talking out in the open, the two men went inside. Churchill explained that he was looking for somewhere to rest for a while and to dry his clothes before moving on, but Joseph was clearly uncomfortable about him staying there as he knew the consequences if caught.

It was not the welcome Churchill had expected. It made him wonder if all receptions were going to be the same, but any concerns he might have had were quickly put aside when Joseph's wife, Francine, appeared and gave him the biggest hug. She was so pleased to see him again and did not mind him staying one bit. The cottage next door was vacant and so she made up a bed in there and, as Francine explained, she would always leave a key for the empty cottage should Churchill ever need somewhere to stay, and there was a motorboat available should he need to get away.

Later that afternoon, Churchill went on his way. As he walked down to the Rue d'Antibes he felt refreshed. He had slept, been fed, and he was dry, and he was pleased to have been able to leave some francs from his money-belt as a way of thanking Francine for what she had done. He was planning to catch a bus for the last part of his journey, but having watched one after another go past, each full to the brim, he decided to walk to the terminus where he would stand a better chance.

Churchill eventually boarded a bus, but by the time it pulled into the ancient coastal town of Antibes it was early evening and too late for him to make his first contact with the doctor known as PHILIPPE. It would certainly arouse suspicion if he was to turn up at his surgery out of hours. Instead, Churchill went straight to the Nouvel Hôtel. It was a small and rather unattractive place just off the main square. His room was small and cold, and there was no heating, but the hotel was quiet enough not to attract any unwanted attention.

It did not take Churchill long the following morning to walk to the Boulevard Maréchal Foch. He found the doctor's surgery at number 31 easily enough. The surgery was also PHILIPPE's home. A maid answered the door. She was Polish but spoke perfect French. She explained to Churchill that the doctor was not there, but he would be back after lunch.

Churchill left a note in French, underlining four letters of the name Jacques, and took a stroll down towards the sea. It gave him an opportunity to see if there was a suitable landing place there should he ever return by sea, which there was. There were low-lying rocks and a set of steps leading up from the shore. It was perfect, he thought, and would save a long journey along the coast like he had just endured.

It was soon time to return to the surgery. The man Churchill had been sent to meet was 46-year-old Dr Élie Lévy, a middle-aged Jewish physician. After serving in the First World War, he had studied medicine and settled in Antibes with his wife and two daughters. Lévy had been recruited the previous summer by de Guélis and arrests elsewhere meant he was now one of just a handful of SOE contacts still operating in the south of France.

It was a crucial time for SOE and Lévy was a vital link, his surgery having become an important reception centre for agents sent to the south of France. He had also helped another SOE agent set up an embryonic circuit called URCHIN (also known as OLIVE URCHIN), one of only a handful of SOE circuits operating in France at that time.

The agent Lévy had helped was 38-year-old Francis Basin, codenamed OLIVE, who had returned to France the previous September. He had been dropped with three others on a beach near Perpignan from HMS *Fidelity*, a clandestine vessel posing as a Spanish and Portuguese freighter. Basin had been sent to Cannes to establish a link with a man called André Girard (codename CARTE), who was setting up his own network of resistance groups in Aix, Cannes and Nice. Basin was immediately arrested at his hotel for being a 'suspicious' person but was not held for very long. He had then found Lévy and together they established the circuit.

Churchill knew of Basin, of course, and had hoped to see him during his brief visit to France, but, as Lévy explained, Basin was not in Cannes at the time. Churchill still hoped to meet up with him before returning to Britain, but for now that would have to wait. Lévy then produced a typed sheet containing his latest report for London. He was about to send it by the normal courier route through Spain and Portugal, but Lévy thought it a good opportunity to show it to Churchill first.

The report was much as Churchill had expected. The group needed money to keep it going and a trained wireless operator; the only way of communicating with London was by courier, which was always risky and slow. For urgent messages there was an occasional motor launch that could be called upon, which connected Marseille with Gibraltar, from where a message could be sent to London, but it was not always available.

While Churchill could not instantly provide a trained wireless operator, he was able to produce some money and gave Lévy 400,000 francs to keep the OLIVE network going. The first part of his mission was effectively done, and so Churchill wrote a telegram – ANNABELLE QUITE RECOVERED AND SENDS LOVE AND KISSES – and handed it to Lévy, asking for it to be sent to one of his British addresses as soon as possible.

Lévy also arranged for Churchill to meet André Girard, who was in fact a patriotic painter by profession who lived nearby. Girard's contacts reportedly spread far and wide across the Vichy south, as well as into the Occupied Zone, and included important links with senior French officials. Girard also boasted that he had thousands of trained soldiers on hand and an effective intelligence network capable of transmitting across Europe.

As far as F Section was concerned, Girard potentially had a ready-made army in the making; all he would need, it seemed, was money and weapons. Lévy also introduced Churchill to a tall, bearded man called BERNARD. This was 42-year-old Baron Emmanuel d'Astier de la Vigerie, a mercurial left-wing poet and journalist, and one of the founders of an early resistance group in the Unoccupied Zone that grew to become known as LIBÉRATION-SUD (Liberation South). In its early days the group had produced an underground newspaper and distributed thousands of propaganda leaflets, but resistance had now progressed to acts of sabotage against the railways, one recent example being at the station in Cannes.

Churchill's mission debrief report included his own assessment of those he met while in Antibes, and the groups they were involved with. Under the title *Groupes de Resistance*, the report includes:

> Levy's and OLIVE's organisations are now quite separate. Levy has a great many men in his organisation who produce military and political information. It is probably correct to say that he has given up sabotage to OLIVE. They both work together very well.
>
> OLIVE's seventeen cells have five or six people in each. They are under the direct control of OLIVE, and getting bigger and bigger, spread over the area of Antibes/Cannes/Nice, and a totally new organisation is being arranged in Marseille. OLIVE has covered the whole of the Riviera. There are undoubtedly many other organisations in being without our knowledge. It was by chance more than anything that our men had come across those they knew of.
>
> D'Astier – knows addresses for people arriving in France, where they can be put up. D'Astier can be contacted through Levy. Churchill believes d'Astier to be a newspaper man, has his own political views. He is a younger brother of the general. He will obviously expect to fit into the political picture after the war. Is about 39 years old, has been in the Navy, submarines, and is a very fine figurehead for the movement, good-looking, tall, etc. He is a very well-known character and is therefore

> always liable to be picked up. His brother has already been picked up.
>
> Girard – an artist and well-known painter, is the '*eminence grise*' of the Groupes de Resistance. He is a man of absolutely no political ambitions, does not wish his work for France to be recognised after the war, only wishes to return to his pictures. He is not a man who takes money easily, and in fact feels insulted if offered something to cover expenditure. He is not a figurehead himself, but knows everyone worth knowing in France, and has many people who will work for France for the love of it and nothing else. They will do anything to expel the Germans from France. Girard lives 150 yards from PHILIPPE's house, is a first-class man. He has such influential friends as the secretary to Pétain, who can send full reports of meetings with those such as Goering, etc. . . . Girard has been of immense value to OLIVE, giving him a perfect picture of the political situation, and helping him to meet people of interest in Marseille, Périgueux, Nimes, Cannes, Nice. We can have complete confidence in him. If there is something to be done, it is done quickly and efficiently, whereas d'Astier is more of a dreamer. D'Astier directs LIBERATION in Unoccupied France.
>
> LIBERATION – appears to be alright.

In the report, Churchill also offered a word of warning when it came to matters of security, although he was more positive when commenting on their political views:

> The security of these three groups is not good, they have no imagination for tricks to show things are all right or dangerous and so forth. They get caught easily as a consequence . . . The groups do excellent work and have a tremendous organisation behind them. They are agitating very strongly for cooperation with us . . . With regard to their attitude towards de Gaulle, they are obviously pro-de Gaulle and pro-English in a way, but first of all pro-France, and they are afraid that after the war the British will insist on having a finger in the pie there, whereas they wish to be left to their own devices, have their own quarrels and troubles and overcome them without outside interference, and work out their own internal policy.

> They very definitely want to work with the British and have directives from Great Britain, even though some are 100% patriotic Frenchmen, they give all their own money to further the cause. They must be given financial aid from here.

Churchill was next off to Lyon. D'Astier was heading that way too, and so suggested they travel together, although they would have to board the train separately. There was a night train leaving Cannes later that evening.

Having bid farewell to his hosts, Churchill made his way to the station. The Lévy family had left a lasting impression on him. He arrived to find the Gare de Cannes busy. With the Germans occupying the north of the country, many French people had fled south to the Unoccupied Zone and with there being few cars and buses about, it was to the railway network they turned to travel between the main cities and towns.

A busy railway station was good. It meant Churchill could easily blend into the crowd and he did not have long to wait before boarding the train. It was hot and stuffy inside and the carriages were overcrowded, but he found d'Astier easily enough at their agreed meeting point and made their way to the seats they had reserved. Although their compartment was packed, they were able to converse quietly against the background noise.

When the train reached Marseille there was a break in the journey of half an hour. As there were no further stops until they reached Lyon, they stepped off the train on to the crowded platform and made their way to the buffet for a drink. Churchill also used the break to speak to the attendant in the sleeping carriage to see if there were any empty bunks. It was a long way to Lyon, and he did not fancy spending several more hours in the crowded compartment. Fortunately, there had been a late cancellation and 400 francs later Churchill and d'Astier were settled for the night.

The city of Lyon is in east-central France, some 480 km south of Paris and 320 km north of Marseille, and lies at the confluence of two large rivers, the Rhône and the Saône. As France's third most populous city, and with the main rail line connecting Paris and Marseille passing through its centre, Lyon was always a place of strategic importance during the Second World War. For those who could neither live with nor collaborate with the Germans, it had become somewhere to gravitate to, and, as the biggest 'free' city in the Vichy south, Lyon soon became the hub of resistance activities in the Unoccupied Zone.

By and large, the Lyonnais were behind the French Resistance but for the Vichy authorities Lyon was a hornets' nest. The size of the city, with its network of narrow streets and interconnecting passageways, derelict buildings, and low standard apartment blocks where many people lived, all made Lyon an ideal refuge for anyone seeking anonymity, including those working for SOE. By January 1942 there was one established circuit, HECKLER, in and around Lyon, while another, SPRUCE, was in its embryonic stage, but the increase in resistance activity meant that Lyon had become heavily policed, with frequent swoops on buildings and regular searches on the streets.

And so, it was against this backdrop that Churchill arrived in Lyon. It was just starting to get light on what was a cold winter's morning when the train pulled into the Gare de Lyon-Perrache. Churchill and d'Astier split up to avoid passing through the exit barrier together. They had agreed to meet up again just outside the station, failing that at a café on the Rue de la République the following day.

Churchill went first as he was unknown to the authorities. D'Astier, however, was known to the police, although he had now grown a beard to help change his appearance. There was a long queue to leave the station. As he got closer to the exit Churchill noticed three men, not in uniform and standing next to the ticket collectors, carefully scrutinising everyone going through the barrier. Although there was a slightly anxious moment when the man ahead of him in the queue was pulled to one side, Churchill calmly passed through the barrier and left the station with ease.

Slushy snow covered the ground, and it was very cold outside. Churchill met up with d'Astier once more – he had also passed through the barrier with ease – and they went to the café opposite the station for coffee, although the coffee was not particularly good and there was no milk. That was how things were in wartime France.

After coffee, d'Astier and Churchill went their separate ways. Both had things to do, but they had an agreed rendezvous point at the café on the Rue de la République. Churchill set off towards the Place Bellacour and walked along the narrow central strip banked on either side by Lyon's rivers, in search of the Hôtel de Verdun on the Rue de la Charité.

It did not take him long to find the hotel. Having registered his details at reception Churchill went up to his room. It was cold and there was no heating or hot water, and no pillow on his bed. After unpacking his things, he set off to find the Grand Nouvel Hôtel on the Rue Grolée where he was to contact a woman known to him as GERMAINE, although to the hotel staff she was Mademoiselle Brigitte Le Contre.

Churchill found the hotel easily enough, only to be told that Le Contre was out and was unlikely to return before 6 p.m. Being so cold outside, he was reluctant to spend the rest of the day wandering around the streets and so he first had a drink in the hotel and then went to the café on the Rue de la République hoping that d'Astier would be there. But he was not, and so Churchill made his way back to his hotel.

It seemed a long day just hanging around, but it gave Churchill the opportunity to check out the local trams and to read what the morning newspapers had to say. Churchill was hungry, though, and had no food tickets. It was still early in the year and so there had been no up-to-date food tickets for him to take with him to France. Indeed, those back in London were relying on him taking back as much as he could as far as food tickets and other up-to-date coupons were concerned, so that agents going into France after him could be better prepared. Hopefully, Le Contre would be able to help.

It was time to set off for her hotel once again. Churchill had waited until 6 p.m. hoping that she would have returned, but she had not. He decided to wait in the bar, but he knew little about Le Contre, other than she was an American woman in her mid-thirties, tall or maybe of medium height who walked with a slight limp, although even the limp was apparently well concealed. He knew she was working as a newspaper correspondent, but that would hardly help him identify her. Other than that, she could be blonde or brunette, or maybe she would have reddish brown hair, as she was known to change her appearance regularly.

He had little to go on, but Churchill waited, and waited. Every half an hour or so he returned to the reception desk to check if she had returned. But she had not. After a couple of hours of thinking what best to do, he decided to keep to what he had been briefed before leaving London and to leave a note for her at reception with the number of his hotel and asking her to get in touch with him as a matter of some urgency, asking if 'she had news of her sister Suzanne'.

Leaving a note was risky, but Churchill had little choice. He simply had to contact Le Contre. He had no food coupons or ration books, and she was to arrange for him to meet his main contact in Lyon, a man known as CHARLES. Besides, he wanted to make sure that Le Contre was alright.

Churchill returned to his hotel once more and was lying on his bed mulling over what to do next when the telephone rang. It was Le Contre. She had news of her sister Suzanne.

The woman known as Le Contre/GERMAINE was the legendary Virginia Hall, the first resident female agent F Section had sent into France. A talented linguist, particularly in French and German, Virginia had been educated at some of the best schools and colleges in America and Europe, but a shooting accident before the war had resulted in her losing the lower part of her left leg. When war broke out, she was living in France and briefly worked with the ambulance service in the south of the country but, horrified by the signing of the armistice, she made her way to Britain via Spain, having crossed the Pyrenees during the cold winter months, and volunteered for service with SOE. As a citizen of the United States, then not at war, Virginia knew that her American nationality would allow her relative freedom to move around France. Leaving Britain in the summer of 1941, she returned to France by a commercial route under the identity of Marie Monin, a correspondent for the *New York Post*. She began writing articles from her hotel room in Lyon, but when America entered the war in December 1941 the situation changed. Although she was living legally in the Unoccupied Zone, it was an entity within a country occupied by a nation that was now at war with the United States. Virginia no longer enjoyed immunity and faced the same risks as all resisters – arrest, imprisonment, torture, and ultimately death.

Virginia Hall had become the focal point for F Section agents operating in the Unoccupied Zone, all looking for help in different ways. Within minutes of her call, Churchill was back in the lobby at the Grand Nouvel Hôtel. At first glance, with her reddish-brown hair, Virginia gave the appearance more of a schoolmistress than the agent she was.

Virginia took Churchill to a black-market restaurant run by a trusted friend where they enjoyed a wonderful meal together. Items such as chicken, fish, coffee, potatoes, and butter were all available in Lyon with enough money and knowing the right place to go. Churchill briefed her on his cover story and why he was in Lyon, while she briefed him on how to get around the city without raising suspicion, particularly when it came to getting food. There were tickets for every essential item, such as bread and cheese, with each ticket being for a specified portion. They also talked about Virginia's own situation in Lyon. Living at the hotel had its advantages, but an increase in the number of her visitors would undoubtedly attract unnecessary attention. It would be far better if she could find somewhere else to live, where visitors could come and go without arousing suspicion.

It was late by the time the two parted company. Virginia had given Churchill enough food tickets to see him through the next couple of days and had agreed to arrange for him to meet CHARLES at a nearby café the following day.

Refreshed from a good night's sleep, Churchill was already at the café when Virginia walked in. A few minutes later they were joined by a tall, slim man whom she introduced as CHARLES, and having made the introductions, Virginia got up and left.

The man known as CHARLES was 34-year-old Georges Duboudin, also codenamed ALAIN. He had been dropped from HMS *Fidelity* with Francis Basin just a few months earlier and was now in the process of establishing SPRUCE. Churchill's arrival in Lyon had provided Duboudin with his first opportunity to tell London what he needed if his circuit was to get going. Like the other embryonic groups forming at that time, he needed money, weapons and, of course, a wireless operator, none of which came as a surprise to Churchill. It was what he had expected.

Churchill had the money belt with him, of course, but there was nothing he could do sitting in the café and so the two men took a tram to Duboudin's house in the suburbs of the city where Churchill gave him 300,000 francs. He also left 500,000 francs for an agent called LUCAS who was operating in the Occupied Zone and told Duboudin to get in touch with his associate, CLAUDE. LUCAS, real name Pierre de Vomécourt, had established AUTOGIRO as one of the first SOE circuits in France, and part of Churchill's brief had been to establish contact with him and to hand over the money for the running of his reception committees. But there was not enough time during Churchill's brief stay in France to arrange for him to cross the demarcation line, and so he decided to leave the money with Duboudin, which CLAUDE would collect the following day.

Churchill also talked with Duboudin about SPRUCE's operating area and what was required when identifying suitable drop zones for supplies and potential landing places for Lysanders. They also talked about the security forces in and around Lyon, and how railwaymen could be used to disrupt the rail network. And they talked about the food coupons currently being used, and about other ration cards required for essential items, such as tobacco and textiles, with Duboudin agreeing to provide Churchill with samples of every type of card and coupon that he could get hold of for him to take back to Britain. These could then be forged and issued to the next group of agents going into France.

It had been an extremely useful meeting, during which they were joined by Duboudin's deputy, Marcel Fox, a 25-year-old Frenchman working at the Département de la Haute Banque, attached to the Credit Lyonnais, on the Rue de la République.

Later that evening the three dined at another black-market restaurant where they were joined by Virginia and Francis Basin, who happened to be passing through Lyon on his way back to Cannes. It provided an opportunity for Churchill and Basin to meet, although such large gatherings were discouraged and went against all they had been taught during training. To have five key players together in one place was unwise, particularly if a raid took place. It would not happen again, but Churchill understood that his visit was both timely and welcome. Operating in France was dangerous work and theirs was a lonely existence; the truth was they had been struggling. His visit had given them contact with the organisation back home. Now, at last, they had the opportunity to listen to what he had to say. He was able to bring them up to date with life in wartime Britain, and his encouraging words about what SOE was doing brought them optimism and hope for the future.

As Churchill left the restaurant and stepped out into the cold night air, he felt glad to have been part of such a wonderful evening. It felt like he had been amongst friends. Professionally, though, it appears he had been left unimpressed by Duboudin and more impressed by Fox, as detailed in Churchill's mission debrief report:

> In Churchill's mind, Fox would work considerably better without ALAIN who is a bully and has a bad influence on Fox. Fox does anything that ALAIN says, up to the point of being his batman! . . . ALAIN has no sabotage groups whatsoever. Churchill told ALAIN everything he knew about sabotage

> with regard to canals, railways and electric pylons etc. V.H. [Virginia Hall] had also on several occasions had interesting and influential people come to meet ALAIN, and he just did not turn up at the rendezvous. V.H. was very disappointed in ALAIN.

The following day, however, Duboudin stuck to his word and provided Churchill with the samples of ration cards and coupons he had promised. In return, Churchill gave him a telegram to send – LEONORE NOW FLOURISHING – which was his message to London confirming the second part of his mission was complete. He was next off to Marseille for his third and final task, before it was time to start thinking about making his way home.

Chapter 7
The Exit

Spread over a large metropolitan area and with its large port, Marseille is the second most populated city in France. During the Second World War it was notorious amongst Allied agents as one of the worst places in which to operate. The Gestapo's presence was always significant and they were in a different league to the Vichy police. They did not wear uniforms and they mingled amongst the crowds, and so the Gestapo agents were not always easy to spot. They went everywhere the locals went – to the railway station and the cafés – and if someone looked or acted suspicious in any way, they were quickly whisked away.

It had been a cold four hours for Churchill before the train finally pulled into Marseille's Gare Saint-Charles. There was no heating in the carriage and like every other train connecting the major cities in the south of France, it was overcrowded, with every seat occupied and the corridors full. Snow was covering the surrounding countryside and the atmosphere on board the train glum. Few had even talked.

Virginia Hall was on the platform to meet Churchill; she had gone ahead on the earlier train. Checks were in place at the barriers, only this time there seemed to be more than the usual number of Gestapo about, and so she led him to the station buffet and out through an unmonitored exit door the Gestapo had yet to discover.

From the station they walked to the Cours Belsunce. The streets were clear of snow, but it was still bitterly cold. Virginia took Churchill to a café in one of the city's squares where Basin was waiting to meet them, having also travelled to Marseille. Basin had found a small and quiet hotel nearby, the Hôtel du Pharo, where Churchill could stay. First, though, Churchill needed to go to a factory on the Rue Montgrand, just a short walk away, to meet the manager, known in London as EMMANUEL.

EMMANUEL was Captain Meric, a former French Army officer and another friend of Jacques de Guélis. Meric was also part of Churchill's cover story as Pierre Chauvet. His task now, though, was to try and persuade Meric to use his influence to help with the release of ten resisters who were believed to be imprisoned at Fort Saint-Nicolas, down in the old port area of Marseille. If Meric was prepared to help, then he would be financially well rewarded, but it was a risky thing for Churchill to do. He had no idea how Meric would react. He might want nothing to do with the idea and throw Churchill out, or he might even turn him in.

Churchill found the factory and Meric easily enough, but the meeting was short. Meric appeared to be sympathetic to the request and seemed genuinely interested in who the ten men were. Churchill had reeled off their names – Pierre Bloch, Jack Hayes, Claude Jumeau, Jean le Harivel, Robert Lyon, Georges Bégué, Philippe Liewer, George Langelaan, François Garel, and Raymond Roche – but Meric had given no reaction to each name, except one – Robert Lyon. Churchill's mission debrief report records the meeting:

> He [Meric] was most cordial to Churchill but when he stated his business, which was in fact to ask if Meric could personally assist our arrested men, through a lawyer, he said that owing to the fact that he was well known, was a big noise in the region, and all his movements were followed, he feared that his intervention would only complicate their case. He however assured Churchill that he would make himself personally responsible for the release and care of Lyon, and also stated that he was willing to help Churchill in his cover story by stating if asked that he had known a person resembling him in the French Mission, of which he was an officer.

With the meeting over, Churchill set off to meet up again with Virginia and Basin, only this time at a different café. They had arrived ahead of Churchill, but then had a close call when a dozen gendarmes stormed into the café and asked everyone to produce their papers, after which several men were led away.

Raids like this were happening regularly as men of working age not in a reserved occupation were being rounded up and sent to Germany to work as forced labourers. Virginia and Basin left the café to warn Churchill before he arrived, and so they moved on to another café several blocks away. Churchill explained his meeting with Meric had not been a success. Virginia, as always, offered hope, suggesting that someone else could take it on, although there was clearly some confusion as to where the prisoners were being held. One of their group, Germaine Poinso-Chapuis, had discovered the arrested men were now being held in Périgueux.

With Meric unwilling to help, the task of getting the men out of prison would now fall to Basin, who would get assistance from André Girard. By then, though, the list had grown to thirteen, including another SOE agent from England, Jerry Morel, a Frenchman called Dormoy and a French woman, Madame Dunais.

Having agreed that Basin would take on the task, Churchill handed him the remaining 800,000 francs, which was to be used to secure the group's release and their passage out of France. In Churchill's mission debrief report, under the title Release of Arrested Men, it reads:

> On the release of the prisoners, arrangements will be made by GIRARD and OLIVE for their departure . . . Churchill emphasises that these men must be got out . . . When the others are released, arrangements will be made for parties of three to leave the country through the organisation known to V. H. [Virginia Hall] and moreover V. H. will let the American Vice-Consul know when they come out and he will send a telegram to Barcelona, advising the British Consul-General they would be coming, and a note should be sent from here giving all the names of these people . . .

Churchill was relieved to know the rescue was left in capable hands, and his mission was complete. He gave Virginia his third, and final, telegram to send – MARIUS FIRST TOOTH ONLY VISIBLE AS YET – to inform London he was done in France and that he would soon be on his way to Spain. London, in turn, would warn their contacts in Spain to expect him soon.

It was time for Churchill to think about making his way home. He had two options: one to cross into Spain by sea and the other to cross the Pyrenees on foot. His preference was to travel by sea. Before he left Britain, de Guélis had given him the name of a trusted friend living in Marseille, Monsieur Iche, who had a brother with a small fishing fleet at Port-Vendres, close to the Spanish border. But now Churchill discovered that the brother was lying low and his fishing boats had been sold. A sea passage was out of the question and so Churchill had little option other than to cross the Pyrenees on foot.

The Pyrenees straddle the border of France and Spain, with the mountain range extending from the Mediterranean to the Bay of Biscay and reaching a height of 3,400 metres (11,000 feet) at the peak of Aneto. To cross the Pyrenees on foot is never easy, let alone in winter, but it had been done before and it would be done many more times before the war was over. It did mean, though, that Churchill would need a trustworthy guide. Again, before leaving Britain, he had been given an address of a contact in Perpignan. There was also a hotel there where he could stay, where Basin and Duboudin had stayed when they had first landed in France.

Virginia insisted Churchill should not travel to Perpignan alone. He would almost certainly stand out on his own whereas a couple travelling together to a coastal town would not draw any unwanted attention. And with that, they planned to meet the following day.

Churchill decided to take a short cut to his hotel, through the narrow passages of the old Vieux Port, where he encountered two officials wearing the white armband of the Vichy police. They stopped him and asked for his papers, and threatened to turn him in, unless he paid his way out of trouble, which he did. A few minutes later Churchill walked free, albeit shaken and 25,000 francs lighter. It was the first time he had felt uncomfortable since arriving in France, and when he and Virginia boarded the morning train, he felt glad to be leaving Marseille behind.

Perpignan is the southernmost city in France, close to the Mediterranean coast and a short distance from the Spanish border. Back in the Second World War it was a smaller place than it is today, and far from the sound of guns, but it soon became a hive of activity as a jumping-off point for anyone crossing into Spain. Mountain guides looking for an opportunity to make a few francs roamed the streets and frequented the bars, while informers and Gestapo agents prowled the same turf in search of their prey.

Getting to Perpignan was easy enough, albeit slow because the route along the Mediterranean coast through Montpellier was a busy one. They changed trains a couple of times, but no one turned a head. A couple travelling together had been an excellent idea and it had provided Churchill with some welcome company along the way.

It was bitterly cold in Perpignan, and dark by the time the train arrived. They caught a tram to the small hotel where they were due to stay. The following morning Churchill talked openly with the proprietor. There were guides about, and trustworthy ones at that, but Churchill would first seek out his contact in Perpignan, the woman known as Madame Dasque, at her shop on the Chemin des Eaux Vives, near the River Têt.

After a little searching, Churchill found the address. It was a small shop. Inside he found Madame Dasque, but his pre-arranged and well-rehearsed opening phrase left her looking rather baffled. In his brief before leaving London, he had been warned that if Madame Dasque behaved in any way other than helpfully then he was to leave immediately as it meant something was wrong, and so Churchill left the shop.

Back at the hotel he talked things through with Virginia. They decided that a trusted guide recommended by the hotel proprietor would be the best way ahead, with a price of 5,000 francs agreed, rather than for Churchill to risk returning to the shop and walking into a trap.

For four days Churchill waited at the hotel for his guide to return from his previous trip then, with his departure imminent, Virginia decided it was time to return to Lyon. Churchill went with her to the station. It was an emotional parting. Churchill felt saddened to see her go, but both of them needed to get back to work.

Churchill returned to the hotel. Later that afternoon there was a knock on his door. It was the man who was arranging his onward journey and two other men: a Spaniard in his mid-twenties who was to be his guide, and a young Frenchman who would also be going to Spain. They would be leaving the following day and were to meet at a café near the bus terminus at 5 p.m.

The following day was spent packing clothes and food into his bag, after which Churchill paid his bill and bade farewell to the proprietor. But shortly before he was to leave the hotel, there was a knock on his door. It was the hotel porter holding a telegram. The only person who knew where Churchill was staying was Virginia. The telegram had to be urgent. Something must be up.

As Churchill suspected, the telegram was from Virginia, and it was to stop him leaving for Spain. He was instead to return to Lyon. Someone needed to see him as a matter of urgency. It was all so frustrating. Churchill was within minutes of leaving. He could have chosen to ignore the message, later claiming it must have arrived too late, but he knew it must be important enough for Virginia to call him back. Of that, he was quite sure. But the first train out of Perpignan was not until early in the morning and so there was just enough time to grab a few hours of sleep.

It was a long journey to Lyon. The first part along the coast to Narbonne went well, but then there was a delay as Churchill had to change trains. And there was another delay at Avignon, this time for a couple of hours, again because of having to change trains. After that it was a slow journey north and so it was early evening by the time Churchill arrived in Lyon. He was tired and anxious to find out what all the fuss was about.

Virginia was there to greet him at one of her chosen meeting points beside a newspaper kiosk outside the station. She explained that an organiser of a neighbouring circuit had heard that Churchill was in France and wanted to see him urgently. He would be waiting for Churchill at the railway station in Clermont-Ferrand at 5 a.m. the following day, and the only train that would get him there in time was due to leave Lyon in a matter of minutes. Two seats had been reserved on the train as Georges Duboudin would be going too.

Churchill was furious at being called back because of this, and just as everything had been put in place for him to make his way home. Virginia was full of apologies, of course, but this request had nothing to do with her. She had become involved simply because she was the only person who knew where Churchill was. But there was no time to talk about it now. Churchill and Duboudin boarded the train, and it was soon pulling out of the station.

Clermont-Ferrand is 160 km west of Lyon, and it took eleven hours for the train to get there, and so it was already past 5 a.m. when it pulled into the station. Churchill and Duboudin went straight to the station restaurant where the man was waiting to meet them.

In *Of Their Own Choice* Churchill refers to the meeting but mentions no name, other than describing the man as 'one of their biggest operators from another zone'. However, Churchill's mission debrief report suggests the meeting was with CLAUDE, the associate of Pierre de Vomécourt. The report states that Churchill met CLAUDE during his time in France and their meeting is recorded in the last paragraph before the report covers Churchill's exit from France. There is no previous mention of Churchill having met CLAUDE in Antibes, Lyon, or Marseille, and CLAUDE was a key player in the Occupied Zone as referred to in Churchill's book. The details in the report also refer to reception committees and money that Churchill had left for CLAUDE. It all fits. The report states:

> Churchill went to see CLAUDE as instructed, and was very impressed by him. CLAUDE complained bitterly of the manner in which our men were sown over France, the pilot in some cases circling overhead for an hour and a half and then dropping the man miles from the point selected, after the whole neighbourhood had been attracted. He said that the 50,000 [*sic*] francs which Churchill had brought with him was a mere drop in the bucket, as his expenses were enormous, he had to have cars for reception committees, lorries for the transport of arms, explosives, etc. petrol which he had to buy on the black market, and so on.

The report then goes on to mention a proposed Lysander pick up for LUCAS, and CLAUDE's concern about a possible German spy operating in France. As for the 50,000 francs mentioned in the report, rather than 500,000 francs, it could either be a typing error in the report or it could be correct. If correct, then it would mean the rest of the 500,000 francs that Churchill had reportedly left for CLAUDE to collect had disappeared.

It was time for Churchill to start his journey home once again. Getting back to Lyon was not a problem, but it would be a few days before he could leave for Spain. He stayed with Duboudin, while Virginia set about planning his exit from France. Having spoken to her colleagues at the American Consulate, she arranged for Churchill to be allocated a guide who would take him across the Pyrenees. All Churchill had to do was to get back to Perpignan and make his way to a café outside the station where he would be met and escorted on his way.

Virginia saw him off from Lyon as he boarded the night train. She had packed enough food and drink to last him for three days. Churchill would later be most complimentary about Virginia Hall, as recorded in his mission debrief report:

> V. H. appears to be doing excellent work, and would have been invaluable to ALAIN in every way, but she complained that he did not take advantage of her help. She however helped Churchill in every possible way, travelled for him, made contacts for him, etc. etc. She knows people in factories, railways, etc. She is in with everyone of importance, and has boundless knowledge.

By the following morning, Churchill was back in Perpignan. His mission debrief report continues:

> Churchill reached Perpignan at 11 o'clock on the 3rd February, and went to the Café Express, which is the second café on the left-hand side of the main street leaving the station. There, according to arrangements, Churchill was at a corner table with in front of him a postcard torn ¾ in half [*sic*]. He was immediately accosted by his future guide.

The guide who approached Churchill was a smartly dressed, fair-haired man in his mid–late twenties, called Garcia, a former major in the Republican Army. He told Churchill they would be leaving that evening, just as it was getting dark. A taxi would take them on the first part of their journey, after which they would walk to the frontier. They would then rest during the day before completing the journey the following night. Another man called Manuelo would be going too. He was to help Garcia take some radio equipment across the border before meeting up with his wife in Barcelona. There was no reason for Garcia to know why Churchill needed to get to Spain, but if asked he would always say he was Squadron Leader Edwards, a bomber pilot in the RAF, and that he had been shot down over France. A fee of 12,000 francs was agreed, and then it was time to rest.

Churchill slept at his hotel for much of the day. Then, at 6 p.m., the taxi arrived. Their journey took them out of Perpignan towards the small town of Le Boulou, the road gradually climbing as they went. Then as now it eventually crossed the border and continued to Figueres in Spain, but they got out well before reaching the frontier.

It took forty-five minutes to drive the 20 km towards the border. The taxi then left the main road and pulled into a quiet country lane. The three got out. It was pitch black. They were seemingly in the middle of nowhere. The group then set off in single file, with Churchill in the middle, and started their climb up through the thick brushland at the foot of the mountains. Their eyes soon adjusted to the dark, enough to keep them moving forward, and by using a small pocket compass they were able to keep heading in a southerly direction, avoiding the regular pathways and tracks. None of them said a word. Armed patrols were known to be about – Vichyites who would not think twice about trading in their fellow countrymen for a few francs.

With the thick brushland behind them, they were soon passing over fields, cutting through hedges, and crossing small streams. There was even a small village to pass silently through, while all the time heading towards the silhouette of the mountains ahead. The slope then steepened, and progress was slow. Churchill's mission debrief report reads:

> They started walking at 8 o'clock and reached a small farm at midnight, 500 yards from the frontier. There was no moon at all, nothing could be seen, which slowed up progress considerably. They stayed the rest of the night at the farm, and the whole of the next day, sleeping in the hay.

They planned to cross into Spain the next night. The farmer, a friend of Garcia, brought hot coffee and plates of eggs. They spent the time talking about their lives and catching up on as much sleep as they could before they had to move on once more, as detailed in Churchill's report:

> They set off again at 9 p.m. and marched solidly for 12 hours, with one break of 10 minutes for a meal. Finally, they ended up in a village S.W. of Figueras, thus getting outside the danger zone. They spent Friday in another barn in hiding because the Guardia Civil decided to call at the farm on that particular day. They were fed there, and a cyclist took a message to one of Garcia's brothers in Bañolas, who immediately came out in a car with a friend, and took Churchill alone to Bañolas. Churchill was to have been put up in a hotel, but one of the two people in the car decided to put him up in his house, and as motor cars are not allowed out from 2 p.m. Saturday until 2 p.m. Monday, Churchill spent the weekend there. The man's name is Francisco Esteva.

Churchill had grown fond of Garcia and Manuelo and was full of admiration for them both. As he bade them farewell, he knew the two Spaniards would soon be crossing the Pyrenees once again, guiding people and smuggling equipment across the border. But it was time for Churchill to continue his journey home. A messenger had been sent on to Barcelona and, with the weekend at Esteva's house over, a car arrived to pick him up.

In Barcelona Churchill met the Consul-General, Harold Farquhar. They dined together that evening and early the following morning set off for Madrid in Farquhar's own Ford V8 to avoid any unwanted encounters with the Guardia Civil. Travelling with them in the car was a Belgian Army officer who had also just crossed the Pyrenees. This was

Albert Guérisse, a 30-year-old member of the Belgian resistance, who organised the escape of downed Allied aircrew under the alias of Patrick O'Leary. His escape line would eventually carry more than 600 evaders across the French border into Spain.

It was a long drive of 65 km, and it took most of the day. Only occasionally did they stop by the roadside for a brief rest and something to eat. By the time they arrived at the British Embassy in Madrid it was late afternoon. They were met by Major Norton-Griffiths, whose job it was to look after escaped prisoners of war and arrange their onward travel. In his mission report, Churchill wrote:

> Major Norton-Griffiths took me into an office and asked me for all details of myself. I was rather reticent, but seeing that I should have been kept in Madrid as a P.O.W. for a minimum of 10 days, I was forced to give him some details of my mission. I did not tell him much, however, and I spent the rest of the day in the P.O.W. shed (an old chapel at the bottom of the garden) and had my meals in the kitchen with a private of the Lancashire Fusiliers and a doubtful Polish character.

The evening was spent at the Embassy, with Churchill and Guérisse sharing a room. They talked as much as they could, without giving anything secret away. Both clearly wanted to move on as quickly as they could, but for now there was little they could do. In his mission report, Churchill wrote:

> On 11th February I managed to see Norton-Griffiths at midday. As he seemed totally disinterested [*sic*] in my case, I impressed on him very strongly the urgency for my immediate repatriation. He put forward the usual arguments about the difficulties of sending one individual either to Lisbon or Gibraltar and said that I was unknown in Madrid, that no notice had come through from London about my possible arrival there, and that the man who dealt with people of my sort was away.

With a steady flow of escapees from France it could be days, weeks even, before Churchill could get away. He would later write:

> Whilst I was held as a Prisoner of War in Madrid, dressed in worn out and filthy clothes, I was given no facilities for

> obtaining fresh clothes and when I suggested the necessity for this, Norton-Griffiths tried to dissuade me and said that in Gibraltar this matter would be far simpler. He said, however, he would advance me money if I managed through my own efforts to get something from outside.

Churchill went shopping to smarten himself up. It was then that he had a stroke of luck when he bumped into an Army colleague, Captain Cockburn. Churchill had sailed to Gibraltar with Cockburn on the *Batory* and their meeting in Madrid was purely by chance. Cockburn told him that he had travelled up from Gibraltar in the courier car with the driver and another official, a man called Prescott. The car was due to return to Gibraltar that evening and there was a spare seat. With the right approval, Cockburn could see no reason why Churchill should not travel with them.

The following evening, Churchill was on his way to Gibraltar. He had been in Madrid for three days, but somehow it had felt much longer. It was another long journey of 650 km in a car, and there was another hurdle to overcome – getting Churchill across the frontier. Although his papers were good, he was effectively an escaped prisoner of war and so there was no reason for him to be travelling in the diplomatic car. Furthermore, there were three in the car when it had left Gibraltar and so any more returning to the Rock would arouse suspicion. Churchill would later write:

> At 6.30 p.m. on February 12th, we left in the Embassy liaison car, stopped the night at Bailin and on the following day Prescott had to be let into the secret of my false identity (that I was an escaped prisoner). He was most helpful about this and arranged to stop near La Linea at his own farm so that I could get into the boot of the car without being seen by anybody. This was accomplished with great ease and the remainder of the journey to Gibraltar – stopping at the British Consulate at La Linea and again at the frontier – was done in record time.

Churchill was safely back in Gibraltar. He was taken to the Rock Hotel and was soon in his uniform once more. Now he needed to arrange his passage home. Later that day he met Morris at the hotel only to be told there was no immediate way home. Churchill would have to be patient, but then came another piece of luck when he bumped into a former instructor of his, Captain van Maurik, who had been in Malta and was also on his way back to Britain. His aircraft had stopped off at Gibraltar to refuel and was due to leave later that night. And, in what seemed like no time at all, arrangements were made for a non-essential pallet to be removed from the aircraft so that Churchill could travel on board.

All that was left for Churchill to do before leaving the Rock was to go to accounts and hand over the 35,000 francs he had left from the 100,000 he had been given for his own personal expenditure prior to leaving for his mission. He then spent the rest of the day with van Maurik and the aircraft's captain, Flight Lieutenant Austin, and his crew.

It was Friday the 13th, not a great day for flying for those who are superstitious, but that was not going to stop Churchill. He was just glad to be on his way home. Later that evening he boarded the Whitley bomber for the flight home, but the starboard engine would not start, which delayed their take-off by a couple of hours. Finally, a little after midnight, the engine crackled into life and the heavily laden Whitley slowly accelerated along Gibraltar's short runway and staggered into the air.

For the next eight hours there was nothing but darkness, and the cold. It was so cold that it was hard to sleep. Then, just as it was starting to get light, the starboard engine spluttered a few times and then finally gave up. Fortunately, by then, the English coastline was already in sight and soon after the Whitley landed safely at Portreath.

Churchill was in Cornwall. He was extremely grateful to the crew. It was 14 February 1942. It had only been a couple of months since he had left Britain's shores, but it felt more like a couple of years.

Chapter 8

HMS *Unbroken*

Churchill was soon back at Orchard Court. De Guélis had met him at Portreath and driven him by staff car to London. Park the porter was there to meet them and as they climbed the stairs up to flat 6, Churchill felt he was starting to get to know the place rather well. Buckmaster was keen to hear about his trip. The telegram system had worked well, and they had been able to track his progress while in France, but now it was time to hear about his mission in more detail.

Over the next few hours, Churchill was asked about what he had been up to in France. He also handed over the ration books and coupons he had brought back with him. These important items would soon be in the hands of forgers and copiers who would reproduce them all.

Churchill's full mission debrief report, typed up over the next couple of days, totals nineteen pages. The pages record everything about his mission – how he got in and out of France, what he did during each of his visits and his assessment of the situation there, his thoughts of those he had met, and anything else that would help future missions. The report also records Churchill's chance meeting with Albert Guérisse in Barcelona, and there is a separate section titled 'Aviators' with suggestions as to what Allied aircrew should do should they come down in occupied France and the methods in place to help them return home. And the report records Churchill's distribution of the 2 million francs:

> 400,000 francs was given to OLIVE and 300,000 francs was given to ALAIN, while 500,000 francs was left for CLAUDE, which he collected the day after Churchill had left. The balance of 800,000 francs Churchill left with OLIVE for the release of the arrested men and for getting them out of France.

As far as future financial arrangements were concerned, Churchill's assessment was that a small resistance cell of (say) a handful of people, would typically need around 1,500 francs per month to operate. This meant a group like OLIVE, for example, with seventeen cells, needed more than 25,000 francs per month to operate in addition to the organiser's personal requirement of 50,000 francs per month. And so, the total cost of running just one group, OLIVE in this case, was around 75,000 francs per month. At an exchange rate of 200 francs to the pound (as it was in 1942), it worked out at £375 per month, equivalent to more than £22,000 per month today. And as far as the others were concerned, Lévy said he would like 130,000 francs per month to run his side of the show, Duboudin wanted 100,000 francs, and Virginia Hall 20,000 francs. Funding resistance groups was expensive.

Churchill was also keen to pass on everything he had learned while in France, such as what equipment and clothing to take, to ensure that agents going into the field in future would be as best prepared as possible. The cold weather he had experienced while away had shown just how unprepared he had been. His mission debrief report includes:

> Anyone being sent out in winter should have a strong thick tweed suit, an overcoat, a Norwegian-kind rucksack, with frame, a strong pair of boots of the ski variety. There should be definite equipment for all men going out, and this should be checked up before he leaves. One pair of town shoes, a change of socks, pants, vests, and dark uniform-colour shirts, blue preferably, with collars attached. All this would look perfectly normal in town, many people even wear ski suits. A second suit should be provided, flannel bags and tweed jacket etc. The ordinary equipment, such as Benzedrine, cigarettes, soap (all invaluable) should be sent, but much stronger Benzedrine tablets should be provided. The best type of English razor, Rolls, Gillette etc. plus English razor blades. These are all in use out there, even with the names in English on them. A small clothes brush is also vital, to clean up on arriving at a town. Some petrol and a rag for cleaning too. A hussif, aspirins, iodine and a soap box.

The report also includes useful points about operating in the south of France. The paragraph on the use of trains, for example, reads:

> TRAINS – When a journey is contemplated, get someone to book a seat under their name in a first-class compartment. If there is any question about identity cards, the least risk is incurred in first-class. This is because Germans and big businessmen travel this way, and the police etc. don't want to annoy them. There

> is generally half a first-class compartment, one whole coach of second-class, and ten of third-class. If one wants to sit down, third-class is the only place where one will find a seat, the two other classes are always full. However, third-class should be avoided by our people. If a sleeping compartment is wanted, ten days notice has to be given, but if no notice has been given and one is needed urgently, there are always two reserved in case some high official or etc. should suddenly decide to travel. By approaching the sleeping-car attendant and promising 100 frs. tip one has a good chance of getting one of these couchettes.

There are similar paragraphs on the use of taxis, the carrying of suitcases, and staying in hotels.

The paragraph on the use of restaurants reads:

> RESTAURANTS – Everything is written up plainly in every restaurant. All meals are served against tickets. A man comes round before the meal is served and collects your ticket, which you bring out and place on the table. Bread – a 50 g ticket for one slice. For 100 g you can eat as much bread as you like. Meat – 90 g for lunch. Matieres Grasses – 10 g lunch and 5 g in the evenings. Cheese – tickets are the same colour as the Matieres Grasses, but bear the number 20. Tips are generally included in the bill. You can give a little extra, but it is quite optional.

The paragraphs after that cover Churchill's thoughts on the black market, the use of money and establishing funds, and the next paragraph gives his advice on the use of the telephone and telegrams:

> TELEPHONE & TELEGRAMS – Both very risky. When telephoning or sending telegrams abroad, you have to give name, address, and details of identity card. You must also have a valid reason. You can telephone locally without any difficulty but conversations are listened to. To send wires from one town to another, you show your identity card and it goes. It would not be good to draw attention to yourself by sending too many wires.

There are then paragraphs covering the curfew in force on the Côte d'Azur, snap controls at railway stations, the police, bribery, and safe houses. As for the forged identity documents in use, Churchill's comments were:

> Our carte d'Identity [*sic*] is very good, the only flaw being that if the number is checked up, it is immediately seen to be false. Against this, there is the risk of the gangsters knowing the names of all our people, but giving correctly registered cards. There is no need to worry about the Carte Nationale. There is no strict tally, the card index gives nothing to fear.

One of the more pressing points from Churchill's debrief report was the urgent need to provide circuits in the south of France with wireless sets and trained operators. Buckmaster explained to Churchill they were working on a better way to insert sets and operators into France, as dropping them from an aircraft had major problems. They had yet to work out how to drop operators and sets together and so they were having to be dropped on separate parachutes and, at night, the result was that sets were often either damaged or lost.

As far as Churchill was concerned, there was an obvious solution to this – to land the wireless operators with their sets from the sea. His submarine drop had been successful and the area near Lévy's surgery in Antibes would be an ideal place for them to go ashore. This would avoid them having the long walk with their equipment to Cannes, as had been the case for him. Not only that, but Churchill was prepared to go along as their guide. The suggestion is recorded in Churchill's debrief report:

> Churchill suggests that the best way of landing two W/T men in France is by submarine. On arrival a short distance outside the bay of Antibes, Churchill will enter one of the two canoes, with the two W/T men in the second canoe, and will lead them up to a spot under the cover of the coastal gardens at Antibes, from which position Churchill will be able to point out to them Levy's house, which is at the corner of the third road leading off the Boulevard Marechal Foch, on the right-hand side. Churchill proposes that arrangements should be made to reach the beach at 8.15 p.m. at which time most of the population is having its dinner. If arrangements can be made through Berne to warn LEVY of the arrival of these two men, Churchill suggests that he should also arrange that the three people, whom Churchill had already seen in Antibes at his house, should be led down to the exact spot on the beach, which can be indicated by the W/T operators, so that they may

> be rowed out to the submarine. If the authorities at this end prefer to return members of our organisation or of the *Groupes de Resistance*, this matter is in their hands entirely.

It was a good idea and could potentially work well for both the insertion and withdrawal of agents from France, but Buckmaster was fully aware they could not always call on the services of one of the Navy's most precious assets. It was, however, worth a shot. They might just be allocated another submarine. The problem was, though, Churchill had only just returned from France and although he was happy to go straight back, Buckmaster insisted all his agents had sufficient time off after returning from the field. In the end, Buckmaster agreed to Churchill having just ten days of leave, less than would normally be the case, before setting out for France. In the meantime, Buckmaster would find two wireless operators to go with him.

Churchill returned from leave a captain, albeit acting, effective from 28 February 1942, his promotion and extra pip a reward for his excellent work. By then, Buckmaster had found two wireless operators, otherwise known within resistance circles as pianists or Georges, and both were ready to leave for France. One was 37-year-old Edward Zeff, known as Georges 53 and codenamed MATTHIEU. Born in Brighton to Jewish parents, he had previously worked in Paris in the family tailoring business. When France fell, he returned to Britain with his French wife and volunteered for SOE. Zeff was now heading for the SPRUCE circuit in Lyon. The other was 25-year-old Isidore Newman, known as Georges 49 and codenamed JULIEN. Born in Leeds to Russian parents, he was a former schoolmaster. He had joined the Army and become a wireless operator and soon came to the attention of SOE, passing through Wanborough on Party 27G, the course after Churchill's, and was now off to join URCHIN.

Churchill met Zeff and Newman at Orchard Court, where the three were issued with up-to-date papers and briefed on their task. They were first to fly to Gibraltar. Arrangements had been made with the Admiralty for a submarine to be made available, which would take them to a suitable dropping-off point along the Côte d'Azur, from where Churchill was to deliver Zeff and Newman and their wireless sets ashore. A message had also been sent to Lévy in Antibes to prepare to receive more visitors. Zeff was then to proceed to Lyon and meet Duboudin, whose task it was to find a suitable landing ground for a

Lysander pick-up, sometime between 25 March and 6 April. Newman, meanwhile, was to stay in Antibes and tell Lévy that Maitre Goeau Brissonnière was willing to represent the arrested agents in prison in Périgueux, and that she could be contacted through the American Embassy, using the name René to establish contact. Churchill's part of the mission was to be quite straightforward and if all went well, he would be away for just a matter of days, as summarised in his written instructions:

> He [Churchill] has been instructed to accompany them [Zeff and Newman] to Gibraltar and from Gibraltar on to Antibes by submarine where he will supervise their disembarkation and will, without going ashore himself, give them all indications to reach the house of PHILIPPE from Antibes Bay . . . As soon as Churchill's mission is terminated, he will proceed with the submarine and probably land at Malta.

On 2 March 1942, Churchill, Zeff and Newman left London by train. They were to fly to Gibraltar from Bristol but would have to wait until a flight became available. It gave them time to relax and rehearse the details of their missions. Then, finally, on 9 March, it was time to go.

The twin-engine Curtiss CW-20 transport aircraft was a welcome change to the long sea voyage Churchill had endured before. When they landed in Gibraltar the ever-reliable Morris was there to meet them and Churchill was soon back at the Rock Hotel. He had only been away a little over three weeks.

Morris was surprised to see Churchill again so soon, but, as Churchill explained, there was no one better to take the two wireless operators to France. Morris was quick to point out that getting a submarine would not be any easier this time, no matter what the Admiralty might have agreed. Every submarine was packed with people and supplies for Malta, and Captain Voelcker was keen to ensure that his precious submarines were not going to be called upon on a regular basis for more cloak and dagger stuff.

The situation was fully understandable, and it was not something that either Churchill or Morris at their level could sort out. But there was no other way of landing Zeff and Newman by sea as all the feluccas (traditional wooden sailing boats) seemed to be full or were destined for other parts of the Mediterranean coast.

There was little Churchill could do other than be patient. He had hoped to leave Gibraltar within a few days, but that was clearly not going to happen, and it was looking increasingly unlikely they would even be allocated a submarine at all. On 21 March, Churchill wrote to Buckmaster to update him on the situation:

> Dear Major Buckmaster,
>
> This letter will reach you through the bag [diplomatic bag], so I can speak or write freely. When I arrived here with my party on 9th March everything seemed set for our originally planned departure for the 12th March. However, we had no sooner reached the office before it started filling with high naval officials (who knew me) who harangued me in unison about the impossibility of using this base as a submarine taxi depot, and explained that all submarines were now booked to carry stores elsewhere of a very important nature. This, I admitted, was more than natural and I added that the request for our transport had been made through the Admiralty as they had previously expressed that it should be. I also said that I had been given to understand that a submarine had been allotted to us for the operation I was here for. However, on turning up the files I see that your No. 6871 to [erased] does not specify a submarine at all. Therefore, I have either misunderstood or been sold a pup.
>
> Now that submarines are definitely off, we are waiting for this blessed motor to be unloaded for our surface craft. All the plans for sunset and moon conditions must be altered and this will, of course, be done. But what upsets me is the delay in delivering my two charges, in view of the advancing Spring, the difficulty of keeping them quiet and happy here, and my natural wish to return for the next job.
>
> And now Le Chene and his mate have come, and it appears more are coming, and still there is but one boat leaving on the date I have so often repeated. If they all go in the boat it will be very tricky depositing them – as I imagine you will agree they should be deposited – at various points near my place. If they don't all accompany the first party, they will be hanging around here for weeks on end. Everyone knows everyone else on this Rock, and it is almost impossible for more than

ten days on end for odd couples to maintain their phoney alibis.

My very best wishes to you and all our friends.

Yours ever,

P. M. Churchill [signed].

Getting a submarine was proving as difficult as Morris had suggested. Churchill was even prepared to travel on the next felucca, if he could find space on one going in his direction. The 'Le Chêne' mentioned in the letter was 50-year-old Henri le Chêne, a former hotel manager and one of three family members working for SOE, who was on his way to Lyon by the April felucca.

All Churchill could do was cling on to the hope that a submarine could be arranged, but his frustration at the thought of more agents joining the party was not helped when he found out that two others were to join his group: one a wireless operator and the other an agent on a special mission. The wireless operator was Marcel Clech, codename BASTIEN, a Breton former taxi driver, whom Churchill knew from their time at Wanborough. Clech was now on his way to Lyon to meet Virginia Hall and set up a radio link for her. The other man, Victor Gerson, codename RENÉ, was also on his way to Lyon. He was to set up an escape line via the Pyrenees, later to become known as the 'Vic Line'. Clech and Gerson were to be dropped off along the French coast as well and would be on the same submarine, assuming one could be made available, although they would have to wait until Churchill's team had gone ashore.

The wait for a submarine went on for nearly a month. Churchill spent the time as best he could, with Zeff and Newman practising with the canoes. The plan was for Churchill to go ashore first in one canoe, taking with him the equipment, after which he would return to the submarine. Zeff and Newman would then paddle ashore in their canoe with Churchill acting as their guide. They first practised on a strip of coastline next to the airfield, handling the canoes as if getting them to and from the submarine's bridge, and then getting them in and out of the water. Because of the difficulty Churchill would face returning to the submarine in the dark, a small compass was fitted into a recess at the front of his canoe. Having gone ashore he would then follow the back-bearing to return him to the vicinity of the submarine. He also fitted his torch into a sling, with a blackout funnel attached, so that only a thin ray of light would show, which could then be seen from the submarine.

There was even time for a dress rehearsal at night from a landing craft off the east side of Gibraltar, which did not go well. Churchill spent hours battling against the current and eventually had to be pulled out of the water, but he was confident the current off the French coast would be less dramatic than he had experienced off the Rock.

Finally, there was some good news. Voelcker had agreed to provide a submarine, although Churchill would still have to wait for one to become available. On 2 April, he wrote to Buckmaster:

> Dear Major Buckmaster,
>
> I cannot tell you how pleased I was to hear that you had made arrangements for our original method of transport to be agreed by the Naval Authorities. This method in my view will assure Nervo and Knox getting there.

It seems that Zeff and Newman had become known in Gibraltar as Nervo and Knox, named after the British comedians Jimmy Nervo and Teddy Knox who formed a double act and were part of the original 'Crazy Gang' comedy group. Then, a few days later, came the news Churchill had been waiting for. A submarine, HMS *Unbroken*, was being made ready to leave.

It was to be *Unbroken*'s first full patrol, having not long arrived at the Rock. Her commander, 27-year-old Lieutenant Alastair Mars, a Canadian pre-war submariner, met with Voelcker in the captain's cabin where he was briefed on his special operation, officially called Operation DELAY II. He was to drop off four agents along the coastline of southern France; two at a predetermined point and the other two at a point Mars deemed suitable. After that he could enjoy a few days of hunting in the Gulf of Genoa before returning to Gibraltar. Mars was also told a bit about Churchill and that he would be travelling on board the submarine to see the first two agents ashore, and he was briefed on how to get the canoes on and off the submarine. And with that, Voelcker instructed Mars to be prepared to leave Gibraltar in a week's time.

Of the submarine's crew, only Mars knew where they would be going. There were many Spanish civilians around the dockyard, and he would need to be discreet and so he ordered charts for the African coast down to Sierra Leone in the hope that any prying eyes would be misled.

Over the next few days, Mars and his crew practised manhandling a canoe on and off the submarine in different sea conditions. Then

Mars was introduced to Churchill. In his book *Unbroken: The Story of a Submarine*, Mars recalled their first meeting:

> If I had expected him to be a blond, titanic Viking in the best traditions of the heroes of the twopenny bloods, I would have been disappointed. Of medium build, dark, and with deep, intelligent eyes, he would only be distinguishable in a crowd by his charm and a certain sense of authority. Here was a strong character, I felt, unassuming and quiet, yet capable of decisive violence should the occasion arise.

Churchill met Mars and Voelcker in the captain's cabin, where the three put together a plan. Mars was concerned about the idea of landing the first two agents at Antibes. Like Churchill, he knew the area from his pre-war days. It was a small bay and there were always plenty of fishing boats about. Although it was now wartime and the number of boats in the area would be lower, it was still a concern and probably meant it would be tricky getting in and out of the bay.

Although Mars expressed his concern, the plan remained intact; the reception committee would be expecting them there. There was just enough time for one final night practice to get used to handling the canoes in the dark.

Churchill and his team went aboard during the late afternoon of 11 April. The five newcomers squeezed into the tiny wardroom as best they could. Then, just as soon as it was dusk, HMS *Unbroken* slipped her moorings from the *Maidstone* and headed out through Algeciras Bay and into the centre of the Strait. Mars knew there would be curious watchers on shore, and so once the submarine was out of sight of prying eyes, he swung *Unbroken* around to east-north-east and entered the Mediterranean Sea. As it was getting dark, the submarine stayed on the surface to begin its zig-zag course to pass to the west of Majorca.

The monotonous passage through the Med was just as Churchill had experienced before, again the journey lasting ten days. Mars tried breaking up the routine by setting regular exercises for his crew. At one stage, as they came out of the lee of the Balearic Islands, they were met by a gale. The submarine rolled like a porpoise and the heavy sea meant progress was slow. For Zeff, the whole experience was an unpleasant one; his claustrophobia got worse with every passing day. Newman, however, seemingly adapted much better to the cramped surroundings.

Once again, the hospitality on board was excellent. Churchill could not have asked for anything more. He and Mars talked at length. Mars had spent his last afternoon before sailing for Gibraltar enjoying a picnic on the shores of Loch Lomond with his wife, Ting, before she returned to their Aldeburgh cottage in Suffolk. She was expecting a child at that time and now his daughter, June, had been born. He could only wonder when he would see her, if at all.

By noon on the 20th, they were approaching the dropping-off point. Mars peered through the periscope towards Antibes. Only a slight breeze was stirring the gentlest of ripples on the placid blue sea, and there was not another vessel in sight. Everything was good to land them that night.

Mars took the submarine back out to sea to wait for nightfall and discussed the plan with Churchill. They would approach the bay from the east and creep to within 700 yards of the steps where Churchill and the others would land. The canoes would then be collected from their stowage and passed out through the forward hatch. Churchill would go ashore first and contact the reception committee. By the time he returned to the submarine, Zeff and Newman would be ready to go. Churchill would lead them to the steps and then return to the submarine, towing their canoe behind, to pick up the rest of the equipment. He would then make one final round trip before boarding the submarine once more. But the plan was not without its risks, as it meant taking the submarine to within 400 yards of the nearest rocks.

That evening, as the sun was beginning to set, it started to rain. The sea state was getting worse, which would make launching the canoes a near impossible task, but they would have to give it a go.

At dusk they made their way back towards the shore, but they soon realised they had drifted a couple of miles west of where they wanted to be, and conditions were far from good. The submarine surfaced amidst thunder and lightning. As they edged into the bay it was pouring with rain. Churchill was on the bridge with Mars. It was 11 p.m. They were due to start going ashore in an hour. Then the wind dropped, and the sky cleared, but there was another problem. A darkened silhouette of another vessel, without any lights, was sighted on the port beam. Mars could not risk being spotted, and their position reported. Then the weather began to turn once again.

With everything seemingly going against them, Mars decided to postpone the landing for twenty-four hours. In his mission debrief report, Churchill later wrote:

> We reached our destination on the night of the 20th April. On this night, when the landing operation should have taken place, Lieutenant Mars, the Captain of P.42 [*Unbroken*], having sighted the exact landing spot through the periscope during daylight, then went out 12 miles and waited for nightfall. At dusk we made our way towards our objective. There was, however, such a strong set that we drifted some 2 miles westward of our position to what appeared to be off the Ile Ste. Marguerite in front of Cannes. This made it necessary to repeat the performance on the following night. During the following day we stayed submerged much closer to the coast and were therefore able to make sure of reaching the right spot.

As frustrating as it was, they stooged around the following day submerged off Nice. That evening, they surfaced once again, this time to find much better weather conditions. They quietly slipped into the bay once more. Churchill went up on the bridge with Mars to view the scene. The Alps were silhouetted against the half-moon night sky and the lights of Antibes could be seen before them. They would wait until the lights went out and the population went to bed as the curfew was enforced. Only then would it be time to go ashore.

It seemed a long wait, but as soon as Antibes plunged into darkness, Mars took *Unbroken* closer towards the shore. The canoes were brought up through the hatch and lowered into the water. Churchill climbed over the rail and felt his way to the steps that would take him down the outside casing of the conning tower. His mission report describes what happened next:

> At 12.30 at night when the moon went down, I got into a canoe loaded up with one radio set and one suitcase. Just at this time the lights of about five fishing boats suddenly appeared in the bay. These lights crossed and recrossed the actual landing point and eventually it was discovered that they were powerful acetylene lamps used by fishermen, whose season, it was subsequently found out, starts at the beginning of April. The submarine crept in to within about 1100 yards of the gardens chosen for landing and I paddled in from there.

From the submarine Mars could only watch as Churchill disappeared into the darkness. He was last seen heading towards two lights.

> As I was nearing my objective, one of these fishing boat lights was suddenly lit about 150 yards from me, forcing me to take cover behind some rocks. I waited for the light to move across and out of my way before proceeding to the gardens. When I got there, I climbed out of the canoe, keeping an eye on two or three sets of lights, and when I noticed that one of these was approaching me and lighting up the shore for some 400 yards, I had to make a quick getaway, taking all the luggage back with me. I paddled out to the submarine, following a back bearing. It appeared that the fishing boat was following me to within about 200 yards of the submarine before moving off to the Old Port.

Churchill did not stop paddling until he felt it safe to do so. He then switched on his torch. Almost miraculously, the dark shape of the submarine appeared. His mission report continues:

> On reaching P.42 I found that Zeff and Newman were already in the second canoe and I decided that, in spite of not having been able to reconnoitre the ground previously, we had better go in together in order to complete the operation before dawn. We were further hampered by the fishermen's lights but, fortunately, as we reached the shore they moved away and disturbed us no longer. On getting to the rocks we climbed out and I lifted the two boats on to the top of the rocks, tying one to the other. I then found some steps leading up the side of a 15 foot concrete wall beyond which lay the gardens. Having deposited the luggage in the gardens, I fetched Zeff and Newman and took them to the gardens, where I left them for about twenty minutes while I was making certain of the whereabouts of PHILIPPE's house, which was more difficult to find in the complete darkness than had been anticipated. When I had found it, I returned to the gardens and pointed out the way to Zeff and Newman, who left me, carrying the first set of luggage, on the understanding that they should return to pick up the next lot, which I would fetch and leave at an agreed spot.

A Frenchman called Guillain de Bénouville witnessed Churchill and the two wireless operators going ashore. Although his recollection differs slightly, his dramatic words are repeated in E.H. Cookridge's *Inside S.O.E.*:

> From our little boat I watched the submarine surface slowly, with tears in my eyes. This little ship, these sailors and the three civilians on the bridge had come from England. They had come to fight on our side, to fight for France. And, please God, one day they might return home. To us Frenchmen the surprise in this was overwhelming, but to them it hardly seemed to be an adventure at all. The sailors threw a rope to us and pulled our boat alongside. The three civilians jumped down, shook hands and stuffed packets of cigarettes into our pockets. We embraced them, patted their shoulders, their faces. You must remember that for us this was the first sign of action against the German conquerors of Europe by our friends, the free Anglo-Saxons. Later, on the shore, I learned that one of the Englishmen was Captain Peter Churchill. He was a charming man, who spoke our language admirably. He was dark and I thought he was Jewish. It was not for some time that I was informed that he belonged to a noble English family . . . He was to serve the cause of Freedom well!

Having successfully put Zeff and Newman ashore, Churchill's mission report described what happened next:

> I then returned to P.42, towing back the spare canoe. I found the submarine had closed in to some 600 yards from the shore and as it had drifted slightly towards some rocks on the western side, my back bearing would have made me miss it, if the Captain had not seen my torch, to which he signalled three times with a blue lamp from the bridge. The spare canoe was unhitched and the rest of the luggage placed in the back of mine. I then returned to the gardens for the third time.

It was already past 3 a.m. by the time Churchill approached the steps once more. This time he could see people moving around, just at the point where he intended to land. He stopped paddling. All possibilities flashed through his mind. He slowly paddled backwards, widening the gap between him and the steps, in case he needed to make his escape. But he knew the importance of the wireless set he had on board. For a while he watched from a distance. From what he could see and hear he became increasingly convinced they were friendly.

Churchill's mission report then continued:

> When I reached the spot I saw several figures coming down the steps and was not surprised to find that PHILIPPE was at the head of them. He asked me if I would take back d'Astier, which I did. I had little conversation of importance with PHILIPPE. On returning to P.42 I found it had still further closed in to the coast and was now a mere 400 yards away. The Captain immediately accepted the new and unexpected guest.

It appears that Francis Basin had arranged for d'Astier to go to London. Basin had reluctantly become involved in the quarrels breaking out between the competing leaders of various resistance organisations in the south of France, some of whom were blinded by their personal ambitions and had seemingly forgotten the cause they were all fighting for. Basin had tried to reconcile these warring patriots by suggesting they form a committee and appoint someone to go to London on their behalf to negotiate with SOE chiefs for support to their groups to be stepped up. And so d'Astier had been appointed as their spokesman and this was the reason for him travelling to Britain. But the quarrelling did not stop there. D'Astier's appointment was not accepted by everyone and so a second man, Henri Frenay, convinced that he should be the spokesman instead, was later sent to London as well, although the outcome was that Frenay then decided to sever his links with SOE and moved to join de Gaulle's camp.

None of this had any impact on Mars, of course, who was not at all bothered by having d'Astier as an extra soul on board. Anyone associated with Churchill's line of business was good enough for him. And no sooner were they safely on board than the canoes were secured, the hatch was closed, and the submarine submerged and went silently on its way.

Churchill spent much of the following day asleep until it was time for the second drop, at the Pointe d'Agay near Fréjus. As there was no precise spot where Clech and Gerson were to go ashore, Mars chose a small beach between clusters of rocks. He took the submarine closer to the shore, until it was just a few hundred yards off the beach.

This time, the drop-off was far more straightforward, using the same procedure as before, as Churchill's mission report states:

> The operation was very simple indeed and made even easier by the fact that P.42 approached to within 300 yards of the landing spot and was never out of sight, owing to the clarity of the night, in spite of it being 2.30 a.m. Only one fishing boat disturbed our work. I left Gerson and Clech with their luggage in that very black bay. This operation was completed in about three-quarters of an hour.

Mars was relieved. Everything, so far, had gone well. Now it was time for his crew to do what they had been trained to do – to hunt and sink enemy ships. They were soon heading for the Italian coast, their chosen hunting ground being a position dominating the approaches to Genoa. The weather and sea conditions were perfect. For now, the submarine remained submerged, although Mars kept surveying the scene from periscope depth. He could see in the distance numerous yachts and schooners, but nothing worthy of an attack.

The following day, a ship was sighted. The crew leapt to action stations. The ship was probably an Italian tramp, although it was still several miles away. It took *Unbroken* fifteen minutes to get about two miles closer. A check on the target's range now put the ship at six miles distant – still too far away to carry out an attack. Another fifteen minutes at full speed brought the range down. They were now close enough to see that the merchantman was around 4,000 tons and some 350 feet in length. It was not exactly big, but it was better than nothing. The range reduced further still. They were now 7,000 yards from the merchantman. Mars estimated it was doing around 10 knots and since it was at long range he decided a salvo of torpedoes would be required, fired at intervals of 45 seconds.

Unbroken fired three torpedoes. With each discharge Churchill felt the pressure on his ears as the compressed air that fired the torpedo vented back into the boat. There was no time to hang around, as they needed to get away as quickly as possible from the tell-tale signs of where the torpedo tracks had started. Then, after several minutes, the unmistakable sound of a torpedo striking home was heard. A couple of minutes later, two deeper explosions were heard, probably the result of the other torpedoes hitting the bottom. Mars looked through the periscope. The merchantman could be seen down by the stern and the next time he looked there was nothing. He would later claim the ship as 'hit, probably sunk', the attack having taken place 20 miles south of Genoa.

A routine submarine patrol lasted around three weeks. *Unbroken* had now been at sea for thirteen days and it would take anything up to ten days to get back to Gibraltar. Mars decided to spend a further thirty-six hours in the Gulf of Genoa, although they found nothing more to attack. It had been a successful first patrol, but now it was time to head back to the Rock.

The drama, though, was not yet over. When 12 miles off Bordighera near the Franco-Italian border, they sighted what looked like an enemy schooner of around 200 tons to the south of San Remo. *Unbroken* fired two torpedoes at it from a range of 800 yards. The first was seen to pass ahead of the schooner, which must have reduced its speed or stopped, but there was no sign of the second until an explosion was heard ahead of the submarine, all but bouncing *Unbroken* out of the water. The torpedo had presumably exploded on the bottom. Churchill was asleep at the time of the attack but was woken by the sound of the explosion, and the sudden jolt of the submarine threw him out of his bunk. Badly shaken, he sheltered beneath the wardroom table, not knowing whether they were still afloat or plunging to their deaths.

It was fortunate that neither torpedo found its target as they had fired at a Portuguese vessel, the *Vale Formosa II*. It was only when Mars ordered the submarine to close in, so that an attack could be made using its gun, that the vessel's neutral nationality was realised. Not wishing for the schooner skipper to report they had been fired upon by a British submarine, Mars called Churchill to the bridge and asked him to speak to the schooner crew in Italian and to tell them they should not have been in the area. Which Churchill did, even though he was still in a state of shock.

The schooner turned away and nothing more was said. Mars later found out that he had summoned Churchill to the bridge immediately after his unpleasant experience of the wayward torpedo. Mars remembered:

> Hearing of this, my admiration of Churchill increased tenfold, for he had given no indication of the nerve-destroying shock he had suffered when he gallantly hectored the skipper of the schooner.

On 2 May, HMS *Unbroken* entered safe waters and surfaced for the last time. The final part of their return to Gibraltar was completed with a naval escort of two motor torpedo boats, before *Unbroken* was secured alongside the *Maidstone*, her crew exhausted. It had been three weeks since they had left the Rock and they could now enjoy some well-earned leave, although they knew it would not be long before they were back at sea once more.

While d'Astier was led away by an intelligence officer, Churchill gathered his belongings and went aboard the *Maidstone*. There was much celebrating that night and the party went on into the early hours of the morning, although Churchill could only wonder what was next in store.

Chapter 9
Saint-Assise

As he approached the entrance to Orchard Court, Churchill was wondering what Buckmaster might have for him next. It was 15 May 1942. Churchill was enjoying what he was doing and hoped he would soon be on his way back to France. First, though, he had to be debriefed on his latest mission and complete his report .

In this latest report, Churchill was full of praise for the part played by Alastair Mars in making the landing of Zeff and Newman a success:

> The operation which had begun at 12.30 ended at 4 a.m. and, had it not been for the very helpful co-operation of Lieutenant Mars in closing in to the coast and not being frightened away by four fishing boats which, at different times during the operation, had lain alongside P. 42 and begun to fish, it would have been impossible to land the two W/T operators so very close to their final destination before daylight. In order to dispel any suspicions on the part of the fisher folk, Lieutenant Mars and myself had arranged that Gerson should stand on the bridge and call out to them in French, giving them the impression that we were a French submarine on manoeuvres. This all worked perfectly.

The rest of Churchill's mission report covered the second drop – that of Gerson and Clech – and the problems he had encountered when taking d'Astier into Gibraltar. It had been an unexpected arrival in port and so it had naturally raised some concerns about security, meaning that d'Astier was not allowed to leave the *Maidstone* until his identity had been fully established. Churchill wrote:

> It seems strange, as d'Astier is a personal friend of mine and I was the only person who could vouch for him, that I was never asked to do so. However, d'Astier was taken off and spent his time waiting for transport to England in [erased] house . . . D'Astier's state of semi-imprisonment on the Rock was

> not made very happy for him because of the general feeling of dislike for the de Gaulle movement . . . It seems that with the presence at Gibraltar of a direct representative of this department, this unnecessary unpleasantness would in future be obviated.

Churchill was also asked to comment on the use of folbots from a submarine:

> The wooden cross-pieces, seat backs and bamboo frames were found to be too delicate for continuous assembling, disassembling and stowing in bags. Several parts broke and some butterfly nuts were lost on this trip. Would it be possible to have an automatically opening aluminium frame for future submarine use? The wooden frame with recesses to take an open compass for following the back bearing to the submarine proved to be most satisfactory and is absolutely indispensable for finding the submarine about 1,000 yards from the shore. The blacked-out French torch gave ample light to be seen from the submarine and owing to its funnel shape the light was invisible from the sides.

With the debriefing of his second mission complete, it was now a matter of finding out what was to come next. Nicolas Bodington got straight to the point. There was something big on, and it had come from the very top. The Chiefs of Staff were at last taking notice of F Section's achievements and had something of an intimate and specialised nature that needed attending to. More than that, Prime Minister Winston Churchill had been briefed and had agreed that Peter Churchill was just the man to carry out the job.

The briefing went on. The Battle of the Atlantic was not going well and losses amongst Allied convoys were high. It had become apparent that German U-boats were acting on long-range radio transmissions coming from somewhere in France, which could be received on board a U-boat without it having to surface. If the transmitter could be put out of action, even for a short while, it would mean the U-boats would be forced to surface to receive instructions, and that would give the Royal Navy a chance to hunt them down. British intelligence believed the only transmitter powerful enough to do this was at Saint-Assise, near Melun, 50 km south of Paris. Aerial bombing of the transmitter would not be accurate enough for such an attack and would risk killing hundreds of civilians. Precision was required, and so the Prime Minister had turned to SOE to put the transmitter out of action.

Churchill was then taken into the next office where a scale model of Saint-Assise had been laid out. It was accurate in all its detail. The transmitter station was a couple of kilometres long and in the centre of the complex was the aerial running between two main masts, with four sets of cables holding up each mast. It was explained to Churchill that only one set of cables would need to be taken out to have the desired effect. If the outside cables could be cut then the mast would fall inwards, helped by the added weight of the aerial which would then be twisted and broken in the fall, putting the station out of action for several weeks, if not months.

The idea of taking out one of the Nazi's most strategic assets right under their noses practically in the suburbs of Paris was an audacious enough plan as it was, but the task was made even harder because each set of cables consisted of three separate steel hawsers attached to the ground by iron rings on top of concrete blocks, some three metres high and positioned a hundred metres or so apart. Although just the top two cables would need to be broken, it still meant scaling two of the concrete blocks. Unless Churchill intended taking an extendable ladder with him, some other way of scaling the blocks would have to be found. Not only that, but the amount of equipment and explosives required to cut the cables would be too much for one man to carry. This was clearly not a one-man job, and it was unlike anything Churchill had previously been considered best suited to do. He was an organiser, not a saboteur.

Churchill was then told about Henry and Alfred Newton, brothers born nearly ten years apart but known within SOE circles as the Twins. They were former cabaret artists and so scaling a high concrete block would be a piece of cake for them. Not only that, but they had lived near Paris before the war and knew the area reasonably well.

As Churchill had been to France twice in recent months and had just returned from his latest mission, he was given forty-eight hours to think about the idea. The training schools were crying out for someone like him or, as Bodington pointed out, he could accept his next appointment in any headquarters or be a welcome addition to the SOE staff. But with the mission approved at the highest level, and with his name having been put forward to lead it, Churchill had in his own mind already accepted the task. For now, though, he jumped into a taxi for Paddington Station and caught a train home to Malvern to think things over and take some well-earned leave.

When thinking deeper about what he had been told, Churchill was left with many unanswered questions. He assumed they would be dropped from an aircraft somewhere within reach of the transmitter station, but he had no idea of how many guards there would be at the complex; there was a German Army headquarters in the nearby forest of Fontainebleau, just a stone's throw from Saint-Assise. There was also the problem of the Seine River, which flows on three sides of the site of the transmitter station. Bridges were always guarded and so they would need a safe house on the Saint-Assise side of the river to avoid having to make a crossing. And then there was the matter of how they would deal with cutting the cables with explosives, assuming they could get into the right position in the first place. This would be the most crucial part of the operation. Setting the timers too early would not give them enough margin to get away, while setting them too late could risk the explosives being discovered and removed before they went off.

Saint-Assise would undoubtedly be a huge challenge and there were plenty of unanswered questions, but the following day Churchill telephoned Bodington to say he would take it on. The rest of his leave was spent quietly at home with his parents. They were always keen to know what he had been up to, but Churchill was always careful with what he said and somewhat economical with the truth. With three sons at war, they had enough to worry about as it was.

Leave passed all too quickly. Churchill was soon back in London to discuss the raid with Bodington and de Guélis, and, of course, to meet the Twins. Saint-Assise was just the kind of job the brothers were looking for, particularly because it would give them a chance to hit the German U-boat effort. It was the reason why they had ended up with SOE, after their entire family – their parents, wives, and children – had been lost at sea when the ship they had been travelling on was sunk by a U-boat. Now the Twins were after revenge.

The three went into a room to discuss their thoughts. The plan put together so far was for them to be dropped from two aircraft – Churchill in one and the Twins in the other – on the eastern side of the Seine, a few kilometres from Saint-Assise. By travelling separately, it would mean something might still be possible should anything go wrong with either party on the way to the area. They would then meet up at a designated rendezvous point, just a kilometre or so from the perimeter of the transmitter station. It was believed the complex was not heavily guarded and so Churchill expected it would take them around an hour to get inside and set the explosives.

It was now a matter of planning the raid in its finest detail. Arrangements had been made for them to go to Brickendonbury Manor for some specialist explosives and demolition training. Churchill had been to Brickendonbury before, but only for a couple of days in September prior to going on his first mission. But this time it was different. This raid was to involve explosives. He would effectively be a saboteur, just like the Twins.

That afternoon the three made their way to St Pancras station and were met at Brickendonbury by the Commandant, Major Cecil Clarke. Despite the manor's grandeur, they were accommodated on camp beds on a bare floor. For three days they learned how to become experts in mayhem and sudden death. They were taught precisely where to apply a few pounds of explosive to achieve maximum effect. Plastic explosive, or PE for short, a putty-like material and pale yellow in colour, had changed the way saboteurs operated. It could be cut and moulded into shape and even coloured to help its disguise. All that was needed was a detonator embedded in the mass of the explosive. For the Saint-Assise mission, the quantity of PE required to cut the cables was worked out and then prepared in the right amounts. All they would have to do was to apply the PE in the right places.

There was also time to study aerial reconnaissance photographs of the transmitter and its surroundings. From these images they could work out where the German troop positions were most likely to be and in what strength, and from what direction they should best make their approach. They also planned their escape back to Britain; an aircraft was to retrieve them, after they had laid up for a couple of weeks at a nearby safe house until everything had quietened down.

To help with their preparation, concrete blocks were laid out close to a piece of woodland in the grounds of the estate so they could rehearse the raid. Their first rehearsal was during daylight. Everything they required fitted into a rucksack and after first helping Churchill to scale his block, the Twins then went to theirs. With Henry's help, Alfred went up alone and set the explosives while his brother stayed on the ground to provide cover. The individual packs of PE, each weighing around a pound, had already been shaped to fit around the hawsers, with each pack having a pair of buckles and straps to attach them firmly in place. A fuse ran between the packs, and one end of the packs had a time pencil attached.

They then went through the procedure again, only this time under the cover of darkness and using a reduced amount of PE with ten-minute pencils. Unsurprisingly, they found setting the explosives in the dark more difficult as everything had to be done by feel. Even so, it took just forty-six minutes to complete the job. The explosions went off a minute apart and closer inspection afterwards showed that everything had gone to plan with all the fuse wires blown and each pack of PE having been properly attached.

The following night they carried out another rehearsal. Again, everything went to plan. They then went to the radio transmission station at Hillmorton near Rugby, where the layout of its large very-low-frequency transmitter was much the same as they would encounter at Saint-Assise.

With their training done, it was time to go and do the job for real. They would be leaving in four nights' time, when the moon was half-full, with the raid being carried out during the late evening of 29 May. They were then driven to Tempsford Hall in Bedfordshire, a holding place close to the airfield from where they would depart. They were to spend the final few days there working on their cover stories and being issued with forged documents, and rehearsing in their minds every fine detail they might encounter once they had dropped into France.

During the afternoon of 28 May, Bodington and de Guélis arrived at the hall to go through the mission with Churchill and the Twins for one last time. By all accounts, the weather was forecast to be good. After they finished talking, Churchill handed over a letter he had written to his parents should anything go wrong. But he felt sad for the Twins. They had no such letter to write. They just sat together in the sun. Should they not make it back alive there was no one who would need to be informed. Churchill had been impressed by them and later wrote that, in all his time with SOE, he never met anyone quite like the Twins. These two, he felt, were absolute killers.

Sat in the shade of an old oak tree they all enjoyed afternoon tea together. It was such a peaceful and wonderfully English setting and the perfect way to spend their final hours before leaving for France. It was then time to go across to the storeroom and draw their equipment.

And, as the sun started to go down, it was time for supper – eggs, bacon, chips, toast, and butter.

Finally, it was time to go. Churchill was to leave first; his take-off was planned for 11 p.m. As a car approached the hall, he bade the Twins farewell; he would next see them in France. There were curtains in the back of the car so that no one beyond that point would be able to see who was inside. Bodington also got in. He was to accompany Churchill to the airfield. When it was the Twins' turn, de Guélis would go with them to the airfield, although they still had two hours to wait.

It took fifteen minutes to reach the airfield. The final dispatch point was a barn at Gibraltar Farm in the remote north-east corner of the field and as they pulled up at a Nissen hut, Churchill could make out the silhouette of a four-engine Halifax bomber nearby. An airman helped him into his overalls and a parachute pack was fitted to his back. Spare ammunition clips and rations were packed into pockets wherever there was any space. His Sten gun was then attached to quick-release grips across his chest and finally the rucksack of explosives for the raid was attached to his front. Churchill could barely walk.

But then, just minutes before he was due to board the aircraft, a car could be seen approaching in the distance. At first Churchill thought little of it, but then he started to suspect something might be wrong when in the dim light he could see de Guélis getting out of the car. As he got closer, Churchill could see he had a clouded look on his face. Then de Guélis delivered the bombshell. The mission was off. Churchill was stunned into silence.

The reason given for the cancellation was because the Germans had got wind of a possible raid after an earlier explosion at the transmitter complex. Unbeknown to anyone in F Section, some French patriots, acting it seems on their own, had also decided to try and blow up the transmitter. Using PE inserted in the handles of their bicycles, they had entered the complex and placed the bicycles against one of the main masts. The charges had gone off as planned, but there was only slight damage to the mast and the transmitter aerial remained in working order. And with more German troops now spread across the area, Churchill and the Twins would not have stood a chance.

Whether this somewhat farcical incident happened exactly as it was described to Churchill is not known, but it was the reason given for the cancellation of the raid. If true then it was certainly not the first time, nor would it be the last for that matter, that French patriots and SOE got in each other's way.

For now, Churchill had to put Saint-Assise behind him, although it was initially thought the idea might later resurface. It did not. But there was more frustration for him at the end of May, and it related to his second mission. Firstly, his expenses had come under scrutiny – what he had spent during his week in Bristol, which amounted to £45, and the money he had drawn from accounts in Gibraltar, which was a further £38-10-0. Secondly, a charge was to be brought against him for indiscretion when in France. It was claimed 'that he mentioned in France that rendezvous were kept by submarine' and it was implied that Churchill had previously arranged to take d'Astier back to Gibraltar by submarine.

As for the expenses part, the principle adopted by F Section was for hotel bills to be paid by the organisation, while any other advances drawn by individuals from accounts were to be taken from their salary. In this case, the money spent in Bristol was between three (including Zeff and Newman) and so there was no further action, and only half the money he had drawn from the accounts flight at Gibraltar would eventually be taken from Churchill's pay. As for the charge against him, Buckmaster immediately leapt to Churchill's defence as the charge was based on deduction and presumption, and not facts. However, Buckmaster knew that if the charge could not be quashed then the chances of SOE obtaining a submarine for future operations were slim. Churchill had been asked to make a statement but, again, F Section came to his defence and decided against him submitting a statement. SOE's formal response to Gibraltar includes:

> 1 – The first allegation was that Churchill was asked in France how he arrived and replied 'by submarine from Gibraltar'. This is explained in 583 [a message] as a 'deduction from remarks by A.D.L.V. [d'Astier de la Vigerie] who appeared to know that C [Churchill] has arrived by submarine'. It would be indeed surprising if A.D.L.V. did not know this when he arrived in Gibraltar considering that he accompanied Churchill back by submarine himself. As Churchill spent precisely ¾ hour on French soil, it is difficult to see that he could physically have had much time for spreading the story that he was going about in

submarines, quite apart from his direct statement that he did not do so. On the other hand, it must have been obvious to those whom he contacted there that he had not swum there from Gibraltar.

2 – It is implied that Churchill 'made arrangements to meet A.D.L.V. at Antibes, and take him off by submarine'. This is totally untrue. Neither Churchill nor SOE knew that A.D.L.V. was at Antibes when the submarine arrived. In point of fact A.D.L.V., learning from the doctor [Lévy] mentioned in 583 that bodies were being delivered at Antibes went down there 'on spec' and when the first body reported at the doctor's house, rushed off to join Churchill.

3 – As Churchill spent ¾ hour on French soil and saw only the Doctor and A.D.L.V. himself, the whole allegation falls to the ground.

4 – It is not unnatural that a submarine should be the expected craft. It is the most likely method of operating.

5 – We resent the suggestion that Churchill and A.D.L.V. cooked their story in conjunction. They are both most honourable officers, and would regard such an insinuation as a direct insult.

The incident did not go any further as an official response from Gibraltar, dated 7 June 1942, soon brought the matter to an end:

> Knowing the whole incident from this end at the very beginning and through and through until I was sick of it, it seemed to me to have been magnified out of all proportion and to have been forgotten by everybody here. I was therefore somewhat surprised to find it raked up again . . . So far as Gibraltar is concerned the whole incident has long since been forgotten and, if I may say so, I trust you will not take it up again in the U.K. as it should have died a natural death years ago. It is really just one incident typical of many.

The matter was closed and with the administrative hassles behind him, and with the Saint-Assise idea having disappeared, all Churchill could do now was to wait for his next challenge to come along.

Chapter 10

Spindle

Nothing much happened for Churchill during the next few weeks, certainly as far as an operation was concerned. He was instead sent to RAF Tempsford in Bedfordshire, now home to two Special Duty squadrons, for Lysander training in preparation for his next mission.

With its high-wing monoplane design, short take-off and landing capability, and its robust fixed undercarriage, the Westland Lysander was ideal for carrying agents to and from the field. The biggest advantage of delivering agents in this way, rather than by parachute, was that it ensured pin-point accuracy. Agents sat behind the pilot on a wooden seat facing the tail, giving them an excellent view downwards on both sides. Although the Lysander had no guns to defend itself and its cruising speed was only around 170 mph, half the speed of any marauding night fighters, its stalling speed was around 70 mph, making the aircraft extremely manoeuvrable and evasion its best form of defence. Also, by transiting to and from its destination at between 3,000 and 7,000 feet the Lysander was generally well below the height of any enemy night fighters that were primarily looking for RAF bombers.

Churchill arrived at Tempsford on 16 June 1942, this time using the codename SPINDLE. His training lasted six days. It was an important part of his progression because when he next went into the field, he would be required to organise Lysander drop-offs and pick-ups. He had to understand what the aircraft was capable of, or not, and know what constituted a suitable landing site. He had to know how to prepare a site, the procedures for signalling the pilot from the ground and what lighting was required.

The end of Churchill's training report reads:

> This officer has shown himself completely capable of carrying out a successful operation, and he definitely falls into the above average category.

As far as thoughts about what Churchill's next operation should be, there was the odd idea here and there, but nothing that came to anything; either because it did not meet his expertise, or it could be done equally well by someone already on the ground in France. Churchill later described himself as being bored to distraction during this period. Until now things had constantly moved at pace. There was always something for him, but now he was having to be patient.

Then, in July, Churchill was summoned to Orchard Court. Buckmaster explained to him that he was to return to France. He was to be dropped blind (without a reception committee) near Nîmes and was to proceed by train to a safe house in Cannes. The house belonged to a Monsieur Audouard who would then put Churchill in touch with Francis Basin. Churchill was then briefed on his mission in more detail, the major part being the selection of suitable locations for the dropping of agents and supplies, as summarised in his briefing sheet:

1. In general, to reconnoitre Lysander and dropping grounds in the following areas: Montmorillon (Vienne); N.W. of Confolens (Charente); Allier – river zone; S. of Moulins; Mâcon district in Rhône valley; 5 k.m. N.E. of Gannat.
2. In particular, to pick one or two grounds for picking up the second emissary of the CARTE organisation.

Churchill was also given some messages for Basin. London needed to know details of safe houses where more organisers and W/T operators could be sent during the next moon; this would avoid having to use hotels. Basin was also asked what supplies he would like brought on the next felucca, and where they needed to be landed. The list of messages went on, but once Churchill had done that he was to wait for orders as to how he was to get out of France.

As for when he would be setting off, that should be very soon. An air transport request had been put in for him to leave Tempsford any time during a six-day window starting on 27 July, and he could expect to be dropped into France somewhere around midnight. It was also explained to him that his mission formed part of a larger plan – 'to get large quantities of material within the shortest possible time to those points where it can be best employed'.

It all sounded straightforward enough but once he was briefed and ready to go nothing happened. The six-day window of opportunity passed, meaning Churchill would have to wait for the next suitable moon period the following month.

It was late August by the time Churchill returned to Orchard Court. Much had happened since his last briefing, with the situation in the south of France having become increasingly chaotic following the recent arrest of Basin. Basin had initially gone into hiding after being betrayed by an informer, but, on 18 August, Vichy officials caught up with him. And so, Churchill was to go back to Cannes to take Basin's place and to liaise with André Girard, whose CARTE organisation was seemingly spreading far and wide. Churchill's final instructions, under the codename RAOUL, and dated 26 August, read:

> Captain Churchill will go into the field on the night of [blank] and will be dropped at [blank]. He will then proceed to Cannes where he is to contact ANTOINE at the Villa Isabelle, route de Frejus. There he will ask for BAPTISTE who will be able to put him into contact with PIERROT who will give him the details of his liaison work with the CARTE organisation. Captain Churchill has been given all the available information we have on CARTE, and his organisation and understands perfectly that this is very much out of date and will be completed by PIERROT. If for any reason he has any difficulty in finding the Villa Isabelle – which is unlikely – he can go to Audouard, whose house he knows, and say that he is RAOUL coming rather late in the day *de la part de Jacques*, and ask to see JACQUES who will be able to put him in touch with ANTOINE and thereby with BAPTISTE. This second course is only to be employed if Captain Churchill finds it impossible to make contact with the Villa Isabelle. Captain Churchill is already fully aware of our general principles of work in the field in which he has been briefed several times previously. These have, however, been gone through with him once again. It is to be clearly understood that Captain Churchill is going out on a mission to replace OLIVE [Basin] in his connections with the CARTE organisation and that he is not going into the field permanently. It is to be hoped that his mission will terminate in a month or at the outside in 2 months' time.

Being dropped off by submarine and paddling ashore in the dark was one thing, but this was going to be very different to what Churchill had done before. Until now, he had worked alone, but within a circuit agents worked as a group of three: an organiser to lead; a wireless operator to provide the link with London and others; and a courier to act as a messenger and to make sure things arrived in the right place at the right time.

For a wireless operator, Churchill would have access to Isidore Newman, whom he had earlier taken to France. Newman had been working with URCHIN until Basin's arrest and was now working with Girard, and so he could send and receive messages for Churchill as well. But there was no courier available. Churchill would have to find someone just as soon as he could. He would also have to keep his head below the parapet and delegate accordingly, rather than unnecessarily risk being caught himself. There would be fall-outs and disagreements along the way and Churchill would be required to keep the peace, not only within his own group but with other groups as well. It would be Churchill's greatest challenge.

The SOE official historian M. R. D. Foot later gave his own thoughts on Churchill's suitability for the liaison mission he was being sent on with André Girard's CARTE. In his book *SOE in France* Foot wrote:

> Neither patience nor diplomacy was his [Churchill's] long suit, and his previous clandestine experiences no more fitted him for his liaison work than his capacity as an ice hockey international fitted him to play chess.

Foot's assessment of Churchill seems somewhat harsh considering Buckmaster's confidence in him, but the idea of sending Churchill to work with Girard had been discussed even before Basin's arrest, following a visit to Cannes by Nicolas Bodington the previous month. Bodington had met Girard who boasted a great deal, not least about having a private army some 200,000 strong, many of whom belonged to the French Army of the Armistice and could join up with the Resistance at the right moment to help liberate France. Bodington had been impressed by what Girard had told him and on his return to London arranged with Buckmaster for another SOE officer to be sent to the region; that officer was Churchill, who was considered the perfect choice given he had already been to France. And with Basin now in prison, it was a matter of some priority to get Churchill to France just as soon as this could be arranged.

But Churchill would be returning to France at a difficult time. Firstly, relations with de Gaulle's committee in London were not going well. Secondly, it was a time when the United States' Office of Strategic Services, OSS, which had formed a special operations branch in London to shadow SOE, was sending its first agents into France, with no integration yet between the two organisations. There was a further consideration, too, certainly as far as operations in the unoccupied south of France were concerned. The Allied landings in North Africa were just a matter of weeks away, which would mean a lack of resources available to SOE's operations on the ground.

And so, it was against this rather complex political backdrop that Churchill was to return to France. He would keep his identity card and demobilisation papers in the name of Pierre Chauvet and the plan was for him to be dropped by parachute near the southern city of Montpellier, from where he could catch a train to Cannes. He would be put up at a safe address there. He was required to do many things: organising parachute drops of weapons and other supplies for the CARTE circuit; organising reception committees for agents brought to the south coast of France; finding suitable landing sites for the Lysanders and Hudsons ferrying people in and out of the Unoccupied Zone; and begin preparations for the sabotage of the rail network in the area, although no attacks should be carried out until he was instructed to do so. He was also to arrange for Basin to get out of prison. Furthermore, many young Frenchmen were hiding in the forests and mountains. They would make ideal resisters; all they needed was money and weapons. And as far as money was concerned, Churchill would be responsible for financing the group, which would require around one million francs per month. He would also be required to complete situation reports to keep London informed of progress, and deal with any other matters that needed to be resolved. It was a huge task.

The following day, 27 August, Churchill was back at Tempsford Hall. It was a beautiful late summer day. With him was André Simon, one of SOE's conducting officers, who had just returned from the Unoccupied Zone. It was his job to make sure that Churchill was briefed with any last-minute updates and accompany him to the airfield to help with his equipment before finally boarding the aircraft.

Early that evening Churchill made the now-familiar journey to the airfield where a four-engine Halifax was waiting. He was introduced to the aircraft captain, Flying Officer Walzak, and his Polish crew. Simon helped Churchill with his equipment and parachute, and then attached his suitcase. There was time for a quick briefing with the crew. They were to carry out a leaflet drop on the way, to maximise the sortie, but other than that they would make sure Churchill got to the right place. Looking at the map it became apparent that the planned dropping point was too close to some buildings, and so they all agreed Churchill should be dropped a little more to the north-east. The young dispatcher, Flight Sergeant Madjeski, then explained to Churchill what would happen prior to the drop. And with that, they were off.

It was 8 p.m. The sun was beginning to set. The evening silence was broken by the sound of the engines as they roared into life. The chocks were removed, and the Halifax trundled across the airfield towards the take-off point. Few of the locals would have seen it climb away, although they would have heard it. They had become used to the sound of a lone aircraft climbing into the air at dusk.

With a long transit ahead, Madjeski brought Churchill a flask of hot coffee with rum and some sandwiches to help him settle down. For the next four and a half hours the Halifax droned on through the night. Fortunately, the weather was good, with only a little cloud over Europe, and it was a quiet transit. Their route took them clear of known enemy anti-aircraft positions and any prowling night fighters. Bomber Command was carrying out a large-scale effort against Kassel that night, and so the enemy's defences were likely to be tied up elsewhere. Churchill even managed to get some sleep.

Finally, it was time to prepare for the drop. The Halifax started its gentle descent. Churchill looked at his watch. It was nearly 1 a.m. Madjeski clipped the parachute strap onto the static line running along the length of the fuselage as Churchill sat astride the hole in the fuselage floor. The Halifax was now much closer to the ground, less than a thousand feet beneath. Looking down he could see the moon-lit patchwork of fields and woods below, while all the time keeping an eye on the light panel nearby. But there was no light yet.

Churchill was to jump from a height of around 600 feet, high enough for his parachute to deploy fully but low enough to reduce the amount of time he would spend under the chute, which would only be about fifteen seconds. He could make out the lights of a town, which he assumed was Montpellier. Then the red light flashed on. The dispatcher raised his hand. The aircraft continued to reduce speed. It was now below 150 mph. This was it. Churchill knew that he could not waste any time leaving the aircraft; every second of delay would mean nearly a hundred metres of error on the ground. Then Madjeski shouted 'Go', and his arm swept down. And with that, Churchill was gone. For the next couple of seconds, he was swept through the air before a sudden jerk confirmed his canopy had opened. In his first report back to London, Churchill said:

> Before taking the plunge I stupidly forgot to tighten my harness, so when the sail opened it was like meeting Joe Louis on pay night. The buttock strap slipped half way up my back and as into the bargain I was in a spin I felt like writing to the manufacturers. The moon was a honey so when I ceased pirouetting the three olive trees were very clear indeed. I did not strike any of them but landed like a sack of offal at the corner of a vineyard on a small rock. The harness question wrenched a lot of parts in my left groin which still complain, but this is a matter of no moment at all. Please tell Wooler I kept my puppies together, and also that jumping in triple glasses is perfectly feasible. The Poles [aircraft crew] were A.1. Top marks.

Fortunately, there was no one around. Churchill concealed his parachute in a thicket beneath some trees and set off with his suitcase in hand, albeit with some aches and pains. It was a clear night. He could see the North Star, and the lights of a passing vehicle nearby confirmed where the road must be. On the assumption that he had been dropped in the right place, then Montpellier would be just 10 km away.

When he reached the road, Churchill set off in an easterly direction towards the town. It was not long before he could make out the faint glow of lights in the distance. He decided to leave the road; the curfew would still be in force. But progress through the vines was slow, and he came to a stream he needed to cross. There was no bridge to be found and so he had to wade across. And as he did not want to enter Montpellier until daybreak, he curled up on his raincoat and fell asleep.

Meanwhile, it had taken less than four hours for the Halifax to return home. With another successful drop, the crew filled in the Air Transport Operation Report, giving the sortie codename (SPINDLE I), the date (27 August 1942), the result of the sortie (Completed), the names of the aircraft captain and dispatcher (F/O Walzak and F/Sgt Madjeski), detail/containers (leaflets), key times (all in British Summer Time) –

take-off (2005), drop (0057), and landing (0445) – and the Captain's Report, which read:

> Point found. Man dropped where he wished N.E. of actual pin point on southern margin of road running west of MONTPELLIER. Ground here clear of all obstruction (there were buildings on the agreed point). Jumped from 600 ft a.g.l. [above ground level] flying S – N.

The dispatcher's report simply read: 'Man jumped well and immediately', with the rear gunner's observation confirming that the 'chute had been seen to open. For the Halifax crew it had been a good night's work.

Churchill woke to the rising sun and a cloudless sky. He changed his trousers and opened his wallet to check his tickets and ration book, and then he noticed a glaring error in his preparations. In *Duel of Wits*, Churchill describes how to his horror he found in his wallet a ten-shilling note and *The Times* crossword puzzle, which he had cut out the previous day. Because Churchill was an experienced agent, Simon had skimped over checking his wallet, believing he hardly need inspect the belongings of an old hand like Churchill. It was a schoolboy error, and it was one that Churchill should never have made, but it was a stark reminder of just how easy it was to become complacent. Not only could it have cost him his freedom, but it could also have cost him his life.

Having stuffed the bank note and crossword into a gap in some nearby rocks, Churchill set off along a narrow country lane leading towards the road he had left the night before. Workers would soon be going about their morning business and so Churchill would be able to blend in with the crowd.

By the time he entered the outskirts of Montpellier there were plenty of people about. He was soon on a tram heading to the centre of the town. At the railway station he went into a café for some coffee and bread, and then bought a ticket to Cannes.

The train, as usual, was packed. Churchill had to stand all the way to Marseille, but for the rest of the journey he could relax and enjoy the scene. It was a lovely sunny day and the hazy cloudless sky blended beautifully with the deep blue of the Mediterranean Sea. By midday he was in Cannes. It had only been six months since he was last there. Nothing seemed to have changed, other than that the snowy weather of January had now been replaced by the late summer sun. He caught a bicycle taxi to the Route de Fréjus, where he was to stay at a villa belonging to a man known as ANTOINE. This was Baron Henri Ravel de Malval, a former French naval attaché in London who had retired to Cannes and whose home, the Villa Isabelle, had been used as Basin's headquarters.

The Baron and another man, PIERROT, who had been looking after matters since Basin's arrest, were at the villa to meet Churchill. For the next couple of hours Churchill was briefed on all that was going on. Newman was due to arrive later that evening and they were to meet Girard the following day. There was now a courier in place, a woman called Gisèle, who moved around between Arles, Marseille, and Cannes. Churchill was to meet her on Wednesday at a café in Cannes. As for Basin, he was being held at the St Rock Barracks in Nice. Apparently, he was being treated reasonably well, but the group were trying to find out when he was due to be transferred to Lyon by train, so they could make their move and set him free. Basin's deputy BATISTE was currently out of town but he would get in touch on his return. A flat had been made available for Churchill as it would not be wise for him to stay at the Villa Isabelle for very long. There was money in the safe, some 3 million francs, for him to use until more cash could be sent from England.

That evening Newman arrived. Churchill was pleased to see him again. During their chat Newman made it clear he was not happy with how Girard was using him. He wanted endless messages sent. Not only that, but Newman was having to transmit from the same house every time, which was highly risky as lengthy messages could be intercepted by enemy radio detector vans and traced to the location from where they originated.

It was time to let London know that Churchill had arrived. A cipher message dated 28 August 1942 simply reads: 'FROM DIVIDEND 134. RAOUL ARRIVED SAFE STOP'.

Newman's points were a worry for Churchill and his initial concerns about how CARTE was operating were reinforced the following morning when he met Girard at the Théâtre du Casino. Churchill had met Girard before, albeit briefly during his first mission to France, but now they were going to have to work closely together. Churchill had expected a quiet meeting place, perhaps in an empty office or somewhere else private, but instead he arrived at the theatre to find Girard surrounded by his friends, including a police commissioner and a senior military officer, and Girard was keen to make sure they all knew who Churchill was.

There was much to discuss, although the crowded theatre was probably not the best place to talk about a possible felucca arriving that night. A reception committee would have to be arranged, and so the two agreed to meet for dinner that evening at Girard's house in Antibes where plans could be considered in more detail.

Churchill spent the rest of the morning cycling around Cannes to observe the local scene. He cycled past the port and along the seafront, and then turned into the Rue Pasteur to meet the Baron at a small block of flats off the Croisette where Churchill was to stay. He surveyed the one-bedroom flat on the ground floor. He could hear the noise of everyday life and there was a window, which opened easily and quietly, with a small drop out on to the courtyard. It was ideal should he ever need to make his escape and quickly merge into the world outside. The landlord could be trusted and would not ask any questions. In his first report back to London, Churchill later commented:

> My small flat is ideal. It is leased in someone else's name. It is leased unfurnished and therefore not on any list for perquisitioning [requisitioning]. If, however, this should happen there is a little grille like they have in doubtful nightclubs through which I can check up as to who and how many are knocking. If it is one gendarme I can attend to him thanks to the gorilla's tender instructions at Garramor. If there are two I have only to say wait a minute and collect my suitcase full of papers and blow out of the window into the night air and back alleys.

The flat was perfect, although Churchill would also need a second flat available should he ever need to leave in a hurry.

Next stop was a beautician's, the Salon de Beauté, on the Rue du Canada, just around the corner from the flat, where Churchill was introduced to a woman known as Suzanne. This was Marie-Lou Blanc, a discreet and trusted beauty specialist in her forties. She had a room available. Churchill could set up his headquarters there.

Marie-Lou had lived in Cannes all her life. She knew many people, including most officials, and so Churchill took her on as an assistant. After lunch, he met Newman, who had a message to deliver. A felucca carrying six agents would be arriving that night. Churchill then went to see Francine, who he had briefly stayed with on his first mission, to check the empty cottage was still available should he ever need somewhere to stay. It was, and Francine gave him a warm welcome as always, although Churchill was saddened to hear that Joseph had died. He then set off along the coast road to cycle the 10 km to Girard's home in Antibes.

Girard lived with his wife and four daughters in a modest house just a few hundred metres from where Churchill had landed Newman and Zeff a few months before. By the time Churchill arrived it was early evening. Others were already there, including the local police commissioner from Marseille and members of the CARTE circuit, including Girard's deputy, Henri Frager, known as PAUL and also codenamed LOUBA. Churchill also met a young engineering student from Lancashire called Victor Hazan; he had studied at Manchester University and was now in France to train saboteurs. There was also a tall, young man of immense energy called André Marsac, codenamed END; he was another of Girard's lieutenants. Churchill was also introduced to another friend of the Baron, Colonel Pierre Vautrin; he was an officer in the Armistice Army and the head of the local French counter-espionage service.

After supper, the others left to wait for the felucca, leaving Churchill and Girard to talk some more. Girard explained to Churchill that Basin was due to be taken to Lyon the following morning and that his men would board the train to set him free. Basin would then need to return to Britain as his cover would be blown. They then talked about Newman. It was clear Girard and Newman did not get on, as Newman had already explained, but Girard seemed to have no appreciation of the dangers wireless operators faced. Girard wanted more messages sent, and longer ones at that, all transmitted exactly as he had so verbosely written, whereas Churchill was keen to keep transmissions short. Even then, only urgent messages should ever be sent; couriers should be used for anything else.

It was a point on which the two could not agree. However, as Churchill would need access to a wireless operator, they agreed that Newman would work with him as well, until another 'pianist' could be sent out and allocated to Girard for the sole use of CARTE. But that would take time, probably several weeks, and so Churchill knew that he would have to keep on the right side of Girard.

With their meeting over, Churchill returned to Cannes and went to bed. For now, Newman would stay, although Churchill had already seen the tell-tale signs of strain on the young wireless operator's face and knew that he might have to be replaced before too long. It had been a hectic first day and Churchill was tired, but it was not easy to fall asleep with so many things going on in his mind.

Chapter 11

Enter Odette

Back in London, Buckmaster's staff were following developments on the Côte d'Azur. It was a crucial time. Churchill had quickly settled into life in Cannes. His time was split between meeting Newman, or Marie-Lou Blanc at the salon, and attending the Wednesday meeting at the café with the courier, Gisèle. Churchill and Newman would meet every day, at a different time and in a different place, and through Marie-Lou Churchill secured a second headquarters on the Quai St Pierre, at a flat belonging to a woman known as CATHERINE, but whose real name was Odette des Garets, a Parisian artist in her early fifties.

Churchill had also got to meet the man known as BATISTE, who had been Basin's deputy, but it was a difficult situation from the start. The two did not immediately get on, BATISTE having far too much to say. Churchill felt BATISTE always talked down to him as if he would not understand anything he was saying or have any understanding of what life was like in France. BATISTE wanted to be involved with everything, which was understandable, but he wanted to be involved to the point that he was the one giving the orders, rather than Churchill, which is not the role of a second-in-command.

Rather than being able to pick a deputy of his own, Churchill had inherited one and so it was never really going to work. It also seems that BATISTE was slack when it came to matters of security. In his first report to London, dated 10 September 1942, which was sent by courier the following day through the Spain, Churchill was critical of BATISTE:

> BATISTE is not only a 100% Jew with a death sentence issued in the Z.O. [Zone Occupée], but he talks too much, too often and too loud. BATISTE has a Jewish identity card which he openly waves around on the waterfront cafés. So, whether BATISTE is capable of filling O's [OLIVE's – Francis Basin's] shoes or not, we always live under the sword of Damocles, or shall we say the sign of the Swastika where BATISTE is concerned. There has only to be a mishap in this Jewish household for O's lieut., if

> B is to be O's lieut., which so far I've not settled, to be creased in his turn. Now added to this B took ULYSSE to the Marseille ghetto where, of course, B is very much persona grata owing to the death sentence hanging over his head. But these members of the big mafily [family] would have no part of ULYSSE as he was not on the run, not a Jew and not ostensibly poor. This is no kind of setting for piano study [wireless training], whatever, so after many changes of residence and no appearance of the piano [wireless set], it is not surprising U returned to this town. What kind of work is this? In the train with Yvonne, B was openly bandying PIERROT's real surname, and discussing submarines and parachutes much to the joy of all the citizens in the same compartment. Then B declares to one and all at Y's home town that he has now superseded O. Y claims that he makes a very bad impression wherever he goes outside the ghetto bounds, and I am not surprised at that. Flashy characters full of ballyhoo are not meant for this work. If I can possibly find someone else I shall cut down B's activities to set active jobs which have nothing to do with organising. I will eat my old wool hat if I know what I have done to inherit this quagmire.

Also included in Churchill's first report are details of the failed attempt by Girard's men to release Francis Basin during the train journey from Nice to Lyon. A brief message had been sent to London the day before to deliver the disappointing news as soon as possible, as Churchill's typed report would take several days to reach London. The message, dated 9 September 1942, simply reads: 'FROM RAOUL STOP ATTEMPT OLIVE ESCAPE FAILED NOT CARTES FAULT FEAR OLIVES WORK OVER BUT EVERY HOPE OBTAIN FULL LIST HIS CLIENTS STOP'.

With the message having been sent, Churchill's report provided more details of the failed rescue attempt:

> LOUBA and a heavy posse accompanied O. [Basin] in the train from Nice to Lyon. The former crowded the corridors. Sitting beside O. was his ever-loving sweet pea, a passionate and dangerous red-head. However, during the trip to the Lyon assizes O. managed to hand over to her the addresses of three characters who can be contacted and who have lists of O's organisation. These have been passed to me and when I can

> find someone capable of handling the matter the loose ends will be dealt with. Many bookie signs were exchanged between the confederates in the train, and O. signalled to leave well alone so these heroes beat it at Arles thinking also that maybe they would all be roped in if they went as far as Lyon. So now O. is nothing but a gone gosling, and if he gets out I still maintain he must be shipped home as he is blown wide open.

And so, Basin had not been freed. He was taken to Lyon and held at the old prison of Fort Montluc, used to hold military prisoners and opponents of the Nazi occupation and Vichy regime. But the fact that the planned escape had not been a success would later lead Churchill to question if Basin had even wanted to be released at all. Either way, it made little difference. Just a few weeks later Basin's release was negotiated with the Vichy military command, and he was flown back to Britain.

Churchill would send regular reports to London, usually every week, which he signed off as Damon Runyon. These reports were generally of a routine nature to keep London informed that he was doing fine, although he was still struggling to keep the peace between Girard and Newman, as highlighted in the opening sentence of his seventh report, dated 8 October 1942: 'For weeks that I think are months I keep the peace between JULIEN and CARTE, and although I do the best I can it is of no avail.'

Churchill had become increasingly convinced that Newman needed a rest and made the difficult decision to send him home on the next felucca. It was a decision that upset Newman to the point that on his return to London he made it clear he did not approve of the way Churchill had treated him. Isidore Newman would return to France the following year, this time to work with a circuit in Rouen and Le Havre, but his luck eventually ran out when he was arrested and ended up at the concentration camp at Mauthausen, where he was executed in September 1944.

The decision to return Newman to Britain had been made a little easier by the unexpected arrival of another wireless operator, 24-year-old Adolphe Rabinowitch, codenamed ARNAUD. A Russo-Egyptian Jew and former boxing champion, he parachuted into France around the same time as Churchill with orders to go to Paris, but his aircraft had missed the drop zone and he landed to the north of Grenoble, some 30 km from where he should have been. Temporarily stranded, he had gone into hiding until BATISTE became aware of him through his contacts and arranged for Rabinowitch to go to Cannes. Initially, though, he did not want to stay in Cannes. He considered the Unoccupied Zone too quiet and felt he could be of far more use in Paris, where he should have been. But Churchill managed to persuade Rabinowitch that he would be incredibly useful where he was, explaining that his current wireless operator, Newman, was about to leave.

London had approved Churchill's request for Rabinowitch to stay. Churchill had now settled into a routine that, so far, did not involve any active operations. But some along the Côte d'Azur were becoming frustrated at the lack of any activity against the enemy, although that was not what Churchill had been sent to France to do. In *SOE in France*, M. R. D. Foot wrote:

> Peter Churchill's main role in France was to act as principal liaison officer between CARTE and Baker Street; this may in part explain what so much annoyed his colleagues on the Riviera at the time, why he did no actual sabotage work at all. To do it was only a minor part of his task, for which other preoccupations never left him time . . . That it was part of his task indeed can only be inferred from a couple of indications that microphotographed notes of targets were sent to him in October; and even these may have been for transmission to somebody else.

Although there was plenty going on elsewhere in France at this time, much of F Section's attention was being taken up with CARTE. It had promised so much and was the reason why Churchill had been sent to France, but although Girard was perhaps at the pinnacle of his power, there was nothing to confirm that his boast of a potential army of 200,000 resisters was true.

While Girard was not a military man, he always seemed to say the right things. His diplomacy and charm were the reasons why Churchill and others persevered with him for so long. But even if Girard genuinely had an army of 200,000, the shortage of air transport available to SOE at that time meant it was never going to be possible to equip them with the explosives and arms they would need.

This was a crucial period for the SOE planners back home, if for no other reason than it gave them a true appreciation of the scale of effort required if the resistance groups across France were one day to rise against their Nazi occupiers and fight. But the truth was that Girard was starting to make growing demands of London. In addition to more money and arms, he wanted wireless sets to be operated by his own men, rather than by wireless operators working for SOE. Also, he was starting to quarrel with everyone, including his own deputy, Frager, and Churchill.

Back in London, meanwhile, Churchill's work with SOE had led to him being recommended for the Military Cross. The recommendation, dated 19 October 1942, reads:

> T/Capt. Peter Morland Churchill
> Intelligence Corps
> No: P/162707
>
> This officer has already completed two very successful missions in France and is at present engaged on a third. The first was in December 1941. He was sent to France at a time when our agents in the Unoccupied Zone were almost all on the run. It was his duty to establish contact with several of these men in order to determine their loyalty, a task which brought him into great personal danger. He accomplished this successfully and returned home with a valuable report on which our organisation in Unoccupied France was rebuilt.
>
> Capt. Churchill's second mission in April 1942, was to land three agents on the Mediterranean Coast. He left the craft ahead of his party, made a reconnaissance, during which he was in constant danger of discovery. He then carried out three further journeys from ship to shore in the same night and landed his three comrades safely. His success in the final stages of this operation was entirely due to great courage combined with cool-headed resource.
>
> He has gone on his third mission to France with the same determination to succeed without regard to personal danger which characterises his approach to any duty required of him. His bravery is a constant inspiration to our men.
>
> Recommended for the M.C.

How far this recommendation went up the chain of command is not known, but no award was made. Churchill would have to wait for recognition for the work he was doing in France. He was, however, about to gain another member for SPINDLE and like the circumstances behind him having gained Rabinowitch, it was chance that brought it about. Only this time it was an opportunity that would not only change the course of his war, but would also change the course of his life.

The excellent work conducted by the first women sent into France had convinced F Section to send more into the field. Until that point, Britain had not really contemplated the idea of putting women into any danger. It was considered acceptable to employ women to work on the land or in factories, or even in the armed forces if it was not in the face of the enemy, and so it required a fundamental change in thinking for SOE to employ women in the field. As far as F Section was concerned it made perfect sense. Women of all ages were roaming over France and using all forms of transport, such as bicycles and trains, and were often seen carrying bags or luggage. And so, it was felt that women would not attract suspicion or unwanted attention, especially if operating as couriers. Age would be no barrier. Female agents would range from young women barely out of their teens to those in their forties and fifties. It would never be easy to find suitable female volunteers with all the appropriate skills, but those who were selected came from all levels of society and were clever, quick-witted, and brave.

During the early hours of 2 November, three more women stepped off a felucca at a cove near the small commune of Cassis, to the east of Marseille. These were Mary Herbert, destined for Bordeaux, Marie-Thérèse Le Chêne, who was to travel to Lyon, and 30-year-old Odette Sansom, travelling under the name Odette Meyer and codenamed LISE, who was to travel north to Auxerre in the Occupied Zone. Also dropped from the felucca were three men. These were George Starr (HILAIRE), the leader of the group, who was heading for Lyon to join Duboudin and who would later become F Section's chief organiser in Gascony, and two wireless operators – John Young, codenamed GABRIEL, a former fire insurance surveyor in his thirties, and Marcus Bloom, a burly London cinema director with the codename URBAIN, who was heading to Toulouse.

Marsac met the new arrivals. The plan was for Churchill to look after the onward arrangements for the women, while the Baron offered the use of his villa for the men. It was the first time Churchill was to be involved in looking after female agents passing through Cannes, and so he wanted to make sure everything was right for them to make their stay as short and as comfortable as possible. After eight hungry days at sea followed by a couple of hours on the train, they would need somewhere to relax and freshen up and so he decided it was best for them to stay at the salon with Marie-Lou Blanc.

The women arrived from Marseille on the morning train. Marsac took them straight to the salon, where they were met by Churchill and Marie-Lou. After a short rest and a bath, they all went to a local restaurant for lunch. In *Duel of Wits*, Churchill makes no secret of just how closely he had observed Odette during that first lunch. His thoughts are best described in his own words:

> Her name was Lise and from her mop of light-brown hair, swept back to reveal a rounded forehead, down to a pair of discerning eyes, there emanated a distinct aura of challenge that was only intensified by the determined set of her chin below a somewhat colourless face. A fearless look suggested that not even the thought of the prisons held any terrors for this girl.

Odette was everything SOE was always on the lookout for. Born and raised in Amiens, she was privately educated in France and later settled in London after marrying an Englishman. The couple had three daughters, but the war changed everything. Her husband joined the Army, while she and the children moved to the safety of Somerset. She might even have stayed there, but her heart remained in France and after the Armistice she yearned to do more. She had become aware of SOE after responding to a BBC appeal asking listeners for postcards of towns and villages along the northern coastline of France. Her details were then passed to SOE, and she was invited to attend an interview. Although there was some concern about her suitability to become an agent, because she was a mother of three, Odette was too good to let go and, after leaving her children in the care of a convent school, she joined SOE. Now she was in France.

The following morning, Mary Herbert and Marie-Thérèse le Chêne went on their way. Had Odette been heading for one of the circuits in the Unoccupied Zone then she would have been on her way too. Instead, she would have to wait in Cannes until her papers arrived permitting her to travel to the Occupied Zone. It was a delay that would ultimately change the course of Odette's life.

From the outset there was clearly an affinity between Churchill and Odette, but she was quick to point out to him that she wanted to get moving as soon as possible. She had no desire to sit around with nothing to do. However, as it would take time for her papers to appear and there was plenty that Churchill needed doing, she seemed only too keen to help.

The following day Odette agreed to take some messages to Girard, giving Churchill the time to get on with other things. By the time she cycled back to Cannes, Rabinowitch had joined Churchill at the flat. Her trip had gone impressively well, and in good time too, so they all went off to lunch.

Odette was keen to do more and so Churchill agreed to give her another task. She was to go up to the Baron's villa that afternoon and find out where the newly arrived men were heading. She was then to work out the best train times from Cannes to Marseille the following morning, and then for their onward journeys to their respective destinations. She was to book the train tickets and accompany the men to Marseille. Then, once they were all on their way, she was to find the Hôtel Moderne. There she was to give a password to the reception clerk and introduce herself to a man known as OLIVIER. He would have a suitcase that she needed to bring back to Cannes. Having collected the suitcase, she was to catch a tram to Aix-en-Provence and go to a garage on the Boulevard Zola. She was to ask for Monsieur Gontrand and give him 50,000 francs in return for the garage holding 500 litres of petrol. And once everything was done, she was to return to Marseille and catch the train back to Cannes.

This was a much greater challenge. Marseille was not a good place to work, and Churchill warned Odette of all the potential traps. There was much to remember and a lot to do, but it was a task typically carried out by couriers all over France.

The following day Odette went off. Everything went as it should and she returned to Cannes on the last train the following day, suitcase in hand.

Churchill was impressed and clearly wanted Odette to stay. He told her so over dinner that night, explaining he had no courier of his own and that he could really put her to good use. But Odette remained keen on going to Auxerre. In his book *Odette* Jerrard Tickell described her reaction to being asked to stay in Cannes:

> Cannes has nothing to do with the real France, the France I came to find. I expected a hard, resentful, smouldering France and came to live in and to work in that France. It is my misfortune that I came to the one bit of my country where the war doesn't go on. I wanted very much to be with my true compatriots and to fight the Germans.

Odette clearly wanted to be part of the action in the north, but she did agree that Churchill could at least ask London if she could stay.

At first Churchill's request for Odette to stay in Cannes was refused, the message received back simply instructing Odette to go to Auxerre as planned. But Churchill would not give in, and he ordered Rabinowitch to send the request again. This time London agreed.

Churchill had gone to great lengths to arrange for Odette to stay in Cannes. She moved into the apartment belonging to Odette des Garets and with Odette and Rabinowitch now on board, SPINDLE had taken shape. Things were looking up, particularly as Rabinowitch had found a house high up in the hills on the outskirts of Cannes from where he could operate with relative freedom. Churchill also made sure he had the use of other villas as well, although the high peaks and varying weather conditions would often mean it was difficult to send or receive messages from so far south.

The life of a wireless operator was often a lonely one and for Rabinowitch it was no different. It had also been reported that German radio detection vans had recently crossed into the Unoccupied Zone and so he was limited to one transmission a day, of no more than six consecutive minutes, and only then if two designated lookouts were available. Transmission times were constantly changed to reduce the risk of being caught.

Wireless operators elsewhere were also struggling, most noticeably in Marseille, Arles, and Toulouse, usually the result of unreliability or broken sets. Toulouse, for example, had been out of touch since Churchill arrived in France.

At this point Maurice Pertschuk, codenamed EUGÈNE, the young leader of the PRUNUS circuit, arrived in Cannes to see Churchill. Pertschuk had been born in Paris to British parents of Russian origin. Despite his youth – he was only twenty-one – he had been sent to France to carry out political warfare in and around Toulouse, but he soon found there were more opportunities for sabotage than propaganda. He had weapons and explosives stored in a cellar and had recently gained the use of a wireless operator, Marcus Bloom, who had arrived on the same felucca as Odette and was now based at a farm near Montréjeau, to the south-west of Toulouse. Pertschuk needed approval from London to switch from a role of propaganda to one of sabotage, but Bloom was unable to transmit from his faulty wireless set. And so Pertschuk had come to seek Churchill's help. He was hoping that Churchill could arrange to have his request sent to London and that someone could fix Bloom's set.

The problem was the farm was 600 km from Cannes. Nonetheless, Churchill agreed that Rabinowitch would go there to see what he could do, while trying to fix the sets at Marseille and Arles along the way.

On his return to Cannes, Rabinowitch met Churchill at the Quai St Pierre to report he had managed to fix all three sets. It had been a long couple of days, but at least communications had been restored. Rabinowitch was also able to report that a dozen or more short-wave sets had arrived by felucca and were being held at a farm, although they could not stay there long and needed to be stored in a safe house before being distributed amongst the groups.

It seemed to be good news. The extra sets could speed up communications between the groups but when Churchill arrived at the farm, he was shocked to discover their condition. It seemed they had been dumped with little care on a pile of vegetables on a damp floor in one of the outbuildings. Some had broken from their packing, while others had been ruined by seawater and were already starting to rust.

All the sets seemed to be damaged in some way. Churchill hoped Rabinowitch might be able to salvage something from the pile of bits, but he was disappointed and annoyed. People had risked their lives to transport these precious assets to the south of France. Now most of them seemed irreparable. Not only that, but the farmer's son made it quite clear he wanted the sets gone as soon as possible. He did not want them discovered on his farm.

Churchill went to see Girard who agreed to move the sets, but it was another example of what he later described as 'the daily struggle' of being an organiser.

The daily struggles with Girard went on, but then Churchill received a proposal from Colonel Vautrin, and it was something on a quite different scale to what he had dealt with before.

With rumours of an imminent Allied landing in North Africa circulating, Vautrin informed Churchill of a senior officer in the Armistice Army, called General Jean de Lattre de Tassigny, commander of the 16th Military Division at Montpellier, who was prepared to switch to the Allies with his men. His force of 12,000 men was fully equipped with armour and artillery, and the general was prepared to take them to the Pyrenees and fight the Germans from there, the only condition being that the British would have to re-supply his force from the air. Vautrin was now asking Churchill if he would put the idea to London and to ask if he would be prepared to join the general's staff.

Churchill jumped at the proposal and immediately had a message sent off to London. A reply was received just as quickly, with the War Office approving the idea and confirming that Churchill should join the general's staff as and when the moment came. For now, though, all he could do was to get word to the general in Montpellier that London had given the green light and then wait for him to make his move.

The Allied landings in North Africa, called Operation Torch, commenced on 8 November 1942. In response, German and Italian forces crossed the demarcation line to occupy Vichy territory, ending any semblance of independence in southern France.

Churchill could only watch on as Italian forces swept through the streets of Cannes. As far as he was concerned, though, their arrival did not change things too much. Yes, the felucca landings would have to stop and there would almost certainly be more roadblocks in place, and the curfew would be strictly enforced, but none of that should stop what they were doing. Besides, it was not as if the move had come as a complete surprise. The likely occupation of the south had been the main topic of conversation for many days. There was even talk about blowing up Alpine tunnels to prevent the arrival of the occupying forces, but such enthusiastic ideas were quickly quashed by London, much to the annoyance and frustration of those in France who struggled to understand the reasons why. But then came devastating news. Pro-Nazi French forces had stopped General de Lattre de Tassigny's division on its way to the Pyrenees, and the general had been arrested.

With the Germans and Italians having moved into the south of France, the reality was that cities such as Lyon, Marseille, Cannes, and Nice became even more dangerous places in which to operate. Furthermore, a new law – the Service du Travail Obligatoire (the Compulsory Work

Service Law) – was about to be passed, meaning that any man between the ages of seventeen and fifty-five who was not in a recognised job would be deported to Germany to work in factories there. French manpower was being used as forced labour to replace German workers sent to fight in the war, and this trawl for manpower could include Churchill as his cover story of being a journalist called Pierre Chauvet would not make him exempt.

The occupation of the south did not prevent messages going back and forth as Rabinowitch continued to work the keys of his set. One message came from Buckmaster. Churchill and Girard, along with five French Army officers destined for de Gaulle's staff, were to get ready to go to London. An aircraft would pick them up from Vinon-sur-Verdon and Churchill was instructed to find a suitable landing ground.

The message was brief and did not explain why Churchill and Girard were being called to London. Churchill showed Girard the message, although in typical Girard fashion he wanted to be the one to choose where the aircraft should land. His men had already identified a suitable field near Vinon, which would be just right for such a pick-up. It was next to an S-shaped bend in the Durance, 8 km to the south-west of Manosque, which his men had been watching for the past few weeks.

Girard's response put Churchill in a difficult position. If he insisted on surveying the site for himself then Girard would be insulted. But if he did not, and the pick-up subsequently proved to be a failure, then it would be Churchill held responsible. In the end, Churchill, wishing to keep the peace, agreed to leave it to Girard.

When it was time for Churchill and Girard to leave for London Girard reassured Churchill that everything had been taken care of as far as the landing site was concerned. On the day of the pick-up Churchill caught the train to Marseille. Odette was travelling with him, too, and from Marseille they were driven to the rendezvous point at a farm near Manosque.

It was the night of 25/26 November. Girard was already there, as were the five generals. So, too, was André Marsac with a rather large reception group. There must have been twenty people at the farm, and the noise of their chatting and laughter resembled that of a party more than the clandestine operation that it was.

Finally, the assembled gathering left the farmhouse and made their way across the moonlit field. How long they would have to wait was anyone's guess. Churchill immediately noticed the landing site was a rather unusually shaped field. Not only did it seem narrower than he had expected, but a raised bank ran diagonally across the field and the ground sloped away to the boundary where there were several high trees. The field was not suitable at all. It might have been acceptable for a small aircraft to land, but not for a small bomber-sized aircraft like the Lockheed Hudson that had been sent to pick them up. Churchill was livid. Girard accused him of being overly fussy, but Churchill made it clear that when the aircraft arrived overhead, he would have no choice but to refuse to signal it was safe to land.

In what was called Operation STEWARD, the Hudson that night was from No. 161 Squadron at Tempsford and was being flown by the station commander, Group Captain Edward 'Mouse' Fielden. The evening had not got off to a good start for Fielden. He first had to travel to Tangmere in Sussex to pick up the aircraft, only to find it was unserviceable, and so it was after 8 p.m. (GMT) before he got off the ground. Having finally arrived overhead the field at Vinon, Fielden circled the site, and he then circled it again, but after forty-five minutes of hanging around, and with no sign of any lights from the ground, he finally turned away and headed for home. He landed at 3.31 a.m., after more than seven hours in the air.

Back at the landing ground the assembled gathering had wandered off. It was only when Churchill reached the top of a ridge that he noticed an abandoned airfield stretching out before him. It would have been perfect. But now was not the time to argue or sulk. They would have to try again the following night.

Churchill and Odette stayed in Manosque that night and returned to the farm the following day, this time to prepare the landing ground at the disused airfield nearby. A coded message had confirmed that another attempt would hopefully be made that night, although an aircraft could not be guaranteed.

At 10 p.m. the large gathering assembled once again and, as before, it became a waiting game. It was a clear night and growing steadily colder by the hour, but still no sound came from the air. The temperature plunged below zero, yet still they waited in silence. For four hours they waited until the window of opportunity had closed. No aircraft had arrived. The near-frozen gathering walked dejectedly away. A great opportunity to get the group away to Britain had passed.

It was the closest Churchill would come to returning home for a while. He and Odette went back to Cannes from where he wrote a full report explaining what had happened, sending it via Switzerland. Soon after, Churchill received a message that another attempt would be made, from a known field, designated T12, near Chanoines not far from Arles, during the period of the mid-December moon. Only this time Churchill was to make sure that he was satisfied with the field.

Arles is more than 200 km from Cannes. Churchill had other things to do and so he sent Odette to survey the field. He arranged for her to be met at Arles by a member of their group and taken to T12.

Soon after Odette had left Cannes, Churchill received a visitor at Catherine's flat. It was another SOE agent, XAVIER – real name Richard Heslop – whom Churchill had not met before. Heslop had earlier been arrested while attempting to cross the demarcation line but had just been released from an internment camp after the French commandant had chosen to let him go rather than turn him over to the Germans. Heslop now wanted to contact London and would eventually go on to establish a circuit called MARKSMAN, operating in the Jura and Savoy Alps.

Churchill had become a focal point on the Côte d'Azur. There was other routine business to attend to during the morning, but in the afternoon the Baron arrived at Churchill's flat to inform him that two police inspectors had arrived at his villa asking for Pierre Chauvet. The Baron told Churchill he had fobbed them off, saying the man they were looking for was away on business for a few days, but it was obvious they would be back. Then, later that evening, Marie-Lou Blanc came to Churchill's flat to tell him the two inspectors had also called at her flat asking for him.

It was clearly time for Churchill to leave, and quickly. He gathered his belongings, strapped his case to his bicycle and filled the panniers with as much as he could carry. He then took one last look around the flat, which had served him so well for the past three months, before closing the door for the last time.

Chapter 12
Chaos

It was early December 1942. The CARTE circuit was about to descend into chaos, an event that was triggered by the loss of a briefcase on a train. André Marsac was travelling from Marseille to Paris when the briefcase he had with him, containing the personal details of more than 200 circuit members, fell into the hands of the Abwehr, the German military intelligence service, who were following Marsac at the time. Fortunately, the Germans decided not to act immediately on their find, although it would not be long before they made their move.

The delay was long enough to give members of CARTE a chance to go into hiding or leave, with some choosing to flee across the Spanish frontier. Churchill moved into the flat where Odette was staying, the one belonging to Odette des Garets. It would do for now and, as she was still away in Arles, Churchill was offered the use of her room.

The following day Odette returned with good news. The landing field was perfect. With Odette back in Cannes, Churchill moved into another flat on his own. It had a balcony overlooking the Mediterranean and for the next few days he kept a low profile until things settled down. The weather was pleasantly warm given the time of year and so he could relax in his deck chair observing the tranquil scene.

The period of the mid-December moon came. The pick-up window of opportunity would last fifteen nights before it would become too dark again and, even within the window, a pick-up could only happen on a clear night with little or no cloud. While Rabinowitch stayed in Cannes, Odette went with Churchill to Arles where they checked in at a hotel. Girard had also decided to leave the heat of Cannes and Antibes behind, and for the time being had settled with his family in Arles.

That evening they all discreetly listened to the BBC messages, waiting for the one to confirm the aircraft would be coming that night. But no message came. The following day Churchill and Odette were taken to Chanoines to have a closer look at the field. It was as good as Odette had claimed. They then returned to their hotel in time for the evening messages, but again there was nothing for them.

The days passed and still no message came. Each night was crisp and clear, perfect for a pick-up, but still there was no news. There was nothing Churchill could do. Then came news of the Germans setting up an anti-aircraft battery a kilometre away from the Chanoines field. Not only that, but a German motorcycle unit had established a camp in the vicinity.

It was more a case of the Germans strengthening their defences rather than having gained intelligence that a landing field had been identified nearby. Nonetheless, London had to be informed, although as things were to turn out the news made no difference. The message finally came. The pick-up would take place that night.

It was the evening of 23 December. Most of the group piled into two cars and set off through the streets of Arles, heading for the field but this time Odette stayed at the hotel to await the return of the group. Although it was coming to the end of the moon period, it was a crisp clear night. The reception committee wasted no time in taking up their places, and it was then a matter of waiting in silence for the aircraft to arrive.

It was already a cold night, and by midnight the temperature was several degrees below zero. Again, they waited, and they waited, and they waited, but no aircraft came. At 2 a.m., the latest possible pick-up time, they decided to give it another half an hour, just in case, but after that had passed, they reluctantly gave up. It was time to leave.

The group started walking back towards the cars. It was another hugely disappointing night. But then, in the distance, the sound of an aircraft could be heard. It was coming towards them, but it was well past the latest pick-up time and the sound was coming from the opposite direction to where it had been expected, and so it could easily be a German aircraft they could hear. But the sound got closer and closer. The aircraft was clearly descending and seemingly heading for the field they had just left. Looking back towards the field, they could see the aircraft silhouetted against the bright moon. It was their Hudson.

Churchill felt a mix of rage and painful disappointment, but he knew there was nothing they could do. Three times they had been to the field, on each occasion at some considerable risk, and twice an aircraft had turned up, but to no avail.

The Hudson pilot that night was again Group Captain Fielden, for what was another attempt at Operation STEWARD. With no sign of the reception committee, Fielden decided to hang around for as long as he could and spent an hour loitering above the area, but with nothing seen he reluctantly turned for home. It was another disappointing night for Fielden and his crew. They had flown deep into occupied Europe, at great risk to themselves, only to come away with no result. It happened in wartime, but the sense of annoyance was highlighted in Hugh Verity's book *We Landed by Moonlight* where he wrote how Fielden 'had been frustrated by the absence of correctly identified reception committees on the first two attempts at Hudson pick-ups' in the south of France during November and December.

Rather than risk returning to Arles during the early hours, Churchill and his companions spent the rest of the night at the farm before going back the following day to send a message to London. Dated 24 December 1942, it reads:

> WE WAITED FOR YOU 5 OFFICERS RAOUL AND SELVES WITH COMPLETE COMMITTEE FROM 22 HOURS TO 02 HOURS ABOUT 3.15 AS WE WERE RETURNING THOUGHT WE SAW YOUR PLANE. SHOULD WE CONTINUE TO WAIT. GREETINGS TO ALL. HAPPY CHRISTMAS.

Later that evening they all crowded around their radios once more just in case London decided to give it another go. But no one really expected that to be the case. Besides, it was the last night of the December moon. The window of opportunity was now closed.

The problem for Churchill in this latest case was that the missed pick-up had been entirely his fault. He had not factored in the one-hour time difference between the local time in France and Greenwich Mean Time (GMT); the time by which operations were planned and carried out. So, when the reception committee heard the aircraft approaching at 2.50 a.m. local time, it was 01.50 GMT and therefore just within the pick-up window of 10 p.m. to 2 a.m. It was the most basic of errors and a blow to Churchill's self-confidence that would take him a long time to get over.

Churchill spent Christmas with friends at a restaurant. He was a long way from England, but he felt quite at home. The snow came and the temperature plunged. It was a period of inactivity and so it gave Churchill and Odette an opportunity to enjoy some time in the ancient coastal city of Arles. Apart from the sight of German uniforms, particularly at the tourist spots, the war still seemed to be happening elsewhere.

A new year was about to dawn. Churchill and Odette returned to Cannes, but Girard, who had decided to stay in Arles, wasted no time in blaming Churchill and Odette for all that had gone wrong with the failed pick-up. It annoyed Churchill, and some of Girard's closest followers too, who had become increasingly frustrated at their leader's behaviour and the decisions that he made.

Churchill was tempted to tell Girard just what he thought of him, and to walk away from the situation altogether, but he stopped short of doing that, remembering that he had been sent to France to keep the peace.

On 7 January 1943, Churchill received a message from London:

> FOR RAOUL OLIVE WILL COME BACK WITH BOMBER PLEASE GIVE URGENT SAFE HOUSE PASSWORDS WHERE HE CAN REPORT ARLES MORNING THIRTEENTH STOP

Churchill had an immediate reply sent to London, also dated 7 January, which reads:

> ARE WE TO WAIT FOR NEXT MOON OR CAN YOU FIX SOMETHING SOONER WITH BARCELONA. WE COULD MEET CONSULAR CAR AS PRE ARRANGED. IN THIS CASE WHO IS TO COME OUT AND COULD YOU FIX SWIFT PASSAGE VIA LISBON.

As things were to turn out, Basin did not return to France. Instead, he became an instructor and then a member of Buckmaster's staff, his operational days over. Churchill and Girard, meanwhile, had to wait for the next moon period, only this time the pick-up would be from a small, abandoned airfield at Tournus, nearly 600 km from Cannes and an hour's drive to the north of Mâcon. No reconnaissance was needed as the field had already been well photographed. It was considered perfectly suitable for a pick-up, only this time it would be a Lysander rather than a Hudson, and so there would be no room for the generals.

All Churchill could do was to wait, but the whole CARTE situation was now coming to the boil. A signal to London, dated 15 January 1943, included several paragraphs and comments relating to CARTE:

1. BEING CARTE'S SMALL HAND MAN REGRET TO HAVE TO REPORT HE HAS GONE OFF DEEP END . . .
5. INACTIVITY PLUS CARTE'S EGOISM LACK OF COURTESY LACK OF INTEREST FOR MEN IN DANGER OR DISTRESS CAUSED GENERAL FEELING OF INSECURITY. HE DRIVES TOO HARD GIVES TOO MANY ORDERS QUERIES TOO MUCH. OUR MEN WHO HAVE GIVEN UP SO MUCH ASK FOR SOMETHING ELSE.
6. HERE IS WHY YOU MUST REFUSE YOUR SUPPORT TO CARTE:
   A. HE GETS NO RESULTS DOES NOT NEED ARMS.
   B. INCAPABLE OF ORGANISING RECEPTION (1 PARACHUTE OPERATION IN 5 MONTHS).
   C. INCOMPATIBLE TEMPERAMENT WITH ALL YOUR AGENTS. HE IS ANTI-BRITISH ONLY PRO-CARTE.
   D. HE HAS MEANS OF INTERNAL W/T LIAISON WHICH HE DOES NOT USE.
   E. BAD QUANTITIES UNDER PARA 5 ABOVE CAUSING LOSS OF MEMBERS OF GOODWILL AND RECRUITS.
   F. HE IS UNABLE BRING IN PROMISED MILITARY PERSONAGES . . .
9. FOR OUR SECURITY TRIP TO LONDON ESSENTIAL SO THAT CARTE CAN SHOW HIS OWN FAILURE.
10. ALL THIS IS WITHOUT PERSONAL OR PRESTIGE CONSIDERATIONS.

The CARTE matter had also come to a head in France, with what can only be described as an unofficial court martial involving the various resistance leaders in the south and presided over by a former Army general. Discussions, arguments even, took place as to whether Girard should be allowed to stay as the leader of the group.

The outcome was that Girard was dismissed as the head of the south-east zone, with Frager and Marsac appointed as joint commanders in his place. Churchill took no part in the proceedings, but he was delighted with the outcome as he was on good terms with them both. However, his joy at the thought of working more closely with Frager and Marsac was short-lived. In Girard's normal way he paid little heed to the unfavourable findings of the assembly and simply refused to accept what the court had decided. Instead, he rallied his supporters and decided that he would do his own thing.

There was nothing to stop Girard operating independently, of course, but it did become a problem when his men started turning up at fields to intercept supplies intended for other groups. Unsurprisingly, it led to arguments on the ground, almost as if the different groups saw each other as the enemy, rather than the Germans occupying their country. It was more important than ever for Churchill to return to London to clear up the CARTE mess once and for all. He notified London of the latest problems and that it would now be Frager travelling with him instead of Girard.

As the moon period drew closer, Churchill and Odette went to Tournus to meet up with Frager and other members of the group. But when Churchill inspected the field, he was horrified to find it covered with bricks and rubble, presumably placed there recently by the Germans to prevent the field from being used. There was no chance of shifting the piles in time and so they went off to find somewhere else.

Three suitable fields were identified nearby. Details were sent to London but in the end it made no difference. No pick-up took place. Another opportunity had passed. Churchill and Odette returned to Cannes once more, although it would not be safe to stay there for long.

Again, they exchanged messages with London. There was to be another attempted pick-up, this time from a disused airfield near the village of Basillac, 10 km from Périgueux. The problem was the airfield was 800 km from Cannes and the plan was to conduct the pick-up during what remained of the current moon period, which meant they would have to leave straight away.

It was another long and tiring journey by train. Churchill and Odette met Marsac in Marseille and they travelled together to Périgueux, where they were joined by Frager the following day. While the others stayed elsewhere, Churchill and Odette booked into one of the main hotels in the centre of town. Again, there were plenty of German uniforms about, but it made sense to stay together as they easily passed as a couple and so attracted less attention when they moved about.

Later that day, Churchill and Odette went to Basillac. The airfield was easy to find and there were no aircraft to be seen, although a couple of men were spotted walking around. The airfield was fine as far as getting a Lysander on and off the ground was concerned, but Churchill also had to consider the reception committee and the safety of the new arrivals, which the Lysander would almost certainly bring. They would need time to get away and so the fact that people had been seen at the airfield – whoever they were – was a cause for concern.

Later that evening they huddled together to listen to the broadcast messages. It was never easy listening to a radio in a hotel room, with the volume barely loud enough to hear the messages being read above the crackling sound of the poor reception. If they were caught, their war would be over. But then, the message came – '*Les femmes sont parfois volages*' (which can be translated as 'Women are sometimes fickle'). The pick-up would happen that night, the night of 23/24 January 1943.

There was no time to waste. Churchill and Odette met Frager and one of his men, Jacques Latour, and within the hour all four were on the road to Basillac. They arrived at the airfield in good time, only to find it covered in mist.

Fortunately, the mist soon started to lift and there was no sign of movement coming from the watchtower or surrounding buildings. Churchill paced out the 150 metres required for two lamps and then fifty metres at right-angles to the second lamp. It was all the Lysander pilot would need to land and turn off to the point where Churchill and Frager would be waiting, while Odette and Latour would be watching from the other end of the airfield.

This time they did not have to wait long to hear an aircraft approaching in the distance. They could make out the silhouette of the Lysander, heading straight for them, and then flying directly over the airfield at around 800 feet, Churchill flashed the letter 'Q' in Morse code several times to confirm that the airfield was in safe hands. He then watched and waited for the pilot's response, which was to be the letter 'R', to acknowledge he had seen the signal and would land, but no acknowledgement was seen. Worst still, the engine could be heard powering up as the aircraft climbed away and disappeared into the night.

Churchill could not believe what had just happened. The pilot must have seen his signal and so he hoped the Lysander would return. But then they spotted two men coming out of a building. It was probably the same two they had seen earlier, and the sound of the aircraft overhead had woken them up. They all took cover. There was nothing else they could do. With the two men wandering around they could not risk instructing the Lysander pilot to land. As they quietly left the airfield to head back to Périgueux, they could only watch in disappointment as the Lysander returned, only for the pilot to see no signal from the ground and then climb away again.

Above the airfield, the Lysander pilot, Flying Officer Jimmy 'Mac' McCairns, had finally given up. He flew over the airfield four times during the fifty minutes either side of midnight. In the bright moonlight conditions, he saw two small hangars and the windsock, but he did not see a signal from the ground indicating that it was safe to land and so he reluctantly decided to head for home. After four passes and having been in the area for a while, McCairns had done all that could have been expected of him. Operation MINER, as his mission was called, had not been a success. His entry in the records for the sortie would later read 'No signal. Airfield defended.'

It was yet another disastrous night and the fifth time the pick-up had failed. It was too late to return to Périgueux and so Churchill and Frager laid up until morning. It was bitterly cold. The temperature had plunged to ten degrees below zero, but through sheer exhaustion they managed to sleep. When morning came, they entered the town and were pleased to find the others had made it back safely, but word of an aircraft the night before would be circulating and so it was not safe to hang around.

It was time for Churchill and Odette to leave Périgueux, but rather than risk returning to Cannes, they caught the train to Toulouse. There they met Pertschuk, who explained that the situation in Toulouse was quite stable at that time and so they could stay in a safe house for a while.

The decision not to return to Cannes turned out to be a good one. Passengers arriving on the train from Marseille were being questioned by the Gestapo and those without a valid reason for making the journey, or whose papers were dubious, were detained.

The Germans were now rounding up as many as they could from the list of 200 names discovered in the briefcase that Marsac had earlier lost on the train. Churchill also found out that the Baron had received more visits to his villa asking his whereabouts and that his own flat in Cannes had been raided during his time away. There had been other raids, too, with the only place to have survived for now being the flat belonging to Odette des Garets on the Quai St Pierre, although that would soon be raided as well. There had also been arrests in Marseille, and elsewhere along the Côte d'Azur.

The heat was on, and things were getting hotter by the day. CARTE, indeed, was now in chaos, although many of its members had already gone into hiding or had made their escape. Others, though, would choose to operate elsewhere, although there would have to be a break in activity to give them time to relocate. Frager, for example, would now operate from Montélimar, while Marsac went to the Haute-Savoie in the Western Alps, where the occupation by Italian troops was having little impact on the various resistance groups there.

Churchill knew it was no longer safe to stay on the Côte d'Azur. Not only was it unsafe for him, but should he ever be caught then it would put the rest of his associates at risk as well.

In London, meanwhile, there was talk of getting Churchill, Girard, and Frager out of France via the Pyrenees. On 25 January, Buckmaster issued the following instructions:

> To exfiltrate via Spain with LOUBA [Frager] and, if possible, CARTE [Girard]. RAOUL will presumably use his own route and make himself known to the Consulate at Barcelona as he did before.

But, as it was put to Buckmaster in a memo dated 26 January, there were excessive risks to all three should they be caught:

> I hope therefore that the following facts are fully realised by RAOUL:
>
> That in the event of there being any trouble, i.e., their being caught before reaching the Consulate, Barcelona, we can only give assistance to individuals whom we can satisfy the Spanish authorities are British nationals.
>
> That Frenchmen crossing into Spain clandestinely are being reported to the French cum Spanish authorities and returned over the Frontier.
>
> That if RAOUL is caught in company with these two companions bearing French names the Spanish authorities may hold him as a suspect British agent and not as a P.O.W. In this case we may be able to render him little or no assistance.
>
> I would add that these facts were put to RAOUL by me before his departure but of course present conditions render the situation of individuals caught between the frontier and Barcelona more precarious than they were before he left.

Rather than head for home, the SPINDLE group would have to relocate elsewhere, but while Churchill and Odette were in the relative safety of Toulouse, Rabinowitch was still in Cannes. Churchill wanted to go back there to get him, and his wireless set out, but in the end this risky task was left to another in the group, 25-year-old Jean Riquet, who was not so well known in Cannes and therefore less likely to be caught.

A few days later Riquet and Rabinowitch arrived safely in Toulouse. In the meantime, Marsac suggested to Churchill that he should take his group to a small village in the Haute-Savoie, which he knew well. The village was situated high in the mountains, just a few kilometres from Annecy, and 50 km from Geneva. There was a hotel in the village where Churchill could stay and establish a courier route to Switzerland, while Rabinowitch could operate his set from a neighbouring village. There was also a group of patriots living in Faverges, just 15 km away. It sounded a very good plan. Frager agreed, even suggesting that Marsac should become Churchill's liaison officer.

For Churchill, it was the answer to his prayers. But it was 700 km to the Western Alps, and he had already been in Toulouse for more than a week. It was time to move on. He bade Pertschuk farewell and headed off to the station to catch a train.

Just a couple of months later, the gallant Maurice Pertschuk was arrested, and his short life came to an end at the age of twenty-three, hanged in the crematorium at Buchenwald just days before the camp was liberated at the end of the war. It is yet another sad tale.

Chapter 13
Saint-Jorioz

Situated on the western bank of Lake Annecy, Saint-Jorioz is a commune in the Haute-Savoie department in the Auvergne-Rhône-Alpes region in south-eastern France. Today it has a population of around 6,000, but back in the Second World War it was a quieter and considerably smaller place. Even in wartime Europe the beautiful landscape – the hills and splendid lakes – breathed an atmosphere of peace.

Churchill and Odette arrived in Saint-Jorioz in February 1943. After leaving Toulouse, Churchill first spent a few days at La Bocca wrapping up a few bits and pieces, after which he rejoined Odette. They then travelled to the mountains together and were met off the train at Annecy by Marsac's wife, Michelle, a slim, blonde woman in her thirties. They caught a bus to Saint-Jorioz, where they were to stay at the Hôtel de la Poste with their new identities of Monsieur and Madame Pierre Chambrun, a married couple enjoying a holiday together in the mountains.

The Hôtel de la Poste was at the crossroads in the village. It was run by a trustworthy couple – Jean Cottet, a powerfully built man in his late twenties, and his younger wife, Simone. The Marsacs had already moved into a large villa nearby called Les Tilleuls, which would become the group's meeting point rather than the hotel. Frager, meanwhile, was living with his wife on the other side of the lake, while two of his men – Jean Riquet and Roger Bardet – had also moved to the Haute-Savoie to be his couriers.

The hotel was a friendly one and Saint-Jorioz a beautiful place to stay. The main road connecting Annecy and Albertville passes through the village in a near north–south direction, while the other arms of the crossroads run south-west towards the mountains and north-east to the lake and its beach. Churchill and Odette acquired a couple of bicycles for getting around and they were quickly accepted by the locals as the quiet and somewhat distant couple they were posing as.

One afternoon Churchill cycled with Riquet to Faverges to find somewhere suitable for Rabinowitch to stay. It took a couple of hours to cover the 20 km, but it was a beautiful ride along the banks of the lake and on to the village through the high wooded mountains.

At Faverges they met the leader of the local resistance group, a man called Milleau, a tough, truculent bull of a man, who drove them up the mountain through the snow to a small house amongst a hamlet of farm buildings known as Les Tissots. It was a perfect location for Rabinowitch to set up his radio post. There was only one track up to the hamlet, easily observed from the house, and a gap in the mountains meant a clear line of sight to the north. There was nothing to interfere with his transmissions and it would be all but impossible for an enemy radio detection van to make it up the side of the mountain in the snow. And if a vehicle was seen approaching there were plenty of options should it come to making an escape.

For the next couple of weeks things felt settled. The wireless set was working fine high up in the mountains and with the distance to London shorter than before, messages were flowing back and forth. Les Tilleuls was a hub of activity as couriers came and went, making regular journeys to the major cities in France. Suitable new dropping zones were identified, the rail network was being disrupted by the various groups of saboteurs, and more agents were being landed, while the group at Faverges were an established part of a successful escape line for downed Allied aircrew making their way to Switzerland. Churchill had also heard from Jean Cottet that a large group of patriots had gone into hiding on the nearby Glières Plateau. All they needed was arms. Churchill agreed to inform London and a drop of a hundred-plus containers was arranged for mid-March, although whether the drop would happen remained to be seen.

It would be a while before SOE could arm the *maquis*, as these resisters were known, on a scale never thought possible before, but more and more young men were fleeing to the forests and hills rather than face deportation to work in Germany. Buckmaster, in *They Fought Alone*, later wrote:

> It was Peter Churchill, to the best of my recollection, who first saw the possibility of organising these young men into really efficient fighting forces.

Everything was going well for Churchill at Saint-Jorioz, even better than he might have expected. The heat of Cannes seemed a world away. He was even convinced he was no longer being trailed or under suspicion.

Churchill would later write that he could have spent the rest of the war there.

Saint-Jorioz, the small village in the snow, had quickly become one of SOE's most important outposts in France and might well have become one of its greatest successes, but for a series of events that would eventually lead to disaster. Things first took a nasty turn in early March when Frager told Churchill that many arrests had been made in Arles, although Girard had somehow managed to get to Britain on board a Hudson. Not only was Girard back in London, but it also appeared he was back in favour once again. The news put Churchill in a difficult position. He was doing what he had been instructed to do – to work with Girard's successors – but it seemed that Girard had won over those back in London.

All kinds of things were going through Churchill's mind. He even began to wonder if those in London were using Girard to check up on what he had been doing in France. Churchill felt betrayed and was angry.

Churchill knew he had to get back to London to sort out the mess, preferably with Frager as had previously been planned. He sent a message requesting a return as soon as possible. It did not take long for Churchill to receive a reply. A Lysander would pick up the two of them from the same field at Tournus where an earlier attempt had been made, on a night commencing 14 March, but it was the next part of the message that came as a shock. The Lysander would be dropping off his replacement – an agent called ROGER.

ROGER was the 26-year-old Francis Cammaerts, whose tall stature and small moustache made him look more like the schoolteacher he had once been than the Frenchman he was about to become. Cammaerts had been a pacifist during his university days at Cambridge. Following the outbreak of war he registered as a conscientious objector, this being conditional on his taking on agricultural work. However, the death of his younger brother, an observer with the RAF, changed his views, and as a fluent French speaker, he offered his services to SOE.

For Odette and Rabinowitch the news of Churchill's imminent departure came as no surprise. They knew the score, but they had been with him for five months and struggled with the idea of working for someone else. Churchill was quick to reassure them that his successor would be fully briefed and would be coming to France with the latest instructions for them. Churchill also told them he would soon be back. He would return to Saint-Jorioz at the earliest opportunity.

Having said his farewells, Churchill spent the following week in hiding at a small village near the pick-up point waiting for news of when the Lysander would come. But the Lysander did not come. On the seventh day he got a message telling him that the pick-up would no longer be from Tournus but would instead be from a field near Compiègne, and that he and Frager must get there for the pick-up in three nights' time.

The new landing ground was more than 400 km away. With no time to waste, Churchill, Frager, Riquet and Latour, set off for Compiègne. The first part of their journey was by car and took them across the demarcation line to Chalon-sur-Saône, from where they travelled on to Paris by train. After a night in the city with friends they caught the train to Compiègne. There they spent the night in a small hotel, before completing their journey by horse and trap to a small house belonging to a trusted friend near the field at Estrées-Saint-Denis. Then, having checked the condition of the field, they all returned to Compiègne to wait for the message confirming when the pick-up would take place.

The night of 23/24 March was to be the last Lysander operation of the moon period and a relatively short trip for the pilot, 24-year-old Squadron Leader Hugh Verity. Verity's brief was quite simple. He was to take two passengers to a field in France, land there, pick up two more passengers and return to base. Although Verity knew no names or why they were going to France, one of his outbound passengers was Cammaerts, of course, while the other was Georges Duboudin who was returning to France for his second mission.

Churchill and the others arrived at the field in good time. Then, just before 2 a.m., they heard an aircraft in the distance. It was approaching the field. Churchill switched on his torch and flashed the coded signal into the air and as the aircraft passed overhead the pilot acknowledged. The lamps were then lit to mark the line of approach. Verity later wrote 'The field and flarepath were admirable.' In a matter of minutes, he expertly touched down, bringing the Lysander to a halt just metres from where Churchill and Frager were waiting.

With the Lysander having turned back into wind, Cammaerts and Duboudin quickly jumped out with their luggage and made their way to a car waiting for them, while Churchill and Frager climbed up the short steel ladder into the rear cockpit. And with a thumbs-up from his two new passengers, Verity opened the throttle. The aircraft surged forward and in less than a hundred metres it was airborne once more. It all happened very quickly. No one else saw the Lysander come and go.

It had been a textbook drop-off and pick-up. A feeling of triumph swept over Churchill. At last, after all the frustrations of the previous attempts, the pick-up had been a success. He was finally on his way back to Britain.

Chapter 14
Colonel Henri

The flight back to Britain took a couple of hours and the Lysander landed safely in the early hours of 24 March 1943. Verity had expertly weaved the aircraft across northern France and over the English Channel and, despite some hairy moments when they encountered some fog, he touched down at a blacked-out airfield somewhere in southern England. After a good hearty breakfast and a welcome glass of whisky, Churchill and Frager were whisked off to London.

It was still only 9 a.m. when they walked into Orchard Court. Buckmaster and several of his staff were there to meet them. There was, of course, the normal debriefing to go through. In Churchill's case, his debrief notes stretched across sixteen paragraphs, the opening ones of which covered general information about living in and getting around France to help better prepare the next agents going into the field. These included:

> It is now necessary to have one's identity card validated. The stamp of validation signifies that all the particulars on the card have been checked at the Mairie . . . It is dangerous to move about without the '*carte d'alimintetion*'. Frequent snap controls are made on trains as they arrive in stations, and anyone whose papers are not in order is immediately herded into an ambulance and sent to Germany . . . All railway travel is particularly dangerous at the present time, and it is as well to have advance information as to the stations at which trains will be stopped . . . It is always advisable for the agent to have an alternative address in the town in which he is staying; this address can then be given to the police if the agent is apprehended for some trifling offence and thus avoids the complications which might ensue should the police visit the agent's real address. The address should be that of a friend, to whom the agent is well known.

There were then paragraphs giving Churchill's assessment of the German and Italian presence in the south:

> 6. On the south coast of France, there are concentrations of German troops, Air Force night fighters, and the Gestapo. There are small-bore anti-aircraft guns on the roads, and 2" and 3" cannons facing out to sea. The Germans are using French tanks, and Italian lorries and gun carriers; most of their transport is petrol driven.
> 7. From Geneva to Toulon (excluding these towns), the Italians have the east of France, and the coastline; the rest of the country is in German hands . . .
> 8. The morale of the Italians is very low, at the present time. Some of them have even admitted they will be glad of an allied invasion, and they carry a white flag as part of their equipment . . .
> 9. The German attitude towards the French people is to ignore all acts of attempted sabotage, and to foster the idea that the French people will be free from interference . . .
> 10. No serious difficulties will be encountered from the Garde Mobile; 80% of them are good patriots, and delight in pursuing an obstructionist policy towards the Germans. Most of the controls are directed against the Jews.

There were so many things for a returning agent to comment on; all would help the next agents going into France. There were further paragraphs covering administrative points about agents operating in France, such as how to make telephone calls between one zone and the other, what to wear, and how to change a 5,000 franc note, but there was also a paragraph with Churchill's thoughts about a future invasion:

> Captain Churchill suggests that, if an invasion takes place, an airborne division should be landed in the middle of France. He has seen an excellent site, a field of 5 kms by 5 kms, capable of taking 15 flare paths. There is a river close to it, and a bridge, as means of identification. Particulars of the site have been recorded in his own report.

There was much to discuss, including why the earlier pick-up attempts had been unsuccessful, after which the main topic of discussion was the current situation with Girard. Buckmaster explained to Churchill that he had his reasons for wanting to see Girard in person, although none were for the purpose of getting a report on Churchill's activities in France. Then Buckmaster told him that Girard would not in fact be going back to France. Instead, he would soon be leaving for the United States.

Girard had proved to be something of a fantasist. He had promised much but actually delivered very little. He had persistently made growing demands on London – for money, for arms, and for wireless sets to be operated by his own men – but his relationship with the British had all but broken down. For a while Girard thought about trying to co-operate better with SOE, or perhaps switch his allegiance to de Gaulle, but there was now a third option on the table – to accept American patronage. The Americans had started approaching French Resistance leaders to support their own OSS, whose agents had already begun arriving in France, and so Girard soon left for the USA, where he would spend the rest of his life in self-imposed exile.

CARTE was finished. Its remnants would be split into smaller circuits, run from London, the details of which would be explained to Churchill and Frager before they returned to France.

From his talk with Buckmaster, Churchill also gained a better understanding of the complications faced by those in London. Buckmaster even reassured him that his staff were doing everything they could to give their agents in the field the co-operation to which they were entitled. In *They Fought Alone*, Buckmaster later wrote:

> Churchill was here, there, and everywhere – testing methods of introducing our men into France, recruiting new units, and encouraging existing ones – in short, doing the work of ten men. The story of his work has been told; its value cannot be too highly estimated.

Buckmaster also later included Churchill's name in a short list of agents who were 'tremendously valuable . . . their dynamism and that of others like them held the organisation together'.

Churchill was soon to return to France once more, but he was first given leave and so he went home to see his parents in Malvern. During Churchill's time away, SOE had kept his parents informed that he was alive and well. One example of a short letter sent to his parents was from the War Office at the Hotel Victoria in Northumberland Avenue, London, dated 16 November 1942, which read:

> Dear Mr and Mrs Churchill,
>
> We are very pleased to inform you that we receive news of your son, Capt. P. M. Churchill, regularly and that he is in excellent health.

While Churchill was home on leave he learned of the death of his older brother, Walter. While serving as the station commander of RAF Takali in Malta, he was leading a raid on an enemy airfield in southern Sicily when his Spitfire was hit by flak and crashed in flames. Walter was killed on 27 August 1942, the same day that Peter Churchill had left Tempsford for his latest mission. From *Duel of Wits*, it is clear just how devastating the news of the death of his older brother was to Peter.

With his leave up, it was time for Churchill to return to London. He was pleased to be going back to Saint-Jorioz, but it was hard to leave his grief-stricken parents at such a time. If the loss of his older brother was not enough, Churchill returned to London to discover that during his short time away the situation at Saint-Jorioz had taken a turn for the worse. There had been further arrests.

The first to fall was André Marsac. He had been arrested within forty-eight hours of Churchill and Frager leaving for Britain in what was a simple case of betrayal. Marsac had been caught in a trap involving a small and pretty Irishwoman called Helen James when, during a train journey to Paris, she convinced him that although she knew several German officers, she was really an ardent anti-Nazi and was prepared to offer him information. She arranged to meet Marsac at a small café on the Champs-Elysées and when he went to the café and sat at her table, the Germans made their move.

The man behind Marsac's arrest was Germany's notorious spy-catcher in France, 43-year-old Hugo Ernst Bleicher, a *Feldwebel* (or sergeant) in the Abwehr intelligence service. Bleicher perhaps did more than any other individual to harm the Allied cause in occupied France. His tireless energy, good command of languages (particularly French), remarkable powers of dissimulation, and a double nature, all enabled him to play two roles at once with perfect conviction. But in Bleicher there was also an open dislike for the Nazi regime, which was so genuine that it came over as most convincing in his counter-intelligence work when posing as the 'good German'. Nonetheless, he was ruthless in his pursuit of agents and members of the Resistance, and his usual ultimatum to those who were caught was either to work for him or be turned over to the Gestapo.

For German intelligence, Marsac's arrest marked the start of Operation Grand Duke, the biggest espionage case in France at the time. Marsac was taken to Fresnes prison and was questioned by Bleicher for three days. Marsac initially remained silent, but he did not want to be handed over to the Gestapo and eventually the two men struck up a conversation. Slowly Bleicher gained Marsac's trust and gradually bits about the Resistance came out, such as that Marsac's group was led by a man known as Paul (Henri Frager) and that the whole organisation was directed from London.

Bleicher suspected he was on to something big and that there were bigger fish in the pool, but Marsac was unwilling to say any more. Bleicher even tried a different tack, suggesting he had become disillusioned with the war and that Marsac should arrange for an aircraft to pick them both up so they could travel to Britain together. But as he was seemingly getting nowhere with that idea, Bleicher came up with another. He told Marsac he could get him out of Fresnes but to do so Bleicher would need to convince his superiors that Marsac was prepared to work for the Germans, and so he suggested to Marsac that he should get one of his men to visit him at Fresnes so they could plan their next move.

Marsac was initially unsure of what to do, but the following day he agreed to write two letters – one to his wife and the other to Roger Bardet – explaining that he was being held at Fresnes and that, by chance, he had found a good friend in the interrogating officer who would help him escape. However, as the letter went on to explain, Bardet would first need to visit him in Fresnes so they could sort out a plan and that a German officer, Colonel Henri, the bearer of the letters, would give him the opportunity to escape.

With an address to go to and now posing as Colonel Henri, and with his own cover story of wishing to defect, Bleicher went to Saint-Jorioz where he met Michelle Marsac. Being in possession of her husband's two letters gave him the upper hand and he soon convinced her that he was a trusted friend. Bleicher also met Bardet. After handing him the second letter, Bardet seemed equally taken in by Bleicher and his story and agreed to go to Fresnes the following day. Michelle would go to

Paris, too, and with their meeting over Bleicher went to the Hôtel de la Poste for lunch, as recommended to him by Michelle.

All this happened while Churchill was still in Britain, but things were to take a further turn for the worse now that Bleicher had broken into the scene at Saint-Jorioz. There are various accounts as to where and when Odette and Bleicher first met. In E. H. Cookridge's book *Inside S.O.E.*, the suggestion is that Odette walked into a meeting between Bleicher and Bardet in Annecy having learned of the mystery visitor from Michelle Marsac. Bleicher's own account in *Colonel Henri's Story* says he first saw Odette at the Hôtel de la Poste when he lunched there after his meeting with Michelle Marsac and Bardet, although he supposedly did not actually meet her until the night of her arrest. However, in *Odette*, Jerrard Tickell gives Odette's version of how she and Bleicher first met. She had been to Annecy one morning, and it was during the bus journey back to Saint-Jorioz that she first noticed a man in a dark suit: 'He was of middle height, aged about forty-two or three; his face was oval, his nose longish, his eyes brown and benign behind his spectacles.'

It was of no surprise to Odette when the man in spectacles got off the bus at the same crossroads as her, and so she took a detoured route to the hotel, but after lunch the same man approached her at her table. He introduced himself as Colonel Henri, a German officer, and told her he was carrying a letter from her friend, Marsac, who was being held at Fresnes. Odette read the short letter. It confirmed what Bleicher had already told her and went on to say that he [Marsac] had had several conversations with Colonel Henri whom he believed to be trustworthy, and that Colonel Henri would discuss an important matter with her.

Bleicher explained to Odette he was an officer in the Abwehr whose allegiance was to the German General Staff and emphasised he was not Gestapo whose allegiance was to the Nazi Party. He then told her he would like her to provide him with a wireless set and an appropriate set of codes so that he could contact the British War Office in London with a view to negotiating peace terms on behalf of the German High Command.

Odette told Bleicher she could not provide him with a wireless set, the simple reason being she did not have one. She was also naturally suspicious of Marsac's letter. She had no idea whether it was genuine or if it had been written while under duress. Bleicher suggested she go to

Paris with him and visit Marsac in Fresnes to see for herself, but Odette declined the invitation. She did, however, agree to send Bardet with a food parcel. He could visit Marsac to establish if he was alright and to verify all that had been written and what had been said.

Satisfied that he had at least achieved a way forward, Bleicher left Saint-Jorioz. Odette went straight to Rabinowitch and told him what had happened. It was now a matter of waiting until Bardet returned from Paris before all the facts were known. Then they could send a signal to London.

Bardet soon returned from Paris. He had been to Fresnes and met Marsac alone. Not only was Marsac keeping well, but Bardet had also been able to verify Bleicher's story, although Bleicher had since come up with a more ambitious plan. If Odette could arrange a pick-up, then he would arrange for Marsac to get out of prison, and they could all then fly to London together so that Bleicher could begin negotiating for peace.

Remaining suspicious of the whole Colonel Henri story, and not knowing what was behind it all, Odette knew she had to let London know what was going on. All she could do for now was to stall everything as much as she could, to give herself more time, and so she instructed Bardet to return to Paris to tell Bleicher she was working on a pick-up, although the earliest anything could be done would be 18 April, the last night of the current moon.

Odette updated Rabinowitch, who then sent a message telling London of the man calling himself Colonel Henri and his proposal. In London the story aroused suspicion, but no one connected Colonel Henri with their old adversary Hugo Bleicher. Bleicher, meanwhile, was briefing his own chain of command. He was told to arrest Bardet and Michelle Marsac immediately (they were both in Paris at the time), before they had a chance to send any warning, after which Bleicher was to return to Saint-Jorioz to arrest anyone else he could find linked with the group.

It was the second week of April 1943. Churchill and Frager were preparing to leave London. Churchill (RAOUL) was to parachute back into France somewhere near Saint-Jorioz, while Frager (LOUBA) was to be dropped off by Lysander near Tours. Their general mission briefing, dated 12 April 1943, reads:

> RAOUL AND LOUBA MISSION
>
> The position with regard to the LOUBA organisation has been fully discussed while RAOUL and LOUBA have been in London,

> and the delimitations of its activities made clear. These are roughly in accordance with the sketch map which has been seen by RAOUL and LOUBA.
>
> RAOUL and LOUBA will return to the field in the course of the April moon to take charge of these areas and to develop them as quickly and as securely as possible. The only exceptions are the small outlying elements round Toulouse, Bordeaux, Pau and Perigueux which by agreement with LOUBA will be handed over to our established organisers in these regions. LOUBA will inform us by W/T as soon as possible how and where our appropriate organisers are to contact these elements. He will also warn these elements when such contact has to be made for that purpose.
>
> Neither RAOUL nor LOUBA have any need of further cover stories, and both have been supplied with the extra identity papers for which they asked.

The brief went on to describe their working area – stretching from the south-eastern Mediterranean coast up to a line drawn from Paris to Nancy – and that the area was to be divided into three zones. Zone 1, stated in the brief to be 'the south-eastern border of France, which will subsequently join to its elements in the Montélimar region', was to be managed by ROGER (Francis Cammaerts) who was already in Cannes. Churchill was to be responsible for Zone 2, which consisted of:

> The area which has recently been worked by RAOUL and LOUBA and includes the guerrilla elements in the Haute Savoie, the northern boundary roughly follows the old demarcation line.

Zone 3 was to be Frager's, described as 'stretches from Chalon s/Saône to Paris and across to Nancy and includes the eastern frontier of France'.

The brief also included instructions for wireless operators, couriers, post boxes, dropping grounds, guerrilla forces, and BBC messages, and provided details of when Churchill and Frager should first meet up in France given that they were going separately into the field. Churchill's main instructions were then summarised as follows:

> To be senior British liaison officer to all our personnel in zones between S.E. Mediterranean coast and line Paris–Nancy. To be primarily responsible for circuit in the Haute Savoie. His

> job to be that of giving guidance to our organisers in these zones concerning local problems; seeing that they keep within the limits of these zones; to ensure the equitable distribution of funds between them; to organise an inter-circuit courier service, and to supervise the provision of dropping-grounds, post-boxes, safe-houses in each zone.

Churchill was also briefed on the situation in Saint-Jorioz as it was known at that time. Marsac and his wife had already been arrested, but it was believed that Bardet had so far escaped arrest. He was also shown Rabinowitch's signal warning of Colonel Henri. Churchill's immediate thoughts were that Odette should be told to get out, while Rabinowitch should go into hiding with his set. Buckmaster agreed and even made it clear to Churchill there was no longer a need for him to return to France to clear up the mess. Instead, arrangements could be made to have Odette and Rabinowitch picked up by Lysander, after which Churchill could go and set up another circuit elsewhere.

Churchill's life would almost certainly have followed a different path and might well have had a different outcome if he had stayed in Britain at that point, but he wanted to go back to France. In *Duel of Wits,* he gave his reason for wanting to go back as wishing to work with the patriots gathering on the Glières Plateau, but he must also have been thinking of those he had left behind at Saint-Jorioz, particularly as he had told them he would return at the earliest opportunity.

Churchill really should have stayed in Britain and waited for another opportunity to return to France, but he was determined to go. At this point he was clearly putting his personal feelings ahead of his professional judgement. Equally, Buckmaster could have put a stop to it all, but in the end Buckmaster agreed to let Churchill have it his way. He could return to France.

HQ sent a message to Odette telling her that Churchill would soon return and that a suitable dropping point needed to be found. The message also warned Odette that Colonel Henri was highly dangerous, and that she was to go into hiding across the lake and cut contact with everyone except Rabinowitch, who was to leave with his wireless set.

Odette went straight to the others to warn them to get away. Rabinowitch and Cammaerts left immediately, and Odette really should also have left at that point. But she decided to stay, for a few days at least. She had told Bleicher there was no chance of getting to London before

18 April at the earliest, and so she was convinced in her own mind that Bleicher would not return before then.

Within twenty-four hours of London sending the message, a signal arrived back giving the coordinates of the dropping point; a bleak spot under deep snow high above Saint-Jorioz on the slopes of the Semnoz mountain, which dominated the western shore of Lake Annecy. The exact point picked for the drop was close to an abandoned hotel on a hogback ridge, which at its flattest point measured around a hundred metres square, but there were only three nights remaining of the current moon period and so there was no time to waste.

It was 14 April 1943. Churchill was to return to France that night. He was first driven to Gaynes Hall near St Neots and then in the evening he was taken to the airfield at Tempsford where a Halifax was waiting. After confirming the drop zone with the crew, he climbed aboard and minutes later they were on their way.

More than 600 miles away in the mountains, Odette, Rabinowitch, and the Cottets were already en route to the dropping point. Earlier that evening they had received the coded message – '*Le carabe d'or fait sa toilette de printemps*' ('The golden beetle is performing its spring toilet') – telling them Churchill would be arriving that night. They left the hotel immediately, using Jean Cottet's car to take them as far as they could.

Parking the car out of sight from the road, the four began walking up the steep wooded path. They faced a climb of more than 750 metres to the drop zone, which took them the best part of three hours. At first the going was reasonably good, up a wooded path of oak, elder, and pine, and then along a stony mountain track, twisting and zigzagging through the woods, but then they hit the snow-belt. The moon was rising on the far side of the mountain and so it was very dark, and progress was slow. By midnight they were still short of where they needed to be. Simone had fallen behind, but the other three pressed on until they could see the end of the forest and the snow-covered hogsback stretching out ahead. The last few hundred metres were extremely hard going, but they were driven on by not wanting to miss the drop, although they had no idea when that would be.

The three finally reached the drop zone. They were to guide the aircraft into the drop by a line of bonfires. They had gathered branches the day before and hidden them in a chalet to keep them dry. Although exhausted, they quickly set about dragging the branches from the chalet to prepare the line of bonfires. Back and forth they went until they were ready, at which point they all collapsed in the snow.

Simone now caught up and, no sooner had they finished preparing the bonfires, than an aircraft could be heard in the distance. After a few seconds it was obviously coming their way. It was time to light the fires. Jean Cottet poured petrol over the branches and threw a lighted match and with the aircraft getting closer, the four stood back watching the fires take hold.

From his position in the nose of the Halifax bomber, the Belgian observer could see the bonfires ahead. The dispatcher removed the board covering the hole in the fuselage floor and beckoned Churchill forward. With his parachute static line connected, Churchill sat on the ledge. As he peered down through the hole, he could see the snow-covered mountain rushing past him below. The red warning light was on, but then he was nudged by the dispatcher and told they were going round again to make a better approach.

Those on the mountainside below were watching anxiously, waiting for a parachute to appear. But nothing came. Then the aircraft went into a slow turn and climbed away.

Churchill could see Lake Annecy below. The red light had been out for what seemed like an age before it came on again as they began their second run-in to the drop. They were descending once again, and trees were soon rushing past him below. The sound of the four engines was constantly changing, and then the flaps were lowered to reduce the aircraft's speed further. Churchill could do nothing but wait for the green light to appear, which coincided with the dispatcher's hand flashing down in front of him, at which point he had to jump.

Churchill could make out the silhouettes of figures below. They were standing next to one of the fires, and in a matter of seconds he was on the ground.

There was time for brief handshakes and hugs as friends were reunited once more. Five containers had been dropped, too, more arms for the men on the Glières Plateau. They would be collected later, although they would have to be stored out of sight in the abandoned hotel and the parachutes thrown onto the fire. Rabinowitch would stay and watch over the place before returning to Les Tissots, while the others returned to the hotel.

It took four hours to reach the hotel, during which Odette updated Churchill on all that had gone on while he was away. For Churchill, it felt wonderful to be back amongst friends and believing they had a day or two before the man calling himself Colonel Henri would return to Saint-Jorioz, there seemed to be no apparent rush to get away. In his mission report, Churchill later wrote:

> LISE [Odette] then went into Annecy to contact a Lieutenant Morel [leader of the patriots on the Glières Plateau] so as to get his men to collect the stuff which ARNAUD [Rabinowitch] was guarding. As he was not there in the morning, she went again in the afternoon, suggesting that I should sleep off the effects of the drop and also avoid Annecy, where she feared people might be waiting for me.

Because Odette had seemingly been handling matters so well during his time away, Churchill was content to leave things to her, but they really should have left Saint-Jorioz at that point. With all that had gone before, and knowing that Henri was dangerous and soon to return, they were now pushing their luck.

Churchill's mission report described what happened the following day:

> The following day, we looked at a new place in Monthon on the other side of the lake. I made the mistake here of not insisting that we should pack up and leave for this place immediately. Fortunately, during the course of the afternoon I packed up most of my compromising material, such as all radio parts given to me for four or five operators, about Frs. 300,000 and a Belgian revolver, having given LISE some Frs. 150,000, part of which had to be given to members of the French Organisation immediately. The suitcase containing these things was hidden in the bowels of the Hôtel de la Poste and I believe was never found by the Gestapo.

Unbeknown to Churchill, though, two Italian officers had visited the hotel that same day and had seen him having lunch with Odette on the veranda. The Italians had spoken to the Cottets about an unrelated matter so as not to draw attention to the fact that Bleicher had sent them to the hotel to see if Churchill and Odette were there.

That evening Rabinowitch joined Churchill and Odette at the hotel. They all dined together as a happy group, after which Rabinowitch set off back to Les Tissots while Churchill and Odette retired to their rooms. At that stage, it seemed a perfectly normal, quiet evening at the hotel. The only sign of life was coming from the office where the Cottets were catching up with the accounts. But then the front door opened. It was one of the group's couriers, a man known as Louis le Belge, and then things happened at an alarming pace. Churchill's mission report reads:

> At about half past nine, still being very tired from the past two rather hectic days, we were already asleep when there was a knock on the door and M. and Mme. Cottet came in. M. Cottet said 'There is a strange man downstairs, who says that Henri is talking in Paris.' LISE immediately got up and wished to go down to see him. At this moment, although I said that we should discuss this matter together, I should have insisted that LISE should not go down but make preparations either to be hidden in another room or escape through the balcony. My reflex action at this moment was absolutely nil. LISE went downstairs with the Cottets and I went to sleep.

Having pulled on her dressing gown, Odette calmly went down to the hotel reception. She could see several armed men were standing there, none of whom she recognised, but then the man she instantly recognised as Colonel Henri stepped out of the shadows. Believing Churchill might not be far away, Bleicher told Odette to take him upstairs. Odette thought about shouting a warning, but she was told the hotel was surrounded by more armed troops. She did not want Churchill to be gunned down while attempting some sort of heroic escape. Churchill's mission report continued:

> The next thing I knew was that about six men were leaning over me, one of whom asked me what my name was. I told him 'Chambrun'. He and Henri both drew out revolvers and told me to put up my hands. The former said: 'Your other names are Raoul and Captain Churchill, and you are nothing more than a saboteur, and anyway I can hear your English accent.' LISE was inclined to curse Henri for this trap, but I told her not to say a word.

In *Colonel Henri's Story*, Bleicher also recalled the moment:

> Odette opened the door of her room without a word. I asked her to go in ahead. It was a simple bedroom, such as you find in any country hotel. I ceased to watch Odette and looked into the room next door. There in bed lay a young man, perhaps thirty to thirty-five years old, in an elegant pair of pyjamas . . . I asked for his identity card. Without a sign of nervousness, he asked Odette to hand him his jacket, pulled the card out of a pocket and held it out to me. It read the name Pierre Chambrun. I felt that there could no longer be any doubt, and that this was Peter Churchill, known to us as Pierre Chauvet and more frequently still as Raoul.

When Churchill was debriefed at the end of the war, a paragraph under the heading 'Reasons for Source's Arrest', recorded:

> Source agrees that the incident of the arrival of the Italian officers should have been enough warning for him to clear out immediately, but he was at that time extremely tired and also in a worried state because he had left his mother in England dying. He is particularly anxious to emphasise that it was his own fault and not LISE's that they did not immediately leave the Hôtel de la Poste.

Instead of leaving Saint-Jorioz while they had the chance, Churchill and Odette had indeed pushed their luck, only this time they had gone too far. They now found themselves in a situation that could so easily have been avoided had they done what they were told to do on his return to France. On his personnel file there is an entry, written at the end of the war, which reads:

> On arriving in France, SPINDLE [Churchill] stayed the night at the COTTET hotel with CLOTHIER [Odette] instead of, as they had been told to, going immediately to GLAIEULS and they were both arrested by the Gestapo, 16.4.43.

Yes, they really should have done what they had been told to do, because for Churchill and Odette the war was over.

Chapter 15

The Deception

To a certain extent, Churchill can consider himself unlucky to have been arrested in the way that he was, as Bleicher's game was coming to an end. After intercepting messages to and from London reporting that a senior German officer was trying to escape to Britain with a key Resistance leader, the Gestapo had become involved and so Bleicher had been ordered to wind up his operation. As the closing act he had simply gone to Saint-Jorioz to arrest anyone he could find who might be involved with the group. Bleicher later recalled – 'I did not want to return to Paris empty-handed' – and after finding out that suspects were staying at the Hôtel de la Poste, he had taken with him that night three of his colleagues from the Abwehr headquarters, an Italian intelligence officer and a small security squad from the Italian Field Police to make the arrests.

Bleicher was, of course, delighted with the arrests and hoped to take Churchill and Odette straight to Paris. He was keen to keep them for himself, but they had been arrested in an area under Italian authority and so they were instead taken to an Italian Army barracks at Annecy. All Churchill and Odette could do now was to protect the identities of others. During his arrest at the hotel Churchill had been quick to point out to his captors that the Cottets had played no part in anything, and they had no idea who he was. Whether or not Bleicher believed Churchill is not known, but he left the Cottets alone.

While the arrests of Churchill and Odette had brought an end to Bleicher's mission at Saint-Jorioz, the destruction of the SPINDLE network would have disastrous repercussions elsewhere. Marsac was still languishing in his cell at Fresnes, but any hope that Bleicher had of turning him into a German agent was fading away. Bardet, meanwhile, whom Bleicher had also used in his scheme, was now arrested, and chose to turn traitor rather than be handed over to the Gestapo; he would eventually lead the Abwehr to other SOE circuits and, ultimately, to Henri Frager. In Bleicher's own words many years later, Roger Bardet turned out to be the best assistant he ever had during his time in

France. At his trial after the war, Bardet was sentenced to death, but the sentence was later commuted to twenty years' imprisonment, although he would be released in 1955.

For now, at least, Rabinowitch was safe. Having heard that Churchill and Odette had been captured, he sent a message to London about the arrests and then escaped via the Spanish route. He would return to France a year later with the intention of setting up his own circuit, but his drop zone was in the hands of the Gestapo. Sadly, Adolphe Rabinowitch would meet the same end as so many others. He was deported to Germany and, being Jewish, was put to death in the gas chambers at Gross-Rosen, probably during the autumn of 1944. Peter Churchill's second book, *Duel of Wits*, is dedicated to him.

When he arrived at the Italian barracks, Churchill found his cell to be a squalid mess. There were no blankets and no toilet, and all he had for a bed was a wooden board. Churchill's heart sank into his boots.

From the darkness of his cell, Churchill relived the events of the night of his arrest. Time and time again things went through his mind. He wondered if there was anything that he might have left in his room, or in his pockets, which could be of use to his captors. He had noticed his wallet was missing. It had been in the pocket of the jacket he was wearing. Now it had gone.

The thought of the wallet being in the hands of the enemy made Churchill feel quite sick. In his mission debrief report, he disclosed that he believed a small calendar of his had been found 'in which the only three compromising things were the telephone numbers of CATHERINE [Odette des Garets], MARIE-LOU [Marie-Lou Blanc] and DE MALVAL [Baron Henri Ravel de Malval]'.

Churchill thought of nothing else that first night in his cell, as he later explained in his mission report:

> During that night I kept fearing that they would set a trap for the three people whose telephone numbers might have been discovered, although of course there was no mention of towns attached to the numbers and except in the case for MARIE-LOU, the names were war names.

There was nothing Churchill could do about his wallet now and as sleep was out of the question, his thoughts turned to how he might escape. He knew that his best chance was while he was being held by the Italians and so if he was to get out then he would have to make the attempt soon.

The guards outside his cell came and went as the first night slowly passed. In the morning coffee arrived and after lunch Churchill was taken out of his cell and into the yard, after which he was transferred to a larger cell, which had the luxury of its own toilet. He had noticed a bar attached to the wall outside, about two metres above the ground, beyond which was the street, and it gave him the idea that he might be able to escape over the wall by using the bar.

That night in his cell Churchill repeatedly rehearsed his plan in his mind. He would make his escape in the morning. His mission report describes what happened:

> On the following morning at a quarter to seven, as there was only one guard, I called him to the door and asked him for a light through the hole in the door. He opened the door and at the moment I was prepared to give him a heavy blow he brought out his own cigarette case and offered me a cigarette. This action damped down my aggressive intention, and instead of hitting him I pushed him inside the cell, but owing to his *alpini* rubber boots, he did not slide, and then a fight ensued, during which in self-defence I broke his rifle, and after what seemed a considerable time, during which he kept shouting for help, I managed to knock him out. By this time I was somewhat exhausted, and as I was planning to jump on to the bar, the first of the guard arrived, and I slammed the courtyard door in his face. I then jumped at the bar, but before I could get my legs over the whole guard was on to me, and had me pinned against the wall with their bayonets a few inches away.

His attempted escape was over in minutes and Churchill was soon back inside his cell with the door locked. All he had achieved was to gain a black eye from the fist of one of the guards. His punishment was to go without food for two days, although there was the occasional beating with the butt of a rifle along the way, as guards returned to his cell seeking some form of revenge for their colleague who had suffered during the fight.

The hours dragged on and turned into days. Churchill's thoughts were all over the place. He thought about those back in London and wondered what they would do now he was off the chart. He thought about his parents and the friends he had made since being in France, and, of course, he thought about Odette and wondered what she was having to endure.

After several days Churchill was allowed to shave and freshen up. That evening, he was taken from his cell to a truck waiting outside in the yard. Some of the guards were there to see him off, some even wishing him a fond farewell and good luck. It was as if they knew what lay ahead. Churchill's mission report takes up the story:

> After five or six days in Annecy, LISE and I were taken to Grenoble by truck. My wrists were chained, but LISE was free. At Grenoble my bad reputation caused me to be put into another foul cell, my glasses were taken away from me, also my shoes, and my ankles were chained.

The journey to Grenoble took two hours. Although there were Italian guards inside the truck, Churchill and Odette were allowed to sit together and talk. She had some cigarettes, acquired from her guards, and so she shared them with him. They talked about how they had been betrayed and who they felt had been responsible, both agreeing that it must have been Bardet behind the man known as Louis le Belge. She could see Churchill's cuts and bruises and made him promise not to try and escape again. They also promised each other they would battle through whatever lay ahead. She would be thinking of him and praying for him every day, but particularly at 6 p.m., when they could both think of each other at the same time. Churchill sensed that for some reason Odette felt his chances of survival were better than hers.

At Grenoble they were separated once more. In his cell he laid down on the straw that was his bed, thinking of nothing other than Odette. In *The Spirit in the Cage*, Churchill explained – 'Not until now had I fully realised the extent of my admiration and love for her.'

The following morning Churchill had his chains removed. He was taken outside so that he could walk around. There was a water tap where he could freshen up. As he stood there, he could only wonder what the future might hold, but the reality was he was now at the beginning of an all-too-familiar and well-trodden path for captured SOE agents – capture, interrogation, deportation to a concentration camp, and ultimately death.

However, during the following day the probable outcome of his war, and his life, took a dramatic turn. At first there was nothing unusual when Churchill's cell door was opened, but on this occasion several officers walked in rather than one of the guards. Initially there followed a familiar line of questions asking Churchill who he was, to which he stuck with his usual answer of Pierre Chambrun, but what came next took Churchill by surprise. The Italian asking the questions told him they knew he was not Pierre Chambrun, but his real name was Peter Churchill and that he was related to Winston Churchill, the British Prime Minister. Churchill was stunned. He even asked his captors why they would think that, but they would not reveal how they knew.

Until that point, Churchill had hoped that his French identity would keep him alive, but now he was being taken as a relative of one of the most hated men of the Axis powers, which could easily bring an early end to his life. He could only wonder how all of this had come about.

For now, no more was said about Churchill being related to the British Prime Minister and, again, the days slowly passed by. Spending so long in darkness and isolation was hard, not helped by never knowing just how long he was to be held in one place. Then, on his fifth day at Grenoble, Churchill was handcuffed and put on a truck. Odette was already seated inside, only this time the two were not allowed to talk. They were taken to the railway station where they boarded a train, in separate compartments with their guards, and with no idea of where they were heading.

Their destination was Turin, a journey that lasted several hours. When they arrived, they were held in a waiting room, and this time they were able to talk. Odette was quick to tell Churchill that it had been she who had told an Italian officer his real name and that he was the nephew of Winston Churchill. She knew the Italian would be unable to keep the news to himself and should they be handed over to the Germans at some point then she was convinced they would hold him hostage, as he could be of use as a bargaining tool at some point in the future. At least it might mean he would be kept safe for the rest of the war. Not only that, but Odette had also told the Italian officer that she was Peter Churchill's wife, and they had been married since 1941.

Giving up their identities was a huge gamble, probably the biggest gamble of them all, but it might just work. The Italians seemed to have fallen for the deception – so far – but would the Germans? Would they be more thorough in trying to establish the truth, or would they simply accept the word of a captured agent? But the mere possibility that Churchill was related to Britain's Prime Minister might just be enough to keep him alive. And if they were to think there was a possibility that Churchill was related to the Prime Minister then they could hardly take a chance with Odette. The possibility that she might really be Peter Churchill's wife might just keep her alive as well. If there was some doubt in their captors' minds, any doubt at all, then they both stood a chance.

It would prove to be a brilliant idea. At the time, Churchill thought it a good idea too. They would either survive together or not. Odette did point out, though, that the scheme was a wartime measure only, although Churchill already had other ideas.

They were soon joined in the waiting room by an Italian guard and so there was no time for Churchill and Odette to refine their story in detail. They would have to wait until the next time they were together, assuming there would be a next time, but unless they could get their story straight their idea would fall at the first hurdle.

That next opportunity to chat came during a train journey to Nice after leaving Turin. They agreed they had been married on 24 December 1941 in London, at a registry office on Baker Street, and who their witnesses were. They exchanged names and addresses of key members of their families and agreed on other more minor matters just in case they were ever questioned. They kept things as simple as they could, constantly checking each other's memory, and agreed to keep up the story until the bitter end.

At Nice, Churchill and Odette were taken to a villa high up in the hills, which was being used as a temporary prison; she was held in a room upstairs and he in the cellars. Churchill would later describe the facilities as excellent and if he had to spend the rest of the war locked up, then being at the villa under Italian authority was about as good as it could get. He even recognised one of the prisoners being held there. It was Doctor Élie Lévy from Antibes, but he knew better than to let it be known that the two knew each other. That would suggest they had worked together and that would not be good for either of them. Lévy had not long been arrested. After the débâcle on the Côte d'Azur the previous summer he had gone into hiding, but he had later returned to Antibes where, unfortunately for him, he had been picked up by the

Italian police. He had also recognised Churchill at the villa, but he also knew not to let on. Lévy would later be deported to Germany and being Jewish ended up at Auschwitz where he endured fifteen months of hell before his life came to an end during the infamous death march, after he had fallen exhausted and was probably shot.

After ten days at the villa, Churchill and Odette were taken by truck along the Mediterranean coastline to Toulon. It was a long and familiar journey, as it took them along roads they had used freely only a matter of months before. Then at Toulon, after some three weeks in the hands of the Italians, they were handed over to two members of the SS. Suddenly it dawned on them. Churchill and Odette were at the beginning of the ill-trodden path to Germany.

Chapter 16
Fresnes

Built in the late nineteenth century, Fresnes Prison is still in use today. With 1,200 cells for men and a smaller section for women, it is the second-largest prison in Paris, behind Fleury-Merogis, the largest prison in Europe. Back in the Second World War, though, the whole teeming labyrinth of Fresnes – its cells, chapels, kitchens, dungeons, and corridors – was used by the Germans to house captured SOE agents and members of the French Resistance. Kept in horrific conditions, some 3,000 prisoners were held at Fresnes at any one time, many of whom died there during the Nazi occupation.

For Churchill and Odette, Fresnes was to be their next stop. After being handed over to the Germans, they were driven by car to Marseille and then put on a night train for Paris. Bleicher was at the Gare de Lyon to meet them. He already knew, of course, that Churchill was supposedly the nephew of Winston Churchill, but it seems that Bleicher might well have heard this story earlier than first thought. Following Marsac's arrest and Bleicher's subsequent conversations with him at Fresnes, which took place before Churchill returned to France, Bleicher remembered that he had heard from Marsac that a nephew of Winston Churchill was working for the organisation with his wife.

At that stage Bleicher did not know who that person was and believed Marsac's suggestion that the reason the agent had claimed 'that he was a close relative of Winston Churchill was spread about to give him greater prestige in the French Resistance, as well as a safeguard if he fell into the hands of the Germans'. Churchill would later deny that he had used this cover story earlier, and in the same book there is a footnote acknowledging Churchill's comment that, 'It was only after our arrest that we pretended to be married.'

From the Gare de Lyon, Churchill and Odette were driven through the southern suburbs of Paris. It was the morning of 8 May 1943 and the height of spring, but everywhere looked drab, people seemed miserable, and it was not the vibrant capital that it had once been.

As they drove through the iron gates and pulled into the inner courtyard at Fresnes, the massive, forbidding prison had a grim appearance. Churchill was separated from Odette. From now on they were on their own, and he was soon being hustled through the sombre underground passages that seemed to stretch to infinity, the darkness only being broken every now and then by an occasional electric lamp set in the vaulted roof. The dirty smell of Fresnes would last for ever with those who had walked those steps.

Prisoners were held in one of three divisions, each block containing five floors. Churchill was held on the second floor of the second division, in cell number 220, where the walls had been marked by previous occupants, with a wide range of 'artwork' on display. There was a double window of frosted glass, one pane of which was broken, with a plain glass over-window above, allowing some light into the cell and opened or closed by a lever. Through the broken frosted glass window, the building of another division could be seen, and the courtyard below. There was a lavatory and a tap, an iron bed with a straw mattress, three blankets and a sheet, a wooden table, and a stool. A slot in the cell door allowed guards to pass things to the prisoner, and a spy hole allowed him to look out, although there was very little to see.

It was against the rules to shout, sing, or tap the pipes, but it all happened anyway and so it was noisy inside Fresnes. Some inmates shouted words of encouragement while others shared what they were having to endure, with the occasional scream of pain. New prisoners were arriving every day and provided regular updates on how the war was going; it did not take long for word to pass around. The walls and pipes could be used for Morse tapping and the design of the prison plumbing meant there was a hollow between the adjoining corners of cells, containing the pipes for the taps and toilets. By speaking through the holes that housed the taps prisoners were able to communicate. It was known as 'talking through the tap' and all part of the background noise at Fresnes.

Churchill had only been at Fresnes a matter of hours when he was taken from his cell. His mission debrief report reads:

> About three hours after my arrival I was called down to see Henri. He was extremely affable and did his best to get something out of me, but I would not talk. He showed me several sheets of closely-typed paper and read out some of the things that Marsac had said about me and our organisation.

> From what I gathered, no single thought, action or hope of mine had been omitted. There was a table showing the names of officers from Col. Buckmaster downwards, with a line to me in France, including besides my name, that of LISE, GERVAIS, ARNAUD, EUGENE, GIL, GISELLE and some others. The line I took, both with Henri and subsequently at Gestapo Headquarters was that Marsac, who had been so simply fooled by Henri, had through *folie des grandeurs* made out that the organisation was far more important than in fact it was. Henri warned me that the Gestapo would probably not be put off by such talk. He then said: "Do you think that your Government would be willing to exchange you against Rudolph HESS?" Knowing Marsac, I was sure that he had not only given my real name away but had also exaggerated the relationship between the Prime Minister and myself, which in point of fact I believe is sixty-second cousin. I told Henri that I was only distantly related, and his reply was: 'I advise you to say that you are closely related, as it may do you some good.'

The two men also talked about political matters and the way the war was going. Hess was Hitler's former deputy and had been in British hands for the past two years. The idea of a possible exchange amused Churchill, although he was sure that no one in Britain would see it as a fair swap – not even the British Prime Minister. Bleicher then left Churchill some cigarettes and walked out of the cell, saying he would return in a few days.

The meeting with Bleicher so soon after arriving at Fresnes took Churchill by surprise, although it did suggest that the idea of him being the nephew of the British Prime Minister was at least being taken seriously. That was fine, of course, great news even, providing the Germans did not go to any great lengths to establish the truth.

For most new prisoners at Fresnes, the biggest battle was isolation. Although the prison was desperately overcrowded, putting the new arrivals into solitary confinement was a way of breaking them down psychologically. They had to exercise as best they could within the confines of their cell. Once a week the guards brought razors from cell to cell, but the soap was bad, the brushes thin, and the blades usually blunt because they were passed from man to man. The rations were barely enough to keep a man alive, yet liberal enough not to help him die.

Coffee, if it could be called that, was brought around in the morning, but the highlight of the day was at midday when soup, usually cabbage, was served with a chunk of bread and a minute piece of fat, a sliver of liver sausage, or a small piece of cheese. Hunger was all part of the inhumane game. The evening came in on a relieved stomach, if not on a full one. Sleep depended on eating, but the only thing to eat was any bread that had been saved from lunch, because to lie awake at night on an empty stomach was something to avoid.

Being alone in a cell meant Churchill soon lost all sense of time. He could only guess when it was 6 p.m., the time Odette had told him she would be thinking of him. The only indication of daytime was from the light coming through his window, and it was not long before he started to lose track of what day it was, and so he scratched a calendar on the wall and started crossing off the days. There was nothing to help pass the time as he had nothing to read. Reading material would only come as a privilege, and earning privileges only came with good behaviour over time. But by communicating through whatever means they could, prisoners were able to find out who else was in their immediate surroundings. Churchill discovered he was being held on the same division as Marsac and Riquet, and the Newton Twins. They had been captured a couple of weeks before Churchill. Now they were all at Fresnes at the same time.

It was not long before Bleicher came to meet Churchill again. They met in an empty cell on the floor below, where they smoked together and talked. Bleicher asked Churchill if he knew anyone in Paris who could supply him with a few extra luxuries, such as fresh linen and additional food. Churchill gave him the name of Charles Fol who lived at the Chaussée de la Muette, although he made it clear that he had not had any contact with Fol since before the war and that Fol was completely unaware of Churchill's wartime activities.

Bleicher also warned Churchill that his interrogation would start soon, although the idea of a prisoner exchange had been put forward to Berlin. He also asked Churchill why he had not declared that he was married to Odette until after they had been captured, to which Churchill gave his well-rehearsed reply that they had decided to keep it to themselves and not to share the information with anyone while they were working together in France. Then came the best bit. Odette walked into the cell.

Unconcerned by Bleicher's presence, Churchill and Odette embraced. They had fifteen priceless minutes together in the cell, although with Bleicher there they could not talk as freely as they would have liked.

After his visit to Churchill, Bleicher drove to the Chaussée de la Muette to meet Charles Fol, introducing himself as a German officer by the name of Captain Johann Verbeck. Having updated Fol on Churchill's health and whereabouts, Bleicher returned to Fresnes with a package of clothing and food.

Churchill was delighted to receive the package, but it was time to prepare for the interrogation that Bleicher had warned him would come. In his mission report, Churchill commented:

> As I had plenty of time to think out my attitude during these interrogations, and as I had fortunately remembered something of what was taught me at Beaulieu, I decided to adopt the attitude of someone whose brain works very slowly, and to show absolutely no enthusiasm or give any signs of insistence whether I was telling a lie or the truth.

Churchill decided not to deny everything. That, he thought, would be madness. But he was certainly not going to give anyone away and so he would respond to each question in the same monotonous voice, not wishing to reveal any emotion or hint as to what the truth was and what was not. Whether the Germans would believe him remained to be seen, but he would certainly require courage to get through whatever lay ahead. Unlike others, though, he had no religious faith to fall back on. For his inner strength he chose to remember his brother, Walter, the courageous fighter pilot, who had a hero's death leading his men against the enemy. That was how he, Peter Churchill, would have wanted to die, and not in the conditions that he now faced. He imagined joining his brother in the hereafter. It was a pivotal moment of his captivity.

Churchill did not have much longer to wait for his interrogation. One day he was taken from his cell, put into a black van, and driven to a building in the centre of Paris.

The Avenue Foch connects the Arc de Triomphe with Port Dauphine. At the western end is number 84 Avenue Foch, a rather ordinary-looking five-storey building now containing a handful of privately owned apartments. Back in 1943, though, it was the French headquarters of the Sicherheitsdienst.

The Sicherheitsdienst (SD) had been established in 1931 as the intelligence agency of the SS and the Nazi Party. It was separate from the Gestapo (formed in 1933) and during the Second World War its Paris headquarters was established at 84 Avenue Foch under the command of Sturmbannführer (Colonel) Josef Kieffer, the senior German intelligence officer in Paris. All captured SOE agents were taken there for interrogation, under the authority of Standartenführer (Major) Helmut Knochen, whose jurisdiction stretched across northern France.

Churchill was taken to a room on the fourth floor, where he was told to sit down opposite a man behind a desk. Churchill would later describe him as a tall man wearing a dark suit, of maybe forty, with a high forehead, protruding ears, and a grey intelligent face, with cold eyes that gave him the shivers. From similar descriptions given by other agents after the war, this was almost certainly Sonderführer Ernst Vogt, a Swiss-German civilian attached to the SD and one of its senior interrogators and French interpreters. Churchill's mission debrief report described what happened during his interrogation:

> A most intelligent man, whose name I do not know, and whose French was faultless, was in charge of my case. His first question was: 'When did you last see Dr Levy?". In answer to his question, I said I had never heard of this man. The Gestapo man simply roared with laughter, and I maintained a dull and stupid look. He then said: 'You know, Dr Levy, 33 Boulevard Maréchal Foch' and I replied: 'I am very sorry, I know no-one at Paris of that name.'

Churchill refers to his interrogator as being from the Gestapo whereas he was, in fact, a member of the SD, though that would have been unknown to Churchill. Besides, it made no difference to those under interrogation what organisation the interrogator was a part of. It was all the same as far as a captured SOE agent was concerned. Churchill knew full well, of course, that Boulevard Maréchal Foch was in Antibes and not in Paris, and of course he knew Doctor Lévy, but he had not expected the interrogation to start in such a way and so he was pleased when it changed tack:

> He [the interrogator] passed the matter off with a sarcastic laugh. We then went through the usual routine of my life story, all of which I related in the same dull tones, as slowly

> as possible, omitting the fact that I was a member of the Intelligence Corps, and saying in its place that I was in the Commandos. I was then asked in what schools I had been trained, and naturally refused to divulge these. In reply to questions about Colonel Buckmaster and other officers, I was very vague and refused to admit knowing General Gubbins [the Head of SOE], whom I know quite well. I was attacked about my various operations and I managed to speak about my first mission without mentioning anyone's name, as can be proved if copies of this interrogation are available. I did not mention my third operation of landing the two radio men at Antibes. With regard to my second visit I spoke a great deal in most detrimental terms about CARTE, knowing that he was in England, and having been assured that he would not be sent out to France again. I was then asked where PAUL [Frager] was, as it was perfectly well known that we had travelled back together by Lysander in March 1943. I said that as we knew that Marsac had given the show away it had been decided that PAUL should not be sent back. I was asked about pretty well every member of the organisation actually in the Field and so ably given away by Marsac. I disclaimed knowledge of most of these, my case being that my own particular organisation was extremely small and that Marsac knew several other organisations of whose existence I was completely unaware and that as he wished to impress Henri with the importance of my organisation in the hope that he would get out of prison, he had joined all these organisations on to mine, and said that I was in charge of them all. I was asked about GERVAIS: I said I had never heard of him. I was told that ARNAUD was arrested, that GERVAIS, ROGER, who was then at Cannes, and most of the names who had been mentioned by Marsac as belonging to the organisation, had also been arrested, and that it would be a very simple matter for them to prove conclusively that since all these people knew me, that I was a complete liar. I must admit that at this moment, I did not feel very strong, but nevertheless I persisted in my dull and negative attitude.

The next line of questioning was about the arming of the resistance groups in the Savoie mountains. Churchill confirmed that he had sent a telegram announcing these people's presence but, other than that, said he had nothing to do with arming them. The interrogator's previously calm personality suddenly changed as he stormed around the room, shouting at Churchill, and accusing him of taking him for an idiot – 'Do you take us people for a bunch of imbecile children?' he shouted.

Churchill was also asked about Odette, to which he replied – 'She was of no importance in the organisation, but merely looked after the supplying of food for ourselves and that she spent her time finding flats and new bicycles for me and ARNAUD.' That was it. The questions then stopped, the interrogator simply warning Churchill that his stubborn attitude would do him no good.

As Churchill left the Avenue Foch, everything about what he had just endured went through his mind. There had been none of the brutal methods he had heard so much about. Many had been tortured there, but not him. Perhaps that would come next time, or perhaps the Germans were starting to believe that he really was the nephew of the British Prime Minister or, at least, there was sufficient doubt in their minds.

Whatever the case, Churchill would have to remember everything he had said during that first interrogation. Back in his cell he went through it all again, as he would do every day. It was important to stick to his story. He had noticed during questioning there had been some inconsistencies and omissions as to what the Germans really did know, and so it was not as if they held all the cards.

Not long after his interrogation at the Avenue Foch Churchill received another visit from Bleicher. Again, they talked about all sorts of things, and it seemed the Germans were believing Churchill's story. And, for the second time that month, there was another meeting with Odette.

Through Bleicher, Churchill was getting privileges that very few at Fresnes were able to enjoy. He was receiving regular food and clothing parcels, not only from Charles Fol but also from a family friend, Mlle Jeanne Laurent, who lived on the Rue du Bac. He was also receiving books from the library and the occasional Red Cross parcel containing biscuits as an extra treat. And he was kept in the same cell throughout his time at Fresnes, whereas other prisoners were often moved about and even crammed three or four into cells originally intended for one man.

The weeks drifted by, albeit very slowly. At times, life seemed almost bearable as Churchill got used to the Fresnes way of life. Then he spotted someone he recognised, as included in his mission report:

> Some time in the Summer, as I was looking through the slit of my door, I saw to my horror someone whom I was sure was de Malval. He was going for a walk and passed in front of my door. I saw him return from the walk. Believing that his imprisonment must certainly be due to the unfortunate note-book which I was guilty of having on me at the moment of my arrest, I was terribly upset . . . Some weeks later, I was having a shower and de Malval was standing opposite me. I managed to get into the showers before he came out and although watched by a guard I managed to whisper to him: 'How did you get here?' He said: 'It is through you, you swine.' I worried over this matter for days.

Churchill's brief conversation with de Malval was a terrible reminder of the missing wallet, and of the horrific consequences if it had been found.

Then, in early August, a quite remarkable event took place. Churchill was taken from his cell to the main doors of the prison where Bleicher was waiting for him. Having told the guards that he was taking Churchill for further questioning, Bleicher then drove him through the streets of Paris. The sun was shining, and it all seemed unreal. They stopped at Bleicher's flat to freshen up before going on to see the Fols and have dinner, after which Churchill was taken back to Fresnes.

This quite extraordinary event is included in Churchill's mission debrief report, which reads:

> On about 4th August [1943], Henri [Bleicher] took Source to see the Fols: the pretence was that Source was to be taken out of Fresnes for interrogation. On the way Henri took Source to his flat which was situated in a turning out of Avenue Foch. Here Source met Henri's mistress, Suzanne. He had a bath, shave and some drinks. Suzanne he described as being a dark girl of average height; aged 30; plumpish and not very well shaped legs; sallow olive complexion, with a lot of dark hair; brown eyes and not very good teeth. She told Henri that Source was a double-agent. From the flat they went on to the Fols – both Henri and Suzanne came. Suzanne brought some fruit. Before their arrival, the Fols had sent their children away by way of precaution. Henri and Source both played two pianos at the same time, and spent a pleasant time at the Fols. Source had

> said to the Fols: 'Look after Henri. He can be useful but he is a dangerous man, and you must give nothing away to him.' This was the only reason why they received Henri. The Fols' sole contact with Henri was therefore upon Source's introduction, and it was maintained solely at Source's request, as Henri might be useful.

When Churchill returned to his cell he must have wondered if it had all been a dream. It really was a most bizarre event, and it was a strange game that Bleicher continued to play. While Bleicher clearly relished the praise of having caught the nephew of Winston Churchill, he was astute enough to realise that one day he might rely on Churchill's help. He even asked if Churchill could arrange an aircraft to fly him to London, which Churchill declined to do, but he did offer the German a chance of a safe passage to Britain via the Pyrenees. All Bleicher had to do was drive them to the Spanish border. But Bleicher admitted it would be impossible to get Churchill out of Fresnes and through all the required checkpoints, however much he might have thought it a good idea. In which case, Churchill said, he would just have to sweat it out inside.

Churchill also took the opportunity to ask Bleicher about de Malval:

> I decided to lay the cards on the table over the de Malval question and asked him point-blank whether he had laid a trap for de Malval through finding my diary. His reply was: 'No, never, no-one went down to Cannes.' I was mystified by this and as it pained me considerably to think of a man his age in prison I decided to mention the matter at my next interrogation in Ave. Foch.

News of Churchill having been seen outside Fresnes soon got back to SOE. Churchill's London friend Madame Fol telephoned F Section to say she had received a message from her brother-in-law Charles Fol in Paris and to pass on the fact that Churchill had been seen safe and well, although there were no further details at that time.

Presumably, Churchill's family would have been kept informed, but all this happened soon after his mother died. She had hated the war and had every reason to do so.

Churchill's second visit to the Avenue Foch came during October. He was well prepared for it, having repeated over and over in his own mind every likely question and his chosen answer for each. Fortunately for him, this second ordeal was nowhere near as traumatic as his first, the interrogator choosing a far easier line of questioning to deal with and so he learned nothing new. In his mission report, Churchill later explained:

> In this interrogation, I allowed myself to relax a bit and told rather more than previously. I mentioned such names as OLIVE, MARIE, ALAIN, confidently hoping that ALAIN had changed his name and realising that OLIVE and MARIE were out of the country. I hope and believe that I caused no damage or harm to anyone by what I said in this interrogation.

As to the matter of de Malval, Churchill wrote:

> The way I tackled the de Malval subject was this. I informed the Gestapo interrogator that I had seen him at Fresnes, and could not imagine what he was there for. I wondered if someone else, like Marsac had mentioned de Malval as being a member of the organisation, and told the interrogator that de Malval in point of fact was an acquaintance of mine, that I had stayed at his house, and that somehow or other I had known of his address, but that he had nothing to do with our work, that in November 1942 when the Italians came in I had told de Malval who I really was and warned him that it was dangerous to know someone like myself, and that therefore he should cut himself off entirely from even knowing me. I would be very interested to know the truth and full details of what actually happened to de Malval.

As things were to turn out, de Malval left Fresnes soon after Churchill's interrogation and would survive the war, although it would not be the last Churchill would hear of him.

The late autumn winds sweeping through the stone prison had taken with them the last of the warmth stored through the summer months. A prisoner would suddenly be gone, only to be replaced by another and the same cycle of getting to know someone else through whatever form of communicating started all over again. It all highlighted one of the biggest problems for those imprisoned at Fresnes. No one knew how long they would be there. They would only be at Fresnes for as long as the Germans wanted to keep them there. But then, in November, there was suddenly hope for Churchill that he might soon be on his way home, as detailed in his mission report:

> Henri came to see me about the 10th November 1943 in a great state of assumed or real excitement, and said that a special envoy had been sent down from Gestapo HQ in Berlin, to find out if I was willing to be exchanged, with another British officer, against a German agent caught in England and risking the death penalty. He said that a telegram would be sent that very day to the War Office and that should London play he did not give me eight more days in Fresnes before being sent home. Of course, nothing happened. When the question was put to me I did not feel that I was in a position to bargain with the Gestapo about insisting on taking LISE out, but if this was a trap to see whether I would refuse to go without her and so be able to use this to torment LISE, it was certainly successful.

During November Churchill was also amongst a group of prisoners taken to a building in the Rue des Saussaies to be photographed and fingerprinted. Odette was there too. They were held in a large open pen while waiting their turn and had a moment together. She had also endured interrogations and had been questioned on their story. Churchill mentioned his conversation with de Malval and his worry about the missing wallet. But she was able to reassure him. Knowing what the wallet contained, she had been quick to remove it from his jacket pocket at the time of their arrests. She had hidden it under her dress, but not wishing to have it in her possession when later searched, she had disposed of it beneath the seat of the car that had taken her to the barracks. They could only guess what might have happened to the wallet after that.

This was the last time Churchill saw Odette at Fresnes. Christmas came and went. While attempts by the Red Cross to send the prisoners a few home comforts merely added to the luxuries for many German guards at the prison, Churchill was fortunate to receive his. Then it was the new year, although that started slowly too.

Churchill had now been at Fresnes for nine months, but just as it was looking like he might be lucky enough to spend the rest of the war there, his cell door opened, and the guard told him to pick up his belongings. He was to leave at once.

It was around midday when Churchill arrived at the Avenue Foch. A Gestapo officer told him he was to be exchanged. Churchill thought it a joke, but the German insisted not, saying that he was first to go to Berlin and from there he would make his way home, either through Switzerland or Sweden. Churchill wanted Odette, as his wife, to be allowed to travel with him, but it was not to be. Orders were that Churchill was to be brought to Berlin alone. It was 13 February 1944.

Chapter 17
Sachsenhausen

Most prisoners leaving Fresnes were sent to a concentration camp in Germany, via the Royallieu-Compiègne internment and deportation camp, but not Churchill. He was instead taken straight to the Gare de l'Est, with an escort of two civilian guards to board the night train to Berlin.

It was the depth of a cold winter. Daylight revealed grey skies and a dismal wintry countryside, and as the train headed deeper into war-torn Germany the effects of the Allied bombing offensive could be seen; at the railway marshalling yards, on the factories, and on the houses. With two changes of train, it took all that day and night to reach Berlin, but it was a journey that Churchill would later describe as having been completed 'in great style'.

It was dark when the train pulled in to the Anhalter Bahnhof, one of Berlin's most important stations and one that had been heavily bombed. There Churchill was met by an officer of the Gestapo who took him to the headquarters on the Prinz-Albrecht-Strasse, where, during the early hours of the morning, he was taken to the office of a senior Gestapo figure.

Churchill must have still been in a state of shock. Only a day or two before he had been in his cramped, dirty cell at Fresnes and now he was in a large office in one of the most important buildings in Nazi Germany. Sat behind a table was an older man. Behind him in the centre of the far wall was a large framed picture of Heinrich Himmler, Reichsführer-SS, and one of the most powerful men in the Nazi Party. There were others in uniform in the office as well, but instead of being asked more questions, or being told anything about a possible exchange, Churchill was sent straight to a cell in the basement.

Churchill was so tired he fell asleep. Other than being taken to a washroom later that morning, nothing else happened that day. Or the next. He started to wonder if there was to be an exchange.

The slow routine prison way of life began all over again. This time, though, there was not the noise and camaraderie of Fresnes. Instead, the place was silent. But the silence was suddenly broken one night by the sound of exploding bombs. Bomber Command had dispatched nearly 900 aircraft to the city, the largest force yet sent to Berlin. More than 2,600 tons of bombs were dropped, a record tonnage, some of which fell around the Prinz-Albrecht-Strasse and caused heavy damage to the nearby centre and south-western districts of the city. For Churchill his life could have ended there and then, the result of bombing by his own side.

The days dragged on. Churchill's mission report states he was held in Berlin for sixteen days. Any thoughts of a prisoner exchange seemed to have long disappeared. Either both sides could not agree the terms, or it could be that Churchill's idea of deceiving the Germans had failed. Perhaps they had been busy checking up on his story, and now they knew it could not be true. Whatever the case, nothing seemed to be happening.

Then, on 2 March, Churchill's cell door opened, and he was told it was time to go. After gathering his belongings, he was put into a van. This time his escorts were more the thuggish type than the two civilians who had escorted him to Berlin.

The van headed north out of the city and signs to Oranienburg soon began to appear. That meant only one thing, and it was not good news. Churchill was being taken to the concentration camp at Sachsenhausen.

Sachsenhausen had opened in 1936 to house political opponents of the Nazi regime and others who had no place in the National Socialist so-called 'people's community', such as criminals, homosexuals, Jehovah's Witnesses, and Jews. During the Second World War, however, it was a labour camp run by the SS, where its inmates were treated inhumanely, fed sparingly, and killed openly, most noticeably the Soviet prisoners of war. At least 30,000 are believed to have died there. But Churchill was to be spared the worst of what Sachsenhausen had to offer.

The camp's inmates also included prominent prisoners of war, such as Joseph Stalin's eldest son, Yakov Dzhugashvili, although he had died at Sachsenhausen before Churchill's arrival after his father had reportedly refused to make a deal to secure his release, and Paul Reynaud, the penultimate pre-occupation Prime Minister of France. Known as *Prominenten*, these high-profile prisoners came from countries across Nazi-occupied Europe and were imprisoned at specific locations, with Sachsenhausen being one. They were being tucked away out of sight ready to be used as valuable pawns with which to barter should the need ever arise.

And so, Churchill became one of Sachsenhausen's privileged few. He was taken straight to a small, enclosed compound outside the main camp perimeter on its northern side. Security was extra tight, with nearly twice as many guards as the small number of prisoners being held. As he was led through the wired gate and into the enclosure, he noticed some were wearing Allied uniforms rather than the striped jackets that he had already seen. Within the compound stood two wooden huts. These were Sonderlager 'A' and Sonderlager 'B', built earlier in the war to accommodate these special prisoners that the Nazi regime had decided to isolate.

Churchill was to be accommodated in the first hut, Sonderlager 'A'. He could not quite believe how lucky he was. Inside his room was a bed, chairs, a table, and a stove. At the end of the room there were large open windows, opening the room to the bright blue sky. Not only that, but he was allocated a senior British non-commissioned officer as his orderly.

After a cup of tea and a British cigarette, and a change of clothes, Churchill spent the rest of the day meeting other prisoners. Each hut had eight rooms, four on either side of a washhouse. In Churchill's hut, the end room closest to the gate was occupied by two NCO orderlies, and the room next to that was shared by two more NCOs. Churchill's room was the third room and next to him were two Polish airmen, while the four rooms beyond the washhouse were occupied by Russians: a lieutenant-general, a major-general, a colonel, and their orderly.

The second hut, Sonderlager 'B', was occupied by Italians. Churchill could walk around the compound whenever he liked. During the following days, he got to meet all his fellow inmates, including the Italians whom he got on with particularly well, helped by his own knowledge of Italian. Even the Poles and the Russians seemed to work around the language barrier in some way, with German often being the common solution. There was food, cigarettes, and even beer, and Churchill received part of a Red Cross parcel every week.

Although Churchill was not free, he could hardly complain. It was impossible, of course, to ignore the suffering in the main camp next door – the smoke rising from the crematorium and the occasional burst of machine-gun fire were constant reminders of that – but for those living in the privileged compound, life went on and the days passed quickly and easily.

Back home, though, there had been no information about Churchill's whereabouts. His family were becoming increasingly worried as to what might have happened to him. The monthly updates to his parents had continued, saying that he was fine, the most recent being dated 7 March 1944, but there had been no news direct from him, and it had been several months since his last visit to Malvern, which was most unusual. With Walter having been killed and with no news of Peter, it was left to the younger brother, Oliver, then serving with Force 133 in the Middle East, to write to London to see what he could find out. Oliver's letter, dated 20 March 1944, reads:

> My brother, Peter Morland Churchill, has been working as a Field officer, I believe, for the French Section for some time now. My father tells me he still receives a monthly note about him. As, however, I have had some experience of sending these notes to next of kin myself, I should be most grateful if you would give me a few facts. As my father is a man of 80, and as I wish to spare him every unnecessary anxiety, you can depend on me not to tell him, nor, naturally, anyone else, anything that you have not been able to say, should you be in a position to give me any news.

Before a formal reply was sent, Oliver Churchill's letter was passed to Buckmaster for comment. Buckmaster's response reads:

> We have an unconfirmed report that Peter Churchill is at Fresnes prison near Paris, and another unconfirmed report from a different source that he has more recently been moved from Fresnes to Germany. There is good evidence to believe, in any case, that he is still alive, although I fear that he will have been put badly through the mill. I can see no objection whatever to informing Captain W. O. Churchill that Peter has been caught and imprisoned, but that he is believed to be still alive.
>
> Our experience is that if he has been sent from FRESNES to Germany he will have got through the worst part of his experiences, and there is no reason why he should not be alive at the end of the war. At least he may have as much chance as any

> normal P. W. For your personal information he was arrested by the Gestapo the night after his arrival (on his third trip) near Annecy, largely I fear because he neglected the precautionary instruction not to return on any account to any place where he was known from his former visit.
>
> Peter is an exceptionally brave, rather reckless young man, who is ideal for leading a smash and grab party, but has not got the clandestine sense which is so much a weapon in the armoury of our best organisers. It was at Peter's own request that the notes to his father have continued, and that they contained no reference to his fate. Peter's idea was to spare the old gentleman unnecessary anxiety at his advanced age. I think there is every justification and reason for telling Peter's brother such part of the truth as you deem permissible from the above facts.

Although there is no copy of the reply sent to Oliver Churchill on file, it can be assumed that a reply was sent, and from Buckmaster's advice the reply most probably included news that Peter Churchill was alive as a prisoner of war. For some reason, though, it was not until 11 July 1944 that an SOE Battle Casualty form was raised for him. Raised by Vera Atkins (Registration No. 275) the form gives the Casualty Date of 16 April 1943, and under the heading 'Nature of the Casualty' the form simply states 'Arrested' while under the 'Source of Report' it reads 'Telegram from Field. Reliable.' And under 'Remarks' it reads 'Later reports from the Field say that he is in Fresnes, 24.7.43.'

By the time the Battle Casualty form was raised in London, Churchill had been at Sachsenhausen four months. At first he was the only British officer in the compound, but now he had a roommate, Major Johnnie Dodge, known as the 'Artful Dodger', an American-born British Army officer, about to turn fifty, and a veteran of the First World War. Dodge had re-enlisted at the outbreak of the Second World War but was taken prisoner in 1940 during the evacuation of France. He had been in prisoner of war camps ever since and had recently taken part in the famous Great Escape from Stalag Luft III, only to have then been caught.

Johnnie Dodge was the first of the Great Escapers to arrive at Sachsenhausen, and soon to follow were three more: Wing Commander Harry 'Wings' Day; Flight Lieutenant Sydney Dowse; and Pilot Officer Jimmy

James. The four were amongst the lucky ones as fifty of the seventy-three captured after the escape were executed on Hitler's orders. Of those to survive, these were the only four sent to Sachsenhausen; others were sent elsewhere, including to Colditz Castle.

The three latest arrivals were accommodated in Sonderlager 'B', although they regularly joined Churchill and Dodge during the day. Having British colleagues around livened up the place, but then word came of the murder of the other escapees. This tragic news should have put off even the most determined of escapers, but at Sachsenhausen it had the opposite effect. The four escapees started another tunnel.

It was decided to keep the tunnel secret from the non-British personnel. Churchill was even invited to join in, but he declined; his reason being he considered it inadvisable given he was being held as a political prisoner and not as a uniformed member of the armed forces, and so he could not expect to be afforded the same treatment under the Geneva Convention should he be caught. It was a reason the others seemed to accept.

Because Dodge was accommodated in a different hut to the others, there was little he could do in the way of digging as his regular absence would likely attract attention, while Day, being older than the other tunnellers and the senior British officer in the compound, was also exempt from the digging. For Dowse and James, though, it was gruelling and filthy work.

While all this was going on, another British officer arrived in the compound, and his name was also Churchill. This was Lieutenant-Colonel Jack Churchill, a commando who had been captured while leading partisans in Yugoslavia. He was no relation of Peter or, for that matter, Winston Churchill, but the Germans were not prepared to take the chance. Believing they might have another relative of the British Prime Minister, the Germans had dealt with Jack Churchill just as they had with Peter.

Jack Churchill was told about the tunnel and immediately jumped at the chance of trying to escape, and so he joined the others in helping to dig. Now there were three diggers and soon the tunnel started to grow. Meanwhile, Dodge and Day dealt with other preparations, which would help them on the outside. The five also formulated their plan and their route, deciding it best to travel in pairs. Day would go with Dowse, while Jack Churchill was to go with James, leaving Dodge to take his chances alone. Even though they knew the Allies had landed in Normandy and were on their way to Berlin, they decided to go ahead with the escape.

On the night of 23 September 1944, the five made their break. Peter Churchill knew they were planning to go shortly before midnight and had stayed awake. But by 2 a.m. there had been no sign of any enemy activity in response and so he finally fell asleep, convinced the breakout had been a success.

Churchill woke around 7 a.m. Then came the chaos. There was shouting everywhere as the compound filled with guards. Both huts were secured, no one was allowed to go anywhere and then the Gestapo arrived.

Within the compound, news of the escape produced a mixed response. While some were delighted, others feared reprisals. In the afternoon Churchill was called for questioning. The questions were everything he had expected – did he know about the plan to escape, why had they felt the need to escape, and why had he not gone with them? He answered each question honestly in turn. Yes, he had known about the escape all along and as to why they had decided to escape, Churchill said it was in their blood and it was the duty of every officer to escape. And the reason for him deciding not to go with them was because he knew that because he was not in uniform he would never be treated the same as the others should he be caught.

With the questions over, Churchill was allowed to return to his room. The Germans had believed there was no way of escaping from the compound, but they had been proved wrong. As for the escape itself, all five were eventually caught and were returned to Sachsenhausen where they were placed in solitary confinement and chained to the floor in the death cells in the main camp, although all five were to be spared execution.

It was now early October 1944. Peter Churchill was again the only British officer in the compound. A new roommate arrived, this time a French officer, and the sight and sound of Allied aircraft overhead brought hope that the war would soon be at an end.

In October F Section received an update on Churchill, and it came out of the blue. The news came from Brigadier Eric Mockler-Ferryman, head of the German section of the Directorate of Military Intelligence in London, who had received a letter from Supreme Headquarters

Allied Expeditionary Force in France, dated 2 October 1944. Mockler-Ferryman wrote:

> Early in March 1944, Churchill was taken to Germany, where he still is. Twice there has been news of him; once some months ago, and again three weeks ago, this time from a woman escapee, who said that Churchill was still alive, and that gossip had it that Von Rundstedt [Generalfeldmarschall Gerd von Rundstedt] himself had taken an interest in his case, and that some arrangements for his exchange for a German prisoner in England were possibly contemplated, although another rumour was current that he was being sent to a fortress.
>
> This all seems rather indefinite, but may be of special interest to Churchill's family, who are unlikely to have had recent news of him. I am assured by M. Fol that throughout his captivity, Churchill was not tortured, nor indeed put to any special interrogation, this apparently being due to Captain Verbeck [Hugo Bleicher], who appears to have befriended him throughout. Would you very kindly see that this information gets to those concerned, if you are able to trace his family. I understand from Mlle Laurent, who literally kept Churchill alive with butter and other provisions from her family home in Brittany, that Captain Churchill is a nephew of Mr. Winston Churchill.

This latest news was passed on to Churchill's brother, Oliver, and, in turn, to his father in Malvern. A letter from Buckmaster to Churchill's father, dated 29 January 1945, reads:

> I know you have in recent months been worried at the lack of news of your son, Capt. P.M. Churchill. You are probably aware of the fact that he volunteered for a dangerous mission in connection with the Resistance movement in France. We now know that he was captured prior to the invasion of France, and that he was held for some time as a political prisoner in a French prison. From there he was sent to a prison camp in Germany. We have heard from different sources that your son is alive and well.
>
> Prior to his departure to the field, Capt. Churchill particularly requested us to continue sending you reassuring news

> of him, even if he were to be taken prisoner or become missing. After discussing this with Major Churchill today, we decided that you would no doubt, prefer to be put more fully in the picture.
>
> I deeply regret the anxiety which this news is bound to cause you, and I would add that we have very good hope of recovering your son at the end of hostilities against Germany. I would like to tell you how greatly I admire your son's efficiency and gallantry. He was held in great esteem by all who know him.
>
> In view of the particular circumstances attaching to this case, I would ask you to refrain from making any enquiries through any other department as this might be most detrimental to his security. We shall of course, let you have any further news that may be received in this office.

There was further confirmation that Churchill had been seen alive, only this time it came from another source in northern Italy. A signal dated 17 February 1945 stated that:

> Contact had been made with an Italian Air Force Colonel who was in ORANIENBURG Gestapo camp from October, 1943, to March, 1944. The Italian Colonel stated that he met there a Captain CHURCHILL who arrived in January, 1944. He said that CHURCHILL wears glasses, has brown hair, black eyes, speaks fluent French and has a French wife. He also said that Churchill was doing intelligence work in France, and that he was treated very badly (presumably by the Germans) but that his health last March was fair. Churchill was said to claim to be a nephew of the Prime Minister. The Italian Colonel promised to inform Churchill's family.

News was now finding its way back to London that he had been seen alive and well, but for Churchill little had changed during this time. Christmas had been and gone, a new year had dawned and by February 1945 news had spread to the compound that the Russian Army was getting close. There was even the sound of battle in the distance.

Then came a big surprise when four of the five British escapees returned to the compound following their time in isolation; the missing member was Dodge, but he was safe and on his way to Berlin. But their return to the compound, and the arrival of more selected prisoners, including five Greek generals, could only mean one thing – the camp was about to be evacuated before the Russian Army arrived. They were all about to be moved elsewhere.

Chapter 18

The Prominenten

It was now 31 March 1945. Churchill had been at Sachsenhausen for nearly a year. The rumble of gunfire had been getting closer by the day as the war entered its final phase. Within the compound, the conversation was all about when they would be moved and where they might go. It was obvious the end of the war was in sight, but the days were starting to drag, and they were still far from being free. Then came news. They were to be ready to move out the following day. They had the evening to pack up their belongings, whatever they were prepared to carry.

The following morning, even before it was light, they were all driven to the station and put on a train. As to where the train was going, they had no idea.

Their journey took all day and all night, plus all the following day as well. They had travelled 500 km south by the time the train pulled in at its destination. They could see they had arrived at another concentration camp. This one was called Flossenbürg, a camp Churchill had not heard of.

Flossenbürg was another pre-war concentration camp but one of the more recent to have been built. Unlike most camps, though, it had been established in a remote area, in the Fichtel Mountains of Bavaria, next to the town of Flossenbürg and close to the pre-war German border with Czechoslovakia. The camp was in a state of disarray. It was the end of the war and Flossenbürg was already overcrowded, but more prisoners were arriving every day as camps were being evacuated elsewhere.

Churchill and the others were taken to the camp hospital, where a ward had been prepared for the new arrivals. In his mission debrief report, Churchill later wrote: 'After spending four days in the main hospital ward, coming into close contact with the dying and the dead, we were moved into the prison section, where we stayed three or four more days.'

Through the windows they could see the smoke rising from the crematorium and endless stretcher parties going back and forth. And yet, even more prisoners kept arriving. At the prison block, there was an exercise yard so they could get out of their cells and walk around, but then there was more chaos as word came that Flossenbürg was also to be evacuated. The Jewish prisoners had already been rounded up and had left. Now it was the turn of the others.

It was time to move on once more, although where to no one knew. They had worked out that they were now closer to the Americans and British than the Russians, and so any negotiations about prisoner exchanges would surely have to take place soon. Alternatively, though, they feared there might be no such negotiations, in which case why had they been kept alive and moved around so much? And who was making the decisions as to where they should go and how they were to be used?

While some were led to a large lorry, Churchill was told to get into a black van. Dowse was in his group too. The van had been designed to transport nine prisoners at a time, and only ever over a short distance, whereas now it was to carry twenty-one, and who knew how long for?

For more than thirty hours they drove, stopping only occasionally for a short break here and there. If the sun had been shining during the day, they could have worked out they were heading further south, but it was not and so they had no idea in which direction they were travelling. Finally, they arrived at their next destination. It was another camp. This time they were at Dachau.

Dachau is to the north-west of Munich in southern Germany and was the first concentration camp to have been built by the Nazis. Churchill and the other new arrivals were led to a large hut, which was already full of political prisoners. This was where all the high-profile prisoners, the *Prominenten*, were being gathered. Amongst them were former statesmen, politicians, political dissidents, priests, selected prisoners of war, and anyone believed to be related to royalty or senior Allied politicians, such as Peter Churchill.

In addition to the military officers that he had already met at Sachsenhausen – the British, the Russians, the Poles, the Italians, and the Greeks – there were plenty of new faces in the hut at Dachau. In his mission debrief report, Churchill would later write:

> At Dachau we were lodged in the brothel, and it was here that I met Squadron Leader Falconer. I also made the acquaintance of General Garibaldi, and his Chief of Staff Col. Ferraro. I also met General d'Estre, who was shot on the following day.

Most of the new faces at Dachau, though, were not military figures. In *The Spirit in the Cage*, Churchill listed many of them. They included Doctor and Frau Erich Heberlein, the anti-Nazi German Ambassador to Madrid and his wife, and the former Mayor of Vienna, Richard Smitz. The Heberleins had been kidnapped from Spain by the Gestapo and then held at various concentration camps, while Smitz had been mayor at the time Austria had been absorbed into the Third Reich and had been arrested for publicly speaking out against the Nazis. Another Austrian was Kurt von Schuschnigg, former Chancellor of Austria, and his wife. Then there was Johannes Baptist Neuhäusler, the Auxiliary Bishop of Munich, and Gabriel Piquet, Bishop of Clermont-Ferrand. There was also Martin Niemöller, a German theologian and Lutheran pastor, who had served in the previous war as a U-boat commander but had then opposed the Nazi regime during the 1930s. And there was Gottfried Wilhelm Flügge, a German engineer, who had been labelled as 'politically unreliable' by the Nazis, and Prince Philipp of Hesse, who had fallen out of favour with Hitler after delivering an honest assessment of the war in Italy. The list went on.

The following day, they were all told to prepare for another move. Churchill had been at Dachau for just one night. The assembled *Prominenten* were put onto coaches and driven through the war-torn streets of Munich, and then on a further 150 km until they reached another camp at Innsbruck. They stayed for about a week at the Innsbruck Straflager where they were joined by others.

The actual number of *Prominenten* assembled was 132, of twenty-two nationalities. Amongst the new arrivals was the French socialist politician Léon Blum and his wife. After the German occupation of France, Blum had been a staunch opponent of the Vichy French. Imprisoned at Buchenwald, he had earlier been sentenced to death, but his life was spared by the authorities in the hope he would be of use. Also amongst the new arrivals was Hjalmar Schacht, President of the Reichsbank under the Weimar Republic, and the former Hungarian Prime Minister, Miklós Kállay, along with members of his cabinet. Then there was a high-ranking officer who had been a supporter of the plot to assassinate Hitler the year before. This was General Alexander von Falkenhausen, a close friend of the conspirators. After the failed attempt he had been relieved of his command to spend the rest of the war in captivity. There were others, too, who had been arrested after the plot. The list went on.

The *Prominenten* were a rare mix of individuals, from many different social backgrounds. Churchill was impressed by them all, none more, though, than Léon Blum.

Amongst the assembled gathering was a German woman called Isa Wermehren, a former cabaret artist who had taunted the Nazi regime. She had come from Ravensbrück, a camp Churchill had not heard of before, a concentration camp in northern Germany exclusively for women. Isa had searched for Churchill amongst the large group in the hope he would be there as she had word from Odette, who had been at Ravensbrück with her, and she was delighted to tell him that Odette was in excellent health and spirits.

It was the first Churchill had heard of Odette since leaving Fresnes, although Isa had not been entirely truthful when she had said Odette was in excellent health. It was very tough at Ravensbrück, as Churchill would later hear. Nonetheless, Odette was alive and that was excellent news for now.

Chapter 19

Liberation

After more days of sitting around, the group were put on buses once again, with their SS guards. The convoy was soon passing through the Brenner Pass, one of the principal passes of the eastern Alps. The route was lined with abandoned vehicles and crowded with trucks heading back towards Germany and Italian soldiers making their way home on foot.

It was dark by the time the convoy headed slowly down the pass towards the Italian frontier. They had reached the Puster Valley, one of the largest valleys running between East Tyrol in Austria and South Tyrol in Italy.

The night was spent in a small town hall. During their journey there were various discussions between members of the group as to what they should do. Their guards seemed less observant and more relaxed, and so one option was to try and make a break, but what would that mean for the safety of the rest of the group? Some were too old or not strong enough to escape. There was a risk their lives might be cut short at such a late stage, simply because others had managed to escape. But where were they all being taken to, and why Italy? Were they about to be executed, as someone had suggested?

They were still in the unpredictable hands of the SS and increasingly concerned about what might happen to them all. At this point the senior German officers present decided to take it upon themselves to try and secure the safety of the group. In *The Spirit in the Cage*, Churchill credits the tough and masterful Oberst Bogislaw von Bonin as the man who achieved this tricky move. Bonin was an officer in the German Army and had served on the staff on the Eastern Front. He had been arrested by the Gestapo after giving a German unit permission to retreat from Warsaw during the Soviet advance, which had been contrary to Hitler's direct order.

In his book, Churchill wrote about Bonin making a telephone call from a post office in the village of Villa Bassa to general headquarters in

Italy, requesting an Army unit be sent to meet the convoy to safeguard the high-profile prisoners. Generalfeldmarschall Albert Kesselring had been the German supreme commander in Italy but had left the previous month to take charge of the Western Front, and so it was almost certainly his successor, Generaloberst Heinrich von Vietinghoff, a former colleague of Bonin's, who agreed to the request.

A signal was sent to a Wehrmacht unit operating nearby, but it would not be able to arrive until the following day. In the meantime, Bonin decided to try and bluff the SS guard commander into believing its arrival was imminent and suggested that he and his guards, if they wanted to survive, should take one of the buses and disappear. It was a trick that might just work, although the SS guards could easily have used that moment to murder their prisoners. What difference would one more atrocity have made?

It was a tense moment, but the bluff came off. The guards boarded a bus and a lorry and vanished. Churchill and the others were free.

Later that evening the Wehrmacht unit – a captain and fifteen soldiers – arrived. They had made good time. The freed prisoners were taken to the Hotel Prags at Wildsee, where they were to stay until the Americans arrived.

Now under the protection of the Army the prisoners could finally feel safe. It was 27 April 1945. Snow covered the landscape, presenting a most tranquil scene. People started to drift away, some to tell the Americans where they were staying and who was at the hotel, while others, particularly some of the Russians, decided to take their chances elsewhere. Churchill opted to stay put. He was quite happy to wait for the Americans to arrive. News then filtered through that Hitler had committed suicide on the 30th. The collapse of Germany was inevitable and soon the war would be over.

A company of the 339th Infantry Regiment, from the 85th Division of the American Fifth Army reached the hotel on 4 May. Churchill was liberated. The German guards were taken prisoner, no doubt thankful their war was over.

Given the high-profile status of those liberated at the hotel, it was not long before newspaper reporters and a film crew arrived, as mentioned in Churchill's mission report:

> At this hotel we were filmed by quite a few American field film units, and also a British unit which I had met at Villabassa,

> which I informed of our presence up the mountains. The Americans allowed very few interviews, understanding the meaning of the Secrets Act, as far as Falconer and myself were concerned.

During the days that followed the one-time prisoners were taken to Verona. Churchill arrived there during the early hours of 9 May. After a good meal and a check-up in a mobile hospital, he was sent to an airfield from where he flew to Naples for clearing.

Gradually, the differing nationalities went their own way. Churchill spent several days in Naples, as he later recalled:

> The Americans' kindness to the entire party was everything that one could have expected, and their efficiency in moving us from point to point and seeing to our welfare left nothing to be desired. In Naples we were housed at the Officers' Mess of the Transport Depot in a district called Rezzina. On my second day in Naples, Falconer and I were sent off to see General Macleod at the Allied Army H.Q. General Macleod passed us on to his Brigadier and two or three Colonels belonging to the Crimes Investigation Departments. Here we were fortunate enough to meet a Lieut. Col. Heddon, one-time Inspector at Scotland Yard. I gave a full report of everything I had taken down from eye-witnesses in regard to our men who were executed at Flossenburg, and immediate steps were taken to apprehend, try and condemn all S.S. men of every rank whose names and addresses I had been able to collect.

While in Naples, Churchill tried to get permission for some of his Polish and Russian friends to travel with him to Britain. They did not want to return to their own countries, but his efforts were to no avail. He also sent telegrams to London announcing where he was, but got no reply.

Then, on 12 May, Churchill flew back to Britain. Vera Atkins was at Northolt to meet him. During the drive into central London Vera brought Churchill up to date with as much as she knew. Odette was alive and well. Not only that, but she was waiting in the office to see him.

Chapter 20

Controversy

Four days after returning, Churchill was back at Orchard Court to begin the long debrief process and to complete his mission report. Titled 'Report by Captain Churchill', it is dated 16 May 1945. Part I is eight pages long and covers the period from when he parachuted back into France in April 1943 until returning in May 1945. Part II, a further six pages, focuses on security, starting with the reasons for Churchill's arrest and includes names of other prisoners he saw during his time in captivity. It also includes a paragraph on Germans favourable to the Allied cause, in which Colonel Henri (Hugo Bleicher) is mentioned. The final part of the debrief report, Part III, was a single page titled War Crimes, which reads:

> Source is in a position to give a very great deal of information about all kinds of brutalities committed in the various camps in which he found himself, and also in Fresnes. As appears earlier in this report, these camps are Sonderlager A, just outside the walls of Sachsenhausen concentration camp, Flossenburg and Dachau. These brutalities include executions, the infliction of torture, and other acts of extreme cruelty. Source after his return, on his way out through Italy, gave full particulars of these matters to Lt Col. Heddon of the Crimes Department of Allied H.Q. Naples. He is in a position to give detailed evidence, including his own eye-witness account of numerous acts of brutality, together with the names and descriptions of those individuals who were involved in their commission.

Exactly what acts of brutality Churchill reported to the Crimes Department as having witnessed at the various camps is not recorded in the report, nor are there any details in other documents on his file.

Another debrief document on file, titled 'Interrogation of Raoul (Real Name Peter Churchill)', is dated 18 May 1945, and provides a summary of Churchill's report:

INTRODUCTION – Source has prepared a lengthy report dated 16th May, 1945 of his experiences during his latest mission to the field and imprisonment. This report is attached to Part I of the following interrogation. Part II of the Interrogation deals with Security matters.

PART I – Source landed in the field on a mountain called Semnoz near Annecy on the 15th April, 1943. He was received by LISE and ARNAUD. His arrest took place as described in his report and in the interrogation of LISE, at the Hôtel de la Poste on the night following that of his arrival. Source was taken to the Barracks at Annecy and after various journeys, described in LISE's interrogation, arrived at Fresnes about 3rd May, 1943. His subsequent movements were as follows:

Remained in Fresnes until 13th February, 1944.

14th February, 1944	Arrived Berlin.
2nd May, 1944	Left Berlin. Arrived Sonderlager A, just outside the walls of Sachsenhausen in a neighbouring village to Oranienburg, 18 miles due north of Berlin.
1st April, 1945	Left Sonderlager A.
2nd April, 1945	Arrived Flossenburg, 50 miles east by south of Bayreuth.
12th April, 1945	Left for Dachau.
14th April, 1945	Left Dachau for Innsbruck (Straflager).
24th April, 1945 (Approx)	Left Innsbruck and went over the Brenner Pass to Villa Bassa (Niederdorf in the Tyrol).
27th April, 1945	Left for Wildsee some 20 km to the south.
4th May, 1945	Liberated by the Americans.

With his debriefing complete, Peter Churchill's war was over. He was first sent on disembarkation leave until 27 June. He initially stayed in London, living in Harcourt Terrace near Earl's Court, and after his leave he briefly took up an intelligence post at the War Office. But Churchill was keen to put his wartime experiences behind him and to be demobilised as soon as possible.

A letter from the Deputy Assistant Adjutant General to A.G.23 (SA), dated 30 June 1945, explained:

> This officer was reported Missing on 16 Apr 43, Casualty list 17/44. He has now returned to the U.K. having been a Prisoner of War in German hands, Casualty list 17/61 cancels the above quoted Casualty list. Captain Churchill is most anxious to be demobilised as soon as possible. It is confirmed that there is no further suitable employment in this branch, and we therefore have to request that sympathetic consideration be given to his wish, and that he be posted from this branch w.e.f. 8 July 1945 for demobilisation.

The request was granted, the official date of Churchill's Termination of Engagement being 18 July 1945. His summary of service card on his personnel file simply reads:

> CHURCHILL, Peter M. – Organiser: RAOUL/SPINDLE Antibes alias RAOUL, SPINDLE, CHAUVET Pierre Marc, EDWARDS Sq/Ldr
> First mission – left for the field 15.12.41 via Gib (Felucca op) to re-establish contact with Antibes group under PHILIPPE and OLIVE.
> Second mission – operation WILLOW, left Gib 1.1.42, arrived Antibes about 13.1.42, returned via Spain as Sq/Ldr EDWARDS, arrived London 10.2.42.
> Third mission – operation DELAY II. Left for Gib 12.3.42 to help land EBONY and DIVIDEND which was done 26.4.42. Brought back d'Astier of LIBERATION. Arrived London 15.5.42.
> Fourth mission – operation SPINDLE, returned to London 23.3.43.
> Fifth mission – operation SPINDLE A. Left for the field 14.4.43. Arrested 16.4.43.

The bottom of the card is signed by Buckmaster, and it is interesting to note the card refers to five missions, although the first two listed are essentially Churchill's first mission to France. There are also some slight variations in the dates recorded on the card to dates recorded in other reports.

Churchill's younger brother Oliver also survived the war. He was awarded the DSO and MC for his bravery. But Peter Churchill was saddened by the grief-stricken state of his elderly father, having lost his wife and eldest son, Walter, during the war. After returning from Italy,

Peter had immediately travelled to the family home in Malvern to find that his father's mind had gone and he was seemingly unable to grasp the fact that two of his sons had survived. His father died in 1947.

In November 1945 it was officially announced that Peter Churchill was to be awarded the DSO for his work in France. Part of the early paperwork proposing the award of the DSO for Churchill included brief details of his missions and a concluding paragraph, titled 'F's Evaluation of Officer', which read:

> Full of dash and verve, but not a diplomat. Grand material for the tough stuff, but no good at finesse. Took unwarranted risks, but by no means was unintelligent. Very realistic and conscientious. Took responsibility and initiative. His history after capture must be studied carefully before making a final pronouncement.

The official recommendation for Churchill's DSO was dated 14 September 1945 and signed by Major-General Colin Gubbins, the power behind SOE during its key wartime years:

> This officer carried out four clandestine missions into France between the end of 1941 and the spring of 1943. He was first landed by submarine in the south of France in December 1941 with the mission of contacting the principal organisers in the Unoccupied Zone, to bring them directives, remedy their various difficulties, improve communications and arrange help for arrested members of the organisation. This involved much travel and dangerous liaison activity, but Churchill carried out the mission with complete success and returned to England early in February 1942.
>
> His second mission was to organise the infiltration of a number of agents by sea into the south of France. Although this involved only a short stay in France, it was nevertheless a delicate and hazardous task. It was mainly due to Churchill's courage and resourcefulness that the operation was successfully carried out.
>
> In April 1942 he was parachuted into France as chief liaison officer to a large resistance group in the south. He worked here for several months organising parachute dropping operations and the reception of agents by sea on the Mediterranean coast.

> His operations were always well organised and he took great personal risks to ensure the safe disposal of infiltrated agents.
>
> In March 1943 Capt. Churchill paid a short visit to England for consultation. Two months after his return to France, in May 1943, he was arrested. By that time he had decentralised the organisation to such an extent that his work could be continued by others. He was released by Allied troops in Germany in May 1945.
>
> Capt. Churchill worked tirelessly and unselfishly over a long period in very trying conditions, showing outstanding courage, leadership and organising ability, which earned him the respect and admiration of all who came in contact with him. It is strongly recommended that he be appointed a Companion in the Distinguished Service Order.

Although there are some inconsistencies in the recommendation as far as dates are concerned, and that Churchill had been liberated in Italy and not Germany, the award of Churchill's DSO was promulgated in the *Supplement* to the *London Gazette* dated 15 November 1945, Page 5574. Quite remarkably, all three Churchill brothers were awarded the DSO.

While Churchill was being recommended for the DSO, he was writing up his own recommendation for the Cottets, as he believed they should receive some form of official recognition for their role in France. Dated 11 October 1945, the recommendation read:

> For about 6 weeks during March and April 1943, M. et Mme. Cottet of the Hôtel de la Poste, St. Jorioz, near Annecy, found themselves very much in the centre of my group's activities. Throughout this time I stayed at this hotel except for various odd periods at which times LISE remained there. The Cottets knew who we were but in spite of the risk to themselves and their commerce they were of great assistance to us, and among the things they did were (a) to allow LISE to remain in the hotel when it was officially closed, (b) they made part of the reception committee which climbed the Semnoz, 6000 feet, to receive me when I was parachuted on 15 April 1943 and (c) their cellar contained radio parts for four different operators, a revolver, a sten gun and quantities of very compromising

> papers on the day LISE and I were arrested. The Cottets kept our private effects on our capture and returned them to us after the war. Throughout they behaved with courage and calm and were of great assistance to both myself, LISE and our organisation. It was through M. Cottet telling me that a large group (the very first) of organised maquisards were in a certain neighbourhood in March 1943 that I was able to telegraph London and obtain arms and stores for them which were actually delivered by parachute from 25 aircraft, 5 of which were brought down. In view of the foregoing I recommend that M. et Mme. Cottet should either receive a decoration or at least a letter of appreciation from an official source as a token of their assistance to the allied war effort.

Whether the Cottets were officially recognised for their work is not known, but the French government did award Peter Churchill the Croix de Guerre and a disability pension for his work in France.

Odette, meanwhile, had come back from the war in a miserable state, having suffered torture and other ill-treatment while under interrogation. By then, she had decided that her marriage was over; it was dissolved in 1946. Little by little, she told Churchill her dreadful story. After Fresnes she had been taken to Ravensbrück where she was kept in isolation and suffered considerable hardship, often without any food. She had been condemned to death but somehow survived her time at the camp. When the Allies advanced to within a few kilometres of Ravensbrück, the camp commandant, Fritz Suhren, drove himself and Odette towards the advancing Americans in the hope that her connection to Britain's Prime Minister would allow him to negotiate freedom. It did not work. Suhren was arrested and would later be found guilty of war crimes and executed.

In August 1946 it was announced that Odette was to be awarded the George Cross for her bravery. The news brought an invasion of reporters and cameramen as she was the first woman to be awarded Britain's highest award for non-operational gallantry, and the only woman to have been awarded it while still alive.

On 19 November, Churchill and Odette received their awards from King George VI at Buckingham Palace. Then, on 15 February 1947, they married at the Kensington Registry Office in London. As far as the British press were concerned it was a fairy-tale story.

Churchill was happy to talk about his time during the Second World War. He took to writing and made his mark as a lecturer, giving presentations about his wartime experiences at schools and societies all over the country, always being received as a distinguished visitor and famous spy wherever he went.

But it was Odette who had been propelled into the public domain, as it was her story that had captured the public's imagination on both sides of the Channel. The War Office was keen to promote her as a national heroine as part of raising public awareness of the work of SOE, and so Major Jerrard Tickell of the Public Relations Department was given the task of describing her achievements, which he did in his book *Odette: The Story of a British Agent*, published in 1949. Then, in 1950, came the film *Odette*, produced, and directed by Herbert Wilcox and starring Anna Neagle as Odette and Trevor Howard as Peter Churchill, based on Tickell's book. Both Odette and Churchill served as advisors during filming, as did Tickell. It premiered at a Royal Command Film Performance before King George VI and Queen Elizabeth at the Plaza Cinema in London on 6 June 1950 and was the fourth most popular film at the British box office that year.

Although the film was well received in many quarters, it was less successful in others, particularly across the Channel in France. The script and production had been backed by a publicity campaign in Britain, particularly as the War Office and former members of F Section had been closely involved in its making, and so the British agents were seen by some as having been portrayed as overly efficient and heroic, whereas the French appeared to be less so. As a result, Odette and Churchill were criticised by some former members of the Resistance.

Churchill decided to write his own wartime memoirs to put across his side of the story, with his three books published during the early 1950s. In these books, Churchill openly admits that mistakes had been made.

Churchill's story was also covered in the *Sunday Chronicle* in 1954. By then, he was living alone in Le Rouret in south-eastern France; his marriage to Odette would soon be over. According to E. H. Cookridge in *Inside S.O.E.*, Churchill's guests at his villa in France included Hugo Bleicher and his wife; Bleicher had been arrested at the end of the war and imprisoned, but had been released by 1954.

In September 1955, Churchill filed for divorce on the grounds of Odette's adultery, alleged to have taken place in a Paris hotel with

Geoffrey McLeod Hallowes; Odette did not contest the case. Again, the news attracted much media attention and was reported in several newspapers, as was the granting of the *decree nisi* in November by Judge Alan Pugh.

In the conclusion of its report on 11 November 1955, the *Western Mail*, wrote:

> The Judge granted Captain Churchill a *decree nisi* and made an order for costs against the co-respondent, the court's discretion being exercised in the husband's favour in respect of his own admitted adultery.

Odette would marry Geoffrey Hallowes, himself a former SOE officer, the following year, while, on 7 June 1956, Churchill married Irene Mary Hoyle, a 42-year-old Australian, in Nice. Irene was described by one newspaper, the *Birmingham Daily Gazette*, as a former London model. The newspaper went on to add: 'The couple met when both were working in the British secret service during the war.'

Churchill continued to write about the war and in 1958 published *By Moonlight*, a novel based on the maquis of the Glières Plateau. However, the controversy about his SOE activities had not gone away, and in November 1958 things came to a head.

With there being so many books and conflicting opinions about SOE appearing in the public domain, several Members of Parliament, headed by Dame Irene Ward, Conservative MP for Tynemouth, demanded an 'authoritative account' of the successes and failures of SOE. They believed that an official statement was essential, following a flow of allegations that the public had been badly misled over the effectiveness of Britain's espionage system during the war. Then, a document signed by members of the French Resistance back in 1950, which had criticised the work of Churchill and Odette during the war and argued that both had received undue credit for their undercover activities, suddenly appeared for publication.

The story was inevitably picked up by the newspapers. The front page of the *Weekly Dispatch* on Sunday 23 November 1958, for example, under the headline 'French Resistance Men Challenge the Exploits of Odette', reads:

> Six prominent members of the French Resistance movement yesterday challenged the war-time bravery of Odette, G.C.,

> and the man who later became her husband, Peter Churchill. In a document, prepared in Paris, the six are asking for proof of the couple's exploits while working for the cloak-and-dagger Special Operations Executive – the British organisation which sent spies into occupied Europe. The document states:
>
> 'We, the undersigned, would be happy to know of, or have confirmed by witnesses of the period . . . one single effective act of sabotage, one single effective act of hostility, one single effective act of damage caused to the enemy in France either by Peter Churchill during the period August 15, 1942 to February 1943, or by Odette between early November 1942 and February 1943.' The top signature on the document is that of Captain Francis Bazin, M.B.E., head of the group with which Peter Churchill and Odette worked. The second signature is that of Baron Henri de Malval, whose villa near Cannes was used as a rendezvous point for British agents.

The signed document had been stuck in a file somewhere for the past eight years, but now it had suddenly and mysteriously appeared. Dame Irene was quick to emphasise in the press that she wanted only to ensure that honour was done to those agents, both men and women, who did not return and that it was not connected to Churchill and Odette.

People were quick to leap to the defence of the SOE agents, particularly Odette who publicly stated that 'the six men were "uneasy" at the prospect of an official investigation into Anglo-French work in occupied France' and that the three named signatories (the third being André Girard) all had a grudge against Churchill.

There followed in the press an exchange of comments between Churchill and Basin regarding the attempted rescue of Basin all those years before. In the exchange Churchill questioned whether Basin had wanted to be liberated or not, whereas Basin defended himself by stating that he had been handcuffed to one of his guards at the time and so had warned off his would-be rescuers from trying anything that might have ended in disaster.

Dame Irene's scrutiny of those who had served with SOE would go on for a while, but amongst those to support publicly the idea of an investigation into the effectiveness of SOE were Maurice Buckmaster, the wartime head of F Section, and Peter Churchill. Because of the controversy caused by the signed document, and because not all six signatories had been publicly named, Churchill also considered demanding a French official enquiry into the recent criticisms of the work of some of those in SOE who had been sent into occupied territory during the war.

For his next book, published in 1960, Churchill avoided writing about the war altogether and instead wrote *All About the French Riviera*, a guidebook for British caravanners and tourists visiting the Côte d'Azur.

Eventually, and for a variety of reasons, and not simply because of Dame Irene's questions in the House of Commons several years before, an official history of SOE appeared. Written by Professor M.R.D. Foot, himself a former member of SOE, his authoritative book *SOE in France* was published in April 1966. As part of the Government Official Histories series, the book was intended to produce a definitive work, compiled by a historian eminent in the field who had been afforded free access to all relevant material in the official archives.

As soon as it was published, *SOE in France* came under the spotlight and immediately prompted controversy. The names of many agents, some of whom were still alive when the book came out, were suddenly propelled into the public domain, whether they wanted to be or not. Not only that, but the book was based solely on official files and reports, some of which were claimed to be conflicting or inaccurate, with Foot having been prevented from interviewing the SOE staff officers and agents involved at the time.

For Churchill and Odette, *SOE in France* revived the controversy of their time together in France during the war. Foot even suggested they had lived a life of luxury at SOE's expense and had accomplished little in the way of military value. The original version of *SOE in France* reads:

> Luxury, in the end, was as much a cause of SPINDLE's undoing as were the stresses in CARTE; Peter Churchill and his courier – Odette Sansom (LISE) – found that life could still be easy for people with plenty of money on the Riviera. Consequently, they fell out with some of their subordinates. After the war, floods of favourable publicity and strong counter-currents of hostile gossip washed round this unfortunate couple, who then married and were later divorced. The truth is that the military value of their mission was slight; though this was not entirely their own fault.

Foot also seemed to back up Baron de Malval's allegation of Churchill's disregard of security regulations, which appears to have been based on information taken from Rabinowitch's interrogation in October 1943 and de Malval's interrogation dated 21 November 1944, when Foot wrote:

> Churchill had a habit of keeping old messages . . . A few messages were found on the captured pair [Churchill and Odette]. Churchill was carrying in a pocketbook in clear the telephone numbers of three of his Riviera sub-agents, one of whom – de Malval – was confronted some months later, when arrested at his flat in Paris, with a message from SOE's home station to SPINDLE which he had seen before; it said, as he later remembered it, 'On reaching the coast of France the agents who have come by felucca will proceed straight to the Baron de Malval, Villa Isabelle, Toute de Fréjus'. Comment is superfluous.

Refusing to accept what had been written about them in *SOE in France*, Churchill and Odette took legal action. As a result, several pages were re-written, and a second impression was published on 15 July 1968. The words suggesting that Churchill and Odette had lived a life of luxury and had accomplished little in the way of military value were removed and as far as the allegation of Churchill's disregard of security was concerned, the first part of the paragraph was changed to read:

> A few messages received that day were successfully concealed by Mrs Sansom [Odette]. Churchill was long worried by the belief that he had jotted down in a pocket-book the telephone numbers of three principal Riviera helpers, but either the Germans never found it, or the numbers were safely encoded.

In all, the text on seven pages of the book was revised, with Churchill accepting an apology and later a financial settlement. Again, the story made the newspapers. In July 1968, on the day the second edition of *SOE in France* was published, the *Belfast Telegraph* reported under the headline 'Apology', a statement from the solicitors representing Churchill:

> The revised edition of '*SOE in France*' published today 'contains substantial alterations to the text on pages 204, 208, 209, 210, 211, 252 and 273. These have been agreed as the result of negotiations between Messrs Oswald Hickson, Collier &

Co, and the Treasury Solicitor acting for Michael Foot and Her Majesty's Stationery Office.'

As for the settlement, one newspaper, the *Birmingham Daily Post*, reported on 28 January 1969 under the headline 'Damages for a Secret Agent':

> A wartime secret agent, Capt. Peter Churchill, is to receive 'very substantial' libel damages for slurs on his reputation in the official book *SOE in France*, the High Court was told yesterday. Aspersions cast on him by the book had been 'hurtful, harmful and entirely unwarranted' his counsel, Mr Brian Neill, QC, said. The first defamatory passage suggested that Capt. Churchill was unsuitable for the task with which he was entrusted. Another passage implied that Capt. Churchill and his courier, Mrs. Odette Sansom, whom he later married, had lived a life of luxury on the French Riviera and had achieved little of military value said counsel. In a later chapter there was an account of the arrest of Capt. Churchill and Mrs. Sansom. It was suggested that he had kept the deciphered texts of over 40 messages exchanged between London and his radio operator, Rabinowitch. The second edition of the book was being corrected to effect complete withdrawal of these aspersions, said Mr. Neill.

By then, Churchill had also received financial compensation for the time he had been held in captivity during the war. After several years of negotiation, the West German state agreed in 1964 to provide the British government with £1 million to distribute as compensation among the British victims of Nazi persecution during the Second World War.

In response to the Foreign Office's request for applications, Churchill submitted his claim in September 1964, listing the camps in which he was imprisoned: Fresnes (1 May 43 to 13 February 44); Sachsenhausen Sonderlager A (March 44 to 3 April 45); Flossenbürg (April 45 for eight days); Dachau (16 April for one night); and Innsbruck (16 April for six days). Under the question asking applicants if they had been interrogated, Churchill answers 'yes, in Annecy and in Paris by the Gestapo', although he states there was no rough treatment, and when asked about escapes attempted, he mentions his failed attempt at Annecy when he tried to climb the prison wall.

Also on his personnel file is an undated covering letter from Churchill, which reads:

> On March 2nd 1944 I entered Sachsenhausen Concentration Camp and was placed in Sonderlager 'A' where, later, I was joined by Group Captain H.M.A. Day D.S.O.; and Flt Lts B.A. James M.C. and Sydney Dowse M.C. – survivors of the Great Escape from Sagan. We were kept as hostages at this camp until the second week of April 1945 when we were transferred to the Concentration Camp at Flossenburg. After some 10 days we were transferred to Dachau where we only spent one night before being evacuated, in front of the advancing Allies, to the Concentration Camp of Innsbruck. At the time of Hitler's assumed suicide we had crossed the Brenner Pass to be rescued at Pragsasee by advanced units of the American Army. The reason for my imprisonment was because I had been captured as a saboteur in Occupied France. When it was too late to use our group as hostages to save Hitler and his associates orders were given for our execution. They were found in the pocket of the SS Commander by Lt. Col. R. H. Stevens on the eve of our rescue. The detailed story of my imprisonment appears in my book *The Spirit in the Cage* published by Hodder & Stoughton.

Churchill's application was one of more than 4,000 received, but by the end of the process the Foreign Office was only able to accept just over a thousand. The compensation pot was limited and so the Foreign Office applied relatively narrow criteria of eligibility for what constituted persecution, although this did typically mean having been held in a concentration camp. However, amongst the claims rejected were those from applicants who had been held in the Sonderlagers at Sachsenhausen, including Churchill, the reason given they had not been subjected to the inhuman and degrading treatment of a 'concentration camp proper'.

Again, the British press took an interest, and one story to attract attention was that of Jimmy James, whose application had been rejected. As a 'Great Escaper' and one of those to have also escaped from Sachsenhausen, James had suffered several months in solitary confinement under harrowing mental and physical conditions, and never knowing when his turn for the firing squad might come. The rejection of his application, and those of others with similar experiences, caused public outrage and triggered a Parliamentary Enquiry, which eventually overturned the decision in 1967.

Finally, more than three years after making his claim, Churchill received a letter from the Foreign Office, dated 6 February 1968, which read:

> You will probably know that the Foreign Secretary informed Parliament of his decision to pay compensation to all claimants whose claims, arising out of imprisonment at Sachsenhausen, had been previously rejected. Your own claim is therefore accepted and a Payable Order for £1,284. 10. 0d. will shortly be sent to you.

Churchill's days of controversy and compensation were finally over, twenty-plus years after the war had ended. He would spend the last years of his life living in Le Rouret overlooking the part of the Mediterranean coast where he had spent his wartime days. When he fell ill with cancer, one of the last to visit him in hospital in Cannes was Odette. Churchill had always publicly supported her even after their marriage was over.

Peter Churchill died on 1 May 1972 at the age of sixty-three. News of his death stretched far and wide, the *New York Times*, for example, covering the story the following day under the headline 'Peter Churchill, British Hero of the French Resistance, Dies'. In Britain, Churchill's obituary appeared in *The Times*, and includes:

> From the point of view of an organiser of underground activities in enemy-occupied territory, he was a 'natural'. His French was perfect, he was quick to grasp the complexities of a problem and, above all, he had an intuitive sense of responsibility and initiative. To say that he was a particularly brave man gives only a superficial description of his character. He was a man who saw, with devastating clarity, the dangers of the work involved and who had the ability to accept these risks without letting them interfere with his judgement. He never took needless chances; his actions were deliberate and balanced. He knew his own ability and used it to the full.

Peter Churchill had lived a quite remarkable life. Whatever people might have thought of him or had said or written of him over the years, there is no other story quite like it. General Dwight D. Eisenhower, the Supreme Commander of the Allied Expeditionary Forces in Europe, said after the Second World War that the operations carried out by SOE, together with those of the French Resistance with whom SOE had been so closely associated, had shortened the war by nine months. Nine months is a long time in war, particularly in terms of lives saved. And if it is true that the war in Europe was shortened by nine months, then the SOE needs no further testimonial. Peter Churchill had served through its most difficult years and had certainly played his part.

In October 2004, Churchill's DSO, still in its case of issue, was sold at auction in London, together with his proof copy of *The Spirit in the Cage* and a hand-drawn map showing his routes travelled in France, and a typed letter of provenance from Churchill's niece confirming all of these belonged to her uncle. The DSO, together with other items of interest, is now on display at the Combined Military Services Museum in Maldon, Essex.

The SOE monument in London, situated on the Albert Embankment and overlooking the Houses of Parliament, states that SOE sent a total of 470 agents into France. According to SOE records, 325 of these were sent into the field by F Section with 125 of them becoming casualties: 12 were killed in action; 45 were executed; 30 became prisoners of war; and 38 are listed as missing. Very few of those sent to concentration camps returned.

Peter Churchill's life could so easily have ended some thirty years earlier than it did. Had the deception over his identity not worked then he would surely have met the same sad and sorry end to his life as so many SOE agents who went to France.

Appendix

Codenames Used by SOE Agents in France

Some agents were known by more than one codename.

ALAIN	Georges Duboudin
ALPHONSE	Tony Brooks
ANTOINE	Baron Henri Ravel de Malval
ARNAUD	Adolphe Rabinowitch
BASTIEN	Marcel Clech
BERNARD	Baron Emmanuel d'Astier de la Vigerie
CARTE	André Girard
CATHERINE	Odette des Garets
EMMANUEL	Captain Meric
END	André Marsac
EUGÈNE	Maurice Pertschuk
GABRIEL	John Young
GERMAINE	Virginia Hall
HILAIRE	George Starr
JULIEN	Isidore Newman
LISE	Odette Sansom
LOUBA	Henri Frager
LUCAS	Pierre de Vomécourt
MATTHIEU	Edward Zeff
OLIVE	Francis Basin
PAUL	Henri Frager
PHILIPPE	Dr Élie Lévy
RAOUL	Peter Churchill
RENÉ	Victor Gerson
ROGER	Francis Cammaerts
SPINDLE	Peter Churchill
SUZANNE	Marie-Lou Blanc
URBAIN	Marcus Bloom
XAVIER	Richard Heslop

Bibliography and References

Published Sources

Binney, Marcus. *Secret War Heroes.* London: Hodder & Stoughton, 2006.
Buckmaster, Maurice. *They Fought Alone.* London: Odhams Press, 1958.
Burney, Christopher. *Solitary Confinement.* London: Clerke & Cockeran, 1952.
Churchill, Peter. *Of Their Own Choice.* London: Hodder & Stoughton, 1952.
Duel of Wits. London: Hodder & Stoughton, 1953.
The Spirit in the Cage. London: Hodder & Stoughton, 1954.
By Moonlight. London: Robert Hale, 1958.
Clark, Freddie. *Agents by Moonlight.* Stroud: Tempus Publishing, 1999.
Colvin, Ian (ed.). *Colonel Henri's Story: The Memoirs of Hugo Bleicher.* London: William Kimber, 1954.
Cookridge, E. H. *Inside S.O.E.* London: Arthur Barker, 1966.
Escott, Beryl E. *The Heroines of SOE.* Stroud: The History Press, 2010.
Foot, M. R. D. *SOE in France.* London: HMSO, 1966.
SOE: The Special Operations Executive 1940–1946. London: Pimlico, 1999.
Fuller, Jean Overton. *German Penetration of SOE: France 1941–44.* London: William Kimber, 1975.
Gleeson, James. *They Feared No Evil.* London: Corgi Books, 1978.
Helm, Sarah. *A Life in Secrets: The Story of Vera Atkins and the Lost Agents of SOE.* London: Little Brown, 2005.
Howarth, Patrick. *Undercover: The Men and Women of the Special Operations Executive.* London: Routledge and Keegan Paul, 1980.
Jacobs, Peter. *Setting France Ablaze: The SOE in France During WWII.* Barnsley: Pen & Sword Books, 2015.
The Twins: The SOE's Brothers of Vengeance. Cheltenham: The History Press, 2020.
Loftis, Larry. *Code Name: Lise.* London: Mirror Books, 2019.

Mackenzie, William. *The Secret History of SOE.* London: St Ermin's Press, 2000.
Mars, Alastair. *Unbroken: The Story of a Submarine.* London: Frederick Muller, 1953.
Middlebrook, Martin, & Chris Everitt. *The Bomber Command War Diaries.* London: Penguin Books, 1990.
Nicholas, Elizabeth. *Death Be Not Proud.* London: White Lion Publishers/Cresset Press, 1958.
Ottaway, Susan. *Sisters, Secrets and Sacrifice.* London: Harper, 2013.
Pearson, Judith L. *The Wolves at the Door: The True Story of America's Greatest Female Spy.* Guildford, Connecticut: The Lyons Press, 2005.
Purnell, Sonia. *A Woman of No Importance: The Untold Story of Virginia Hall.* London: Virago Press, 2019.
Ruby, Marcel. *F Section SOE.* London: Leo Cooper, 1985.
Starns, Penny. *Odette: World War Two's Darling Spy.* Stroud: The History Press, 2009.
Tickell, Jerrard. *Odette.* London: Chapman & Hall, 1949.
Verity, Hugh. *We Landed by Moonlight.* London: Ian Allan, 1978.
Walker, Robyn. *The Women Who Spied for Britain.* Stroud: Amberley Publishing, 2014.
West, Nigel. *Secret War: The Story of SOE.* London: Hodder & Stoughton, 1992.
Wilkinson, Peter, & Joan Bright Astley. *Gubbins & SOE.* London: Leo Cooper, 1997.
Yarnold, Patrick. *Wanborough Manor: School for Secret Agents.* Guildford: Hopfield Publications, 2009.

Documents in the National Archives

FO 950/1307. Nazi Persecution Claim: Mr Peter Morland Churchill.
HS 7/121. Personnel Dropped by F Section.
HS 7/135. SOE Activities in France 1941-44.
HS 7/244. France F Section Diary, July–September 1942.
HS 7/245. France F Section Diary, October–December 1942.
HS 7/246. France RF Section Diary, July–December 1942.
HS 7/247. France RF Section Diary, January-June 1943.
HS 7/249. France RF Section Diary, July–September 1943.
HS 7/250. France RF Section Diary, October–December 1943.

HS 8/895. MEW & SOE Casualties in the Field, January 1943–December 1945.
HS 8/896. MEW & SOE Casualties in the Field, January 1943–December 1945.
HS 8/1002. British Circuits in France by Major Bourne-Patterson.
HS 9/59/2. Personnel File – Vera Atkins.
HS 9/258/5. Personnel File – Francis Charles Albert Cammaerts.
HS 9/314. Personnel File – Peter Morland Churchill (Vol 1).
HS 9/315. Personnel File – Peter Morland Churchill (Vol 2).
HS 9/452/3. Personnel File – Jean Georges Duboudin.
HS 9/536/1. Personnel File – Jacques Henri Frager.
HS 9/648/4. Personnel File – Odette Sansom.
HS 9/1096/8. Personnel File – Alfred Willie Oscar Newton.
HS 9/1097/1. Personnel File – Henry George Rodolfo Newton.
HS 9/1172/7. Personnel File – Maurice Pertschuk.

Index